The Spirit of Breathwork

The Spirit of Breathwork

Edited by Gunnel Minett

First published in volume form in 2001 by
The International Breathwork Foundation

Editorial Office
6 Middlewatch
Swavesey
Cambridge CB4 5RN
England

International Office
Cattenhagestraat 29
NL-1411 CR Naarden Vesting
The Netherlands

For more information about this book please contact:
Public Relations department
Carol Lampman
73091 Country Club Drive
Suite A4-38
Palm Desert, CA 92260
USA
Phone: +1 877 491 3355
Email: bconscious@aol.com

For more contact details and information about the IBF
please see also address list at the back of the book.

British Library CIP Data available

ISBN 0-9540384-0-1

Typeset by Robert Moore and Robert Jones,
Printed in USA.

Contents

Chapter 5 - Body, Breath and Bliss

Chapter 6 - Breathing into Society

Acknowledgements

The International Breathwork Foundation would like to thank the following people whose kind contributions have helped finance the production of this book: Nemi Nath, Denise Burgess, Eirik Balavoine, Lena Kristina Tuulse, Anita Rüegsegger, Marga Parellada, Brigitte Martin-Powell, Yves Kupfermunz, Brigitte Testut, Vicente Macian, Ankara Nygårds, Curt Jonsson, Joy Manné, Robert Alnet, Brigitte Jean, Urs Baumgartner, Tullia Scandolaza, Vivienne Silver-Leigh, Catherine Dowling, May-Joyce Knowles, Claire le Saget, Edward di Maio, Natividad Jimenes Saavedra, Viola Edward, Jim Morningstar, Joan Morningstar, Tilke Platteel-Deur, Judee Gee, Swapana Susanna Hinnawi, Susanna Orsi, Mercedes Márques, Dora M Fucci, Deborah Ostas, Françoise Orhon, Paul Sakey, Eva Maria Molina Figueres, Bo Wahlstroem, Steve Minett.

I would also like to thank all the authors who kindly contributed their lectures, Judee Gee and Vivienne Silver-Leigh who proofread and corrected the text, Cathy Gawlik who gave editorial assistance throughout the project and Annette Waeber who applied her creative talent to designing the cover of the book.

G.M.

Preface

Although breath awareness has been an essential element in spiritual practices since ancient times, the utilisation of conscious breathing as a therapeutic tool in contemporary psychological practice is a relatively recent phenomenon. The emergence of Breathwork as a specific therapeutic method in its own right, claiming a justified place world-wide within the field of holistic medicine, is an even more recent event.

Breathwork is experiencing tremendous success as a tool for personal development. This is no doubt due to its simplicity, power and efficiency as a means to access the inner realms of the psyche. It can heal past traumas and transform personal, limiting belief systems into new paradigms of perception, offering greater individual choice and liberty.

In the world today, there are almost as many different approaches to Breathwork as there are teachers of the method. There are a number of essential principles common to all of the Breathwork methods - principles which act as a foundation for the practice of Breathwork. These certainly serve to sustain the immensely rich discussions, exchanges and debates currently occuring amongst the diversely trained Breathworkers who meet annually under the auspices of the International Breathwork Foundation, and who are presented in the following pages.

Breathworkers are united by their belief in conscious breathing as a fundamental element necessary for physical, psychological and psychic health and well-being.

Breathworkers are also united by their conviction that awareness is a key element in the psychotherapeutic healing process and an important doorway to transcendence of personality.

And breathworkers are additionally united by their understanding that acceptance of what is, in the 'now' moment plays an essential part in the experiences of emotional release, integrational insight and reconciliation with their personal essence, that forms the hallmark of a typical, well conducted Breathwork session.

Breathworkers are pilgrims - pilgrims of the soul. The breath is their pathway. The breath is their guide. And they are endlessly fascinated by the consequences of conscious breathing. They are independant souls, modern day alchemists of the evolution of the human psyche. If we seek them out, we will find them all over the globe practising Breathwork in their own particular corner of the world, and in accordance with their own particular form of divine authority. It has not been an easy task to convince them to address their peers at an international Breathwork conference. But as they speak, we soon realise how devoted they are to their subject - how impassioned they are by conscious breathing and its possibilities as a catalyst for health, healing and well-being. We also note how often their vision not only encompasses the existential challenge of individual healing, but also addresses today's pertinent issues of conscious relationship, family dynamics, community commitment and global ecology.

As you read through this fascinating and very diverse selection of public lectures delivered in six countries scattered across the European continent between 1994 and 1999, know that you are meeting a collection of very original individuals. Many of them have been committed to the profession of Breathwork for well over twenty years.

Many of them are practitioners who have conducted thousands of Breathwork sessions; who have learnt to sit with patience, to watch closely, and to act with great respect for the rightful rhythm of the 'unfolding' breath within each of their clients. These are practitioners who have learnt to listen - to listen to the breath, to listen to the body, to listen to the soul. In listening and through careful observation, these committed practitioners of breath have gained not only knowledge and experience, but also precious understanding.

They share together the understanding that Breathwork is a sacred science; a science because there is a method to it and sacred because it delivers us - time and time again - to the ever-present essence of ourselves that is the fundamental ground of being in which we find true solace.

Thanks to the creation of organisations such as the International Breathwork Foundation which provides an independent platform for breathworkers to share their knowledge and understanding, we can begin to pool the results of Breathwork-related research from around the world. We can now make it available to all who are interested in the method and its potential applications - in clinics, schools, hospitals, corporate businesses, university curricula, and of course in our own homes, and in our own hearts.

Judee Gee
International Breathwork Foundation President
France, November 2000

Introduction

GUNNEL MINETT

Gunnel Minett is an organisational psychologist who has been practising Breathwork since 1979. She trained mainly with Leonard Orr in Sweden and USA and recognises Shri Haidakhan Baba as her spiritual teacher. She is the author of "Shri Haidakhan Wale Baba" and "Breath & Spirit - Rebirthing as a Healing technique". The first Global Inspiration Conference, in Sweden 1994, was her initiative and she co-organised it. She was General Secretary of IBF between 1994-1998 and is now Honorary General Secretary of IBF.

Over the last thirty years there has been a revival of a variety of ancient breathing techniques such as Yoga and Pranayama, Chi Kung and Tai Chi. There has also been a growing interest in old and new Shamanic techniques. A common denominator for this interest has been that breathing techniques lead to altered states of consciousness.

The origin of this revived interest in working with the breath can be traced back to the sixties' and seventies' counterculture era when people around the world started to experiment in a variety of ways to expand their consciousness and to reach altered states of consciousness. People from all groups in society started to experiment with drugs to 'mentally move out of' their everyday social environment, sometimes with quite disastrous effects. Many soon realised what has been an essential part of Eastern teaching for centuries; that the body needs proper preparation if this kind of manipulation of the mind is to have the desired effect in a controlled and safe way. This led to an interest in Yoga, Chi Kung or other safe methods that would give the same results. But given the experiential atmosphere of this time, it also led to the development of a range of new techniques based on the old eastern principles.

Of these new techniques some have survived and changed

with time to become well established in their field, even if they still have a long way to go in some countries before they are properly recognised. One of the best known techniques is Holotropic Breathwork. It was developed during the 1970's by Dr Stanislav Grof, who sought a safe replacement for the LSD research he had conducted since the drug first was developed some twenty years earlier. During the same period Rebirthing was developed by Leonard Orr and others, partly based on Orr's personal experimentation with techniques that would lead to an altered state of consciousness. He shared his experiences with among others Sondra Ray, Jim Leonard, Phil Laut and Jim Morningstar who all later developed their own versions of the same Breathwork technique.

When Rebirthing, Holotropic therapy and other similar breath-oriented therapies were first developed in the 1970's, they meant the beginning of a new approach and a new understanding of the human psyche. Never before had it been possible to get in touch with the earliest period of a person's life, to such an extent and in such an easy and accessible way. By simply changing the normal breathing-pattern slightly, in a very easy-to-learn and safe way, it was possible to obtain very deep relaxation and an opening to the mind. This way people were able to gain access to 'memories' from the first years of their lives, their own birth, and even the period before that, from the time in the womb.

Although this is the very period in our lives, which has the most crucial effect on our development as individual human beings, it had never previously been accessible in such a direct way in the modern western world. Since the brain is still not developed enough to form mental memories during the first years of our lives, conventional psychotherapy, such as psychoanalysissimply does not allow a person to access memories from this time. It is pointless to search the brain for memories that simply aren't there.

The only way to 'remember' this period is through memories stored in the body rather than the brain, which is what Breathwork enables people to do. The way the body stores 'physical memories' is by tensing the body's muscles thus restricting the circulation in this particular part of the body. Because Breathwork aims at relaxing the breath and body, it allows body memories to be released into the body's circulatory system. Once a physical memory is triggered this way we can become aware of it and often also of how and why the memory first was stored in the body.

A large part of our physical memories stem from the actual birth situation. Due to the immense impact the first experiences of life outside the womb have on the new-born baby our first memories often have very simple backgrounds. We may have reacted strongly to loud noises, bright light or a quick drop in temperature. To the new-born baby these may be traumatic experiences that leave a memory, whereas the adult person finds it even difficult to imagine where the potential danger in such minor incidents would lie. Their insignificant origin does not however mean that our first impressions of this life have an insignificant influence on our life. On the contrary - because they were traumatic experiences to the new-born baby, they will be remembered as such until they are released through Breathwork or similar therapy, and we have a chance to discover their true origin. Until then they may well give rise to vague undefined feelings that form part of our individual characteristics. Together they form a large part of our personal outlook on life and determine if we find life 'easy', 'an uphill struggle', or a similar vague feeling of 'this is how life really is'.

Another unique aspect of Breathwork is that rather than being a new form of psychotherapy it is a very versatile tool that can be used for a variety of purposes. In addition to being used as a type of psychotherapy it can be used to improve the physical health. Most adults have some form of restriction in their breathing caused by stress to the body, which can stem from incorrect handling during birth or from any period later on in life. Normally modern people are exposed to so many sources of external stress that when they reach adulthood they suffer from stress stemming from a mixture of sources. The most obvious is environmental pollution in the form of a too hectic lifestyle. There is too much noise in the urban environment and around modern technology. We are exposed to air pollution, chemical pollution in our food or from bad eating habits. On top of all these external sources we also suffer from traumatic experiences that may occur during our lifetime. To re-learn to breathe in a more relaxed way leads to stress reduction which in turns will have a positive effect on the body's ability to heal itself and to stay healthy.

Contrary to western medicine that sees breathing only as a way of bringing oxygen into the body, the eastern philosophies recognise the fact that we also bring in 'life energy' to the body through our breathing. This life energy, called Chi in the

Chinese schools and Prana in the Indian schools, is essential for our physical well-being as well as for our mental and spiritual development. In order to maximise our ability to breathe in and absorb life energy we need to become aware of how we treat our body, what we eat, how much and how we move our body and also the environment in which we live. Most of the modern Breathwork techniques recognise the concept of life energy. They also use the holistic approach in their work and the typical Breathwork training includes advice on nutrition and physical exercises etc. Many also recognise the spiritual aspects even if they do not incorporate them into their training or adhere to any particular religion.

Breathwork can also be used to improve our creativity or our physical performance in a more general way. Today Breathwork or similar exercises are also incorporated in trainings aimed at business people, artwork, dancing or other physical exercises. Last but not least, Breathwork is used in its traditional way as a way to pursue a spiritual path through entering an altered state of consciousness. In short Breathwork has a key role in all human activities.

Because Breathwork is such a versatile and powerful key to our inner selves, the success has followed naturally, although it has often and is still met with a fair share of suspicion, as with most new developments related to the human body and psyche. Still,over the years the various Breathwork techniques have grown to comprise thousands of Breathworkers and practitioners in most parts of the world.

It was with this in mind, that the first Global Inspiration Conference was held in Sweden 1994. There Breathworkers of all kinds, from yoga teachers, to psychiatrists, and modern Breathworkers were invited to come and share their experiences in this new field. An important part of the conference was to lay a foundation for closer international co-operation between Breathworkers. Although many countries have large national organisations for breath-oriented therapies, cross-border activities and global co-operation were and are still only in their first phases of development.

It was to compensate for this that the International Breathwork Foundation was formed with the aim "to provide an opportunity for people world-wide, to learn Breathwork and to use it as a therapeutic and transformational tool to reach health in body, mind and spirit".

Another important task for the International Breathwork

Foundation is to organise the Global Inspiration Conference annually. The conference gives many Breathworkers a chance to present their work and their lectures form an important part of the conference. Each conference has a theme and is held in a different country. At least one or two of the speakers usually live or work in the country where the conference is held.

In this book we have gathered the lectures from the first six conferences. As you will see they cover a wide range of Breathwork applications from Breathwork in psychotherapy, Breathwork as a spiritual path to Breathwork for business. The atmosphere of the Global Inspiration Conference is focused very much on inspiration rather than stringent scientific criteria. This is reflected in the lectures, which range from more conventional academic presentations to rather more challenging claims of what Breathwork can do. It should perhaps also be said that the IBF does not support any one approach to Breathwork but aims to make Breathwork in all its aspects better known. The views in the individual articles are those of the individual writers. The diversity of Breathwork is reflected in the diversity of views expressed in these articles.

The aim of this book is to maintain the open and inspirational approach and leave it up to the reader to get inspired, if not by every article, at least by some of them.

Cambridge April 2000

Gunnel Minett
Honorary General Secretary and founder member of the International Breathwork Foundation

Chapter 1

Global inspiration
– the beginning

The Tree of Life
A system approach to the transformation of consciousness

SERGEI GORSKY

Sergei Gorsky is one of the key organisers in the Russian human potential movement. During the last years, Sergei and his colleagues have carried out extensive research on the medical, physiological and psychological aspects of various forms of Breathwork.

Although people in different times and cultures have developed their own way of describing consciousness in medical, esoteric, mystical, psychological terms, it does not take long to realise that they are all talking about the same thing. The similarities may sometimes be hidden because of a variety of metaphors and terms, and a lot of hidden descriptions. But looking at it from a systematic point of view, we can identify different descriptions of this structure and a subsequent development of that structure. When we see beyond the myths or metaphors, we will see a very simple and yet very beautiful story of who we are. It will also tell us where we are in the evolution of consciousness and why these times are so special and, above all, why Rebirthing is so important for our next step. These are important questions that need to be looked at further.

When we talk about the development of consciousness and the evolution of consciousness we define two definite stages. This division can be taken further, but here we will concentrate on two big stages of evolution, which apply both for the personal evolution of all human beings and for the evolution of humankind.

If these are put into two parallel themes, we can see how the evolution of every human begins to repeat the evolution of humankind at certain stages. There is a beautiful law in biology that says that ontogenesis repeats phylogenesis. The development of each new human being repeats the whole development of the human species that has occurred over time.

The human foetus first looks like a fish, then a frog and then a chimpanzee before it finally looks like a human being. The same is true for our consciousness. As it develops from conception to the adult person, each human being's consciousness goes through all the stages consciousness has been through during millions of years of human evolution.

The structure of consciousness
The first part of our individual evolution is to develop a certain structure of consciousness. Once the structure is fully developed we start to change its form. The first stage, to form the structure, starts at conception and goes on to puberty. From puberty onwards the structure remains the same. The second stage involves changing the form and to develop certain functions.

During the first twelve to fourteen years of our lives, when the structure is formed, we go through very different stages of consciousness. We start with a very beautiful state, which can be called 'holotropic' or 'oneness state' - a state where everything is connected. It can be compared with a page where every bit of information, every experience is written down and is accessed immediately and all at once. This is where we start. As adults we have a very different structure. Over time we develop many different states and end up with a big book of states. Now the book contains many pages, some of which we forget about, and some we don't know how to find. Every time we need to find a bit of information, a bit of experience we go through the whole book, which takes time and energy and gives no guarantee that we'll find it.

Throughout the first twelve or fourteen years of your life consciousness somehow goes all the way from total oneness without any borders, to many different separated states with quite definite borders between them. Although consciousness cannot be reduced to brain activity, the human brain plays a very important role in this phenomenon. Brain activity works as a receiver, tunes to certain layers, to certain stations in our consciousness. The frequency in the diacephallic brain gives access to layers of consciousness with totally different properties and there is a very interesting connection between the frequency of the brain and the structure of the corresponding level of consciousness.

The frequency with very slow brain waves is called the delta frequency. This is where we start. The first period of our lives, i.e. the time in the womb and the first part of our lives, our consciousness operates on delta frequency. Altogether we spend about two years in delta frequency. During this period we have a unified holographic state of consciousness, where we learn about unstructured reality. We don't structure our reality into bits and pieces, we don't separate different arts or qualities, and we simply take in the world in its oneness and its wholeness. It is as if we perceive the flow of life, the unstructured flow of life where everything is connected to everything else.

Around the first year after birth we start to develop a new level of consciousness. It corresponds to a new frequency, the theta frequency. In this level of consciousness we learn about qualities of life. Before we start to separate consciousness as adults and divide life into really small pieces, we first learn about big universal qualities such as love, pain and power, mother and father etc. We start to perceive what Carl Jung called archetypes of life, or archetypes of our collective subconscious. During this period we are not separated from each other. The borders between the various states are still not very well defined. They are almost transparent, which is why it is collective.

At the first level we exist as one. From the second level we exist more as collective consciousness. Here we can see a certain beginning of the personality, a certain beginning of separation although still very closely connected. This is reflected in the old traditions of the world, as for instance the American Indian tradition which describes us all as brothers and sisters and everything as alive. This is a typical message from this level of our consciousness.

On this level the flow of life starts the first step towards separation. The flow divides into qualities. Although the flows are still very connected and together, the child starts to learn that the mother feels different than the father. Here the child also learns about pain, love, fear and joy etc. During this period, which goes from one to two years of age to five or six, the theta frequency is the key. After that we start moving to the next level. This is where the real separation starts. Here we start developing the really separated stages of consciousness. Here we set up a new category for every bit of reality that we see. What we saw as simply a house before, now becomes a building with walls made of wood, covered with red paint etc. At some point we reach the upper side of the spectrum. We started from total oneness without borders and we moved on to a state without oneness, only borders. Here we also have new frequency layers - alpha and beta.

The tree of life
Described in this way consciousness grows into a tree - the tree of life. This is also the most powerful metaphor we have to describe life. The tree of life is a way to describe how reality corresponds to the way we grow through the levels of consciousness. We start at the roots, develop the trunk of the tree during childhood and as adults we spend most of our time in the upper branches of the tree. Like monkeys, we stay out on the branches during the day and return to the trunk of the tree only to sleep. When we start to move down the frequency scale in the evening we fall asleep somewhere between alpha and theta. We have our dreams in theta and when we go even deeper in our sleep we go to delta.

A very important part of the evolution of consciousness is the development of different languages, our main way of communication. To start with, when we are in the lower part of our consciousness, we communicate with sensations, in a very primal way of communication. As we move up we develop images in the theta frequency. These are primarily archetypal images. We can see this development in children, but also if we look back 30 to 40 thousand years, this was still the prevailing level. Then people communicated with each other through images. Only later did words, signs and symbols become the main, and unfortunately for most people, the only way of communication.

Language can therefore be seen as a compensatory mechanism of separation. When the tree grows and develops more separate branches, language is something that holds the different levels together. Language becomes a mechanism for communicating information between the different states. The more separated each level is, the more power, the more time and energy we spend on communication. This is why we have become obsessed with words during the 20th century. The level of separation we have reached is so high that it is very difficult to keep the tree together without words.

While the tree grows it develops the very important function of awareness and self-awareness. To begin with this function is close to zero. The new-born child is not self-aware. We have to develop this ability as we grow. It is only as adults we can feel "yes, that is me, I am aware of different things and that other people are not me". But together with this awareness we also have the separation between subject and object, or matter and spirit.

This brings us to the very interesting point of how we perceive ourselves. What do we mean when we say 'I'? Our consciousness is the whole tree. But if we look at ourselves, it is on all levels that we can say 'I' and 'others' - where we see the difference between subject and object. On the lower levels we don't perceive ourselves as a tree, but as a one unified entity of consciousness. Out on the branches we perceive ourselves as a number of states or personalities with all kinds of tensions and conflicts in between. One part of us may say, "I want coffee in the morning" and another "it is really not healthy to drink coffee, it would be better to have an apple". Whereas the first replies, "but I really want that cup of coffee". This type of dialogue may go on for hours sometimes.

There are all kinds of conflicts and differences in opinion, which cannot be resolved on the level where they occur - out on the branches of the tree. Unless we go deeper there is no way to resolve these conflicts of the ego, the conflicts of personalities. Then again once we go deeper there is nothing to resolve, because here we see it as just the different branches of the tree and all branches have the right to live and be the way they are.

It can be a problem if we are not aware of the different levels. They don't disappear, they are still with us in our consciousness although they are covered by another level of our personality, of our ego. It is still possible to go to the one and unstructured reality. We do so every night although we don't remember how wonderful it is. When we wake up and find ourselves out on the branches, we may try to find the oneness, to find God which may lead us to look everywhere but deep inside.

So the first part of the development of our consciousness is to form the structure, starting from the area of total oneness and eventually reaching the area of total separation and borders. This does not only apply on the personal level but to the whole of humankind. In the beginning of this century the tree of consciousness for humankind grew to its upper limit. From then on it has no more space to grow. How do we know this?

Language
One good indicator of this is to look at language. During this century we have developed a lot of artificial languages in mathematics, sociology, computers, biology etc, with completely defined semantic theories, and with total separation between the sciences. The net we have pulled over reality has become

completely rigid, which is fine, since that is how the tree wanted to grow. It is just that this ends this part of evolution. From now on we need to do something else. We cannot separate ourselves more. We have reached our limit of separation. We need to start our journey back. So let's see how we can do that.

The key function we use for this journey is the function of awareness. Awareness can be seen as a flower in the tree of life, a flower that produces light - light that we can direct into different areas of our life. To begin with we put our awareness outside ourselves. During thousands of years we were involved in exploring our planet, we discovered America, counted insects in Africa or the stars in the sky. We did all kinds of research outside ourselves, developed science and a technical civilisation.

Did this make us happier? Not much! Did it help us to find oneness? No! It only brought us even further from the oneness, further into separation. It is interesting to notice that by the end of the 19th century, scientists thought they had discovered almost everything, that there was nothing more to discover or to be aware of in the outer world. Then Einstein came up with the theory of relativity, which lead to the realisation that the light of awareness could somehow be directed in a different direction. Instead of directing the awareness outward into the external, people started directing it to the small branches, to the area of their personality. Then came Freud and Jung and with them psychology was born. We started to search for complexes, patterns and stereotypes, researching our egos, describing our personalities etc, with as much enthusiasm as we previously had counted insects in Africa.

Did that make us happier? Not much! But it was fun! It was fascinating to research our personalities. And then, after almost exhausting these opportunities, we started to think that we perhaps should dim the light when we tried to become aware of what could be found in the archetypal and transpersonal realms of our consciousness. The moment we decided to do so, after the very first step, we realised that we were on the right path. This was where the lost innocence and lost oneness was to be found. As soon as we directed our awareness to this area we began to experience love, power, joy, oneness etc. To redirect awareness became a new direction in many alternative approaches to transpersonal and humanistic psychology.

We can see this in our personal development. The first thing a child does is to start looking for the outside, to search for experiences, out there. But at some point the child starts to ask 'who am I', 'why am I here'? We try to learn about our personality and then if we go through the stages earnestly we realise that the answer is not out there or in the personality. It is deeper. We start to go deeper into the oneness and we find a surprise. But to understand what this surprise is about, we first need to look at how human consciousness is shaped.

The human consciousness
If we look at a spectrogram or encephalogram of the human brain we see how different frequencies are noted differently in different areas of the encephalogram. We have a strong delta level and a strong alpha level but in between them we have a narrow and weak theta level. After puberty the shape of the average consciousness resembles a mushroom with quite a big head and big stem. The human consciousness consists of two big areas connected with an interface. In one area we have oneness with no awareness, and in the other we have awareness with no oneness. We have unstructured free-flow reality in the base and structured reality in the head, although in effect, reality stays the same. It is just that we have two different ways to interact with it. We spend the day in our personalities, in the head, and we spend the nights in the stem. But we only spend seconds in the area in between. This area is not only narrow but also unstable.

We notice this when we wake up and fall asleep. We can't keep our awareness there. We either wake up completely and move into alpha or beta levels, or fall asleep and go down to theta. This is the story of the needle's eye from the Bible. It is very difficult to get to the kingdom of heaven, which is found in this deeper level.

It is very natural to define three levels of consciousness. The upper one can be called the personal level because on this level we experience ourselves as a personality. Here we say "yes I am me and I know what I am", which also makes it the ego level. The second level is a typical interpersonal level. Here we can't talk about fully transpersonal experiences, since although they occur in dreams, in deep trance, or in deep meditation, we still maintain bits and pieces of our personality. We can experience the connection between people; we can experience that the borders that are so well defined in the ego actually are an illusion, that there are no real borders. So in many senses this is like an intermediate level. It is the real interface. That is why Jung has so many difficulties describing what archetypes are and what they mean. Like a two-faced Janus it serves a connecting purpose. It takes free-flowing and unstructured realities and transfers them to images that are understandable for the mind, the ego, or the personality. It converts the impulses of the flow into the form that our personality can understand.

In the opposite way it takes the products of our personality and communicates them to the transpersonal oneness. This is why Jung has two parts in the definition of the archetypes. He says that archetypal experiences should have a strong emotional aspect and an image aspect. The image aspect interfaces it to the personal and the strong emotional part interfaces it to the transpersonal, since the feelings and sensations of the body is the language of God. The language of the transpersonal is the third level.

The human consciousness' mushroom-shape did not always look the same. If we go back 20 or 50 thousand years or even earlier the shape of consciousness resembled a bump. Over the years from the primal ocean of consciousness, the oneness started to grow and develop a 'bump'. To begin with the archetypal, religious, mythical aspects of culture were very strong for a long period of time, until a few hundred years ago when this narrow point formed very quickly. It took only a couple of hundred years for humankind to create this narrow point.

On the personal level it only takes a couple of years in puberty to form the narrow part. Our consciousness grows and grows and then very quickly it closes. The 12 or 14 year old child suddenly feels that he or she has lost connection with life at the same time as the personality becomes quite obvious. The teenager starts asking questions such as "Who am I?" and "What am I doing here anyway?", "Why did I come here on earth?" Children don't ask these types of questions. They still enjoy the connection to the flow, there is nothing blocking it.

What we see in the 20th century in the social consciousness is simply a reflection of what happens in our consciousness. The destruction of national traditions, of religious tradition, of family tradition are reflections of this narrowing down. It leads many people to question if this really is an evolution or a decline of humankind. What is the meaning of this? Why do we have to go through all this social breakdown? Is there any evolutionary progress in all this? Why do we come to the state we are at the end of the 20th century. What is the evolutionary progress for us as individuals?

The answer is that without this narrow area we would never

develop individual self-awareness to the extent that we have now. It was a very strong evolutionary kick when the mushroom stem became very thin and the head of the mushroom, the ego, became very big. The mushroom began to shake. We started to say "oh my god what is happening". People started to worry about what the world is leading to and to look for alternatives. They didn't know what was wrong but had an idea that something was needed.

So this narrow point has really meant a kick-start to awareness. We are much more aware now than a hundred years ago and much more individual. A hundred years ago, not to mention five hundred or a thousand years ago, the unit of consciousness was not a person, it was a family or tribe, a nation or church but not an individual human being. This was reflected in social rights and many other things. People still existed on the archetypal collective level.

It was to accelerate this process of individualisation and developing of individual self-awareness that this narrow area happened. But we paid the highest possible price for developing self-awareness since it meant almost losing the connection with our higher selves - with God. Five hundred years ago people saw angels every night. They felt their oneness with life directly, in a way that we don't. This is very painful at the same time as it motivates us to find the way back.

A beautiful paradox
Here we meet a beautiful paradox of our evolution. Once we start going back we notice the narrow point but we cannot go through it. It blocks our way to the transpersonal. On one side this narrow area motivates the awareness, on the other it prevents awareness of the experience of oneness.

When we look at a mushroom in the forest we think that each mushroom is a separate plant. It is not. It is not even a plant, the real plant is the invisible little network in the earth. The mushroom is just the visible part.

But let's leave the mushroom here and move on to the next metaphor. This is a metaphor, which also appeared many thousand years ago here and is as ancient as the tree of life. It is the metaphor of the second, or spiritual birth. Instead of seeing our consciousness in the shape of a mushroom, we can see it in the form of a womb, with the birth canal still closed.

On one side we have the outside world, on the other the womb. There is a baby in the womb, the child of God - the human awareness. The baby is growing. It has been growing for thousands of years and so far felt very comfortable inside the womb of the ego, the personality. For thousands of years it did not notice the limits of personality. Like the child, swimming in the womb during the first months, who does not know that it is surrounded by borders, the baby perceives the womb as the primeval ocean of the universe.

The uncomfortable, or should I say urgent, news is that we are now around nine months pregnant. This means, first of all, that there is not enough space in the womb. Our awareness has outgrown our ego. This is a very important point, which has been valid only for the last fifty years on a mass level. Throughout history, there has always been a certain number of people who have felt this way about their awareness, but it is only now that the whole of humankind enters the nine months of pregnancy, when more and more people feel the limitations of their personality. Their awareness starts to notice the invisible womb that surrounds it, which brings the situation to a very different stage.

Fifty years ago only people with wounded ego or womb needed the help of a psychologist or psychiatrist. They needed help because their wombs were so big that they became dysfunctional. They were not able to repair the womb themselves. Now people are much stronger and much more aware and even people with a very healthy personality start noticing that it is uncomfortable. They don't need to be psychotic or neurotic to feel discomfort. A lot of people who feel the discomfort don't need a psychologist or psychiatrist. What they need is a midwife. They need to go through the process of transformation.

So what happens after nine months pregnancy and there is not enough space. The child then triggers a certain hormonal reaction in the mother's body and the body responds with contractions. That is precisely where we are now. The contractions have started but the birth canal is still closed. We are at the second stage of our inner birth. All the turmoil we go through in relationships, jobs, etc. Being very healthy and strong, we are not satisfied with just external success. We feel that something is missing. Life starts kicking its way out from the comfort of our womb. Even people who are quite successful and live comfortable lives sometimes feel that life wants something from them. They get contractions. If you still want to stay in the womb the contractions will become stronger and manifest as physical illness or emotional upset, break up of relationships, the corporation kicks you out of your job. Then you start searching for the midwife.

This is a very difficult time. Anyone who has experienced it in a Rebirthing session will verify this. Grof describes it as second perinatal matrix. The contractions have started but there is nowhere to go. That is where most people are today, especially those who have come into contact with the Rebirthing movement or other similar movements. They have already outgrown their personality but their archetypal level is too narrow for their awareness to grow into the second level. To illustrate this I can give you what probably is the most beautiful results of all the research we have done in Moscow. During Rebirthing the theta activity goes up about 50 %. The theta frequency of the brain and the delta frequency goes up to 200 %. The picture changes, the birth canal opens a little bit we can put our head around and look at this new wide world. So from this point of view you can say that Rebirthing is a rehearsal for enlightenment. We can take five minutes of enlightenment and then come back to the womb again, since it is still too early for the full birth.

A stage of evolution
Although there is a certain discrepancy in the period of evolution, most people are coming into this stage very quickly. Less and less and people can comfortably live with the ego and enjoy it. There are, of course, still people who can go all their life without any motivation to change, but their number is shrinking very quickly, every year. So, in my view, humankind as a whole is coming to the stage of evolution, which corresponds to the second clinical physical stage of birth - the contraction. Some contractions, like those in Russia 1917 or Germany 1939 have been very painful. The 20th century as a whole has been very painful for humankind, but giving birth usually involves pain. So in that sense it gives a very beautiful evolutionary meaning to all the suffering that we still experience.

People in the Rebirthing movement are in a way trained spiritual midwifes. Their experiences in Rebirthing sessions have probably made them more aware, they have developed both the skills and understanding to handle the spiritual birth. This is a metaphorical description of this new profession. A Rebirther is a gardener of the tree of life and a spiritual midwife at the same time. As a gardener you cannot make the tree grow, nor change it. You can only care for it. As a midwife you cannot force the child be born in the fifth month. That is dangerous. You must wait the whole nine months of pregnancy. But when the time is right you can help the person go through the transformation. This is the transformatory side of Rebirthing. Rebirthing has two sides, the therapeutic and the transformatory, which cannot be separated from each other.

The tree of life metaphor has been around for thousands of years. People who do Rebirthing on a continuous basis have stronger theta frequencies. They operate more with images than thought. They become more creative, with more fantasy. Through Rebirthing we practice what Jesus taught us, to be like children. We tune in to other levels of consciousness. This makes Rebirthing unique. The state of consciousness we experience in a Rebirthing session works like a two-way bridge. We cannot just find a lot of suppressed material in our subconscious, but also bring it back and integrate it in our personality, or ego. You can go very deep as in hypnotherapy, but unlike hypnotherapy where you don't remember it and can't integrate it, Rebirthing has a very good balance of both going very deep and bringing the suppressed material up for integration.

The method
The first step we need to take, before our spiritual birth, is to heal the womb. We all suffer from obstetrical or gynaecological problems. There are, above all, two main problems with the womb of our personality. The first problem is that we have holes in the womb, which come from our fights with the ego. Every time we fight with the ego we get holes in the womb. This is a dangerous condition because it can lead to miscarriage or abortion. The second common problem is that the baby's body gets stuck to, or even grows into the walls of the womb. This means, that when the birth is triggered to start, we want to bring the womb with us to enlightenment. To take the ego with us to enlightenment is very painful for the mother - God - and dangerous for the baby, since it can lead to abortion or miscarriage. What I am talking about is a positive identification with the ego, attachment.

These are the two big diseases of the womb; fighting with the ego and attachment to the ego. We need to do a lot of work with these two in order to realise that I am not my ego, but that I live inside my ego. This is closely connected with our identification with the body. The whole tree of life is manifested in the body.

The body is the visual material representation of the tree of life. As long as we fight with the body we damage the womb and as long as we are attached to the body we try to take the body with us to the transpersonal.

So the very first step is getting to know the ego or the personality, which is quite standard in analytical mental work but which also involves a lot of emotional and other work. This is the work required on the personality level. The result is that the womb becomes nice and clean and we become separated. We become aware of ourselves - a pure awareness of being in the body and of living in the personality.

As we know from Rebirthing sessions it is very beautiful to live in the womb. These nine months were probably the best of our lives. It is really safe to live in the womb of mother God, the family aspect of God. When we hear the father calling us "Come its time to come out", we want to say, "No - I want to stay a couple of more weeks, a couple of more days".

Another complication for us at the moment is that we need to repair our womb when the contractions have already started. This is a difficult technical problem for a spiritual midwife. It would be much easier to work with children, to start when we are children and the womb is still healthy. This is why so many societies and cultures are so protective about their children. They are the tree of life that needs to grow without deformation. All little branches should be alive and green. The more pressure we put on the child the more deformed and dry the tree of life will be. That is when we need the therapy.

Once the structure is formed in the child, the situation changes. In many cultures teenagers perform rituals of initiations. They become young adults and society can start putting pressure on them. Although we may train them very hard, teach a lot of endurance, children will always be the flowers of life, which should grow without too much deformation to develop the healthy womb.

With time the birth canal closes and the awareness starts to grow. At least in modern societies, this phase occurs between the age of 14 to around 25 or 30. After that many of us start our spiritual search. We need perhaps around 10 years to go to nine months of pregnancy. It is not necessary to do too radical things if we are not yet ready or lack motivation, but once the contraction starts, once we have healed the womb we go to the second step.

The second step is to open the birth canal. Here the focus of our work moves from the personality to the archetypal level, which involves very different methods. First of all we cannot use the mind, words or structure, because every time we use the mind or words it brings us back to our personality, to our alpha/theta frequency. We need to use images, myths, music, theatre, art etc. Dreams and dreamwork is another extremely important method. It is a very different area of work in this phase.

The more we can stabilise and open up this area of our consciousness, the better we do it, the more it will improve the quality of our spiritual birth. If we have to go through a narrow birth canal to meet God, it would be very frightening and painful but if the birth canal is open we can just walk through and say "Hello God!" At some point it will be easy for all of us to open up our birth canal. The problem we are facing right now is that our generation is a kind of guinea pig for this kind of work. We need to test the different ways and methods, find out what works and what does not. So the second stage is to stabilise the birth canal through working with images as a way of recreating the tradition of the ritual.

The third stage is to actually go through birth. Once again we need to change everything. We need to change the language. Not only is it impossible to use words, we cannot use images after a certain stage. If we want to go further down or closer to the father, we can only do so through bodily sensations. This is a long known fact. The bible talks of two ways to approach God - apathetic and empathetic. One way goes through images but that is a limited way. At some point you need to drop all images of God and reach directly through blind faith and the voice of God. The closer we go to that area, the louder this voice appears, the more distinct it becomes. But it cannot be heard in words. To hear words is already a distortion through our minds. Neither can it be heard or seen in images. The way to get there is through feeling, a very deep feeling.

This is why we need to prepare ourselves. At this stage we need to develop a sensitivity of the body. That is why we need to be aware of how we treat our bodies. We need to be aware of what we eat. If we really want to prepare our body and make it sensitive enough, we need to do a lot of body oriented processes, a lot of exercises to develop the body's sensitivity.

To rephrase this in more formal words we can say that: Awareness, which at present is mainly stuck with the visual perception, should know from the visual perception, the kinaesthetica, that the nervous system should become activated.

Since the tree of life is manifested in the body through the vegetative nervous system, the body becomes like a big ladder perceiving the voice of the father.

Shifting from visual towards kinaesthetic and perceiving life through the body prepares us for birth. It is also essential to be very clear about the fact that at some point all techniques and all models will stop working. The models I have described may be beautiful but at some point we need to drop them as well. The models are just for the mind, for the structured part of the mind.

People often ask me why then we need the models at all. Why can't we go directly? The answer is that we always carry a lot of subconscious models, a whole range of conflicting and incomplete models from society, school, science, from everything and everywhere, which work in us whether we want this or not. There is a possibility, as in Buddhism, to drop everything and go for unstructured reality, but in modern life we use reality to a large extent. Therefore it is easier to have an adequate model of the mind and know that this model will have its limitation.

When we hear the inner voice telling us what we need next, we don't need the models anymore. Then we'll just go through birth. Rebirthing is a very important part of this process, since it works in all three stages. There are many other techniques that work at a certain stage, a lot of mental, analytical, art, therapy, body oriented, therapies. They are all priceless therapies, but when it comes to Rebirthing it is very unique because it works on all levels.

Through Breathwork we heal our womb, we can close the holes, we can stop hating ourselves (actually we don't hate ourselves we hate part of our personality which is not ourselves). We can stop being attached to parts of our personality. Through Rebirthing we realise ourselves as children of God, living in the very safe womb of the body and the personality. Through Rebirthing we open the birth canal. Once the preliminary material is nurtured, once we have healed the ego to some extent, then the energy of the breath reaches further and will open the birth canal. Then people start learning about archetypal codes of life. The womb becomes more and more transparent and opens up. The breath opens our body and makes it more sensitive. It allows us to feel the direction of the father. It is a wonderful exercise to rehearse enlightenment. It would be much more difficult if we had to do it all at one time. In Rebirthing we can get a sense of what to expect. Rebirthing is gymnastics for the womb to keep it flexible.

Talking about our spiritual birth makes it essential to also look at death and the concept of physical immortality. In this context death can be seen as a caesarean birth. It occurs when the womb becomes too rigid and too old or when the child says "I don't want to go out I want to stay here". Then the great midwife comes and performs the caesarean section and takes away the baby. But will the baby survive? I believe that the spiritual birth is along very similar lines to our physical birth. With modern medicine we are now able to save the life of premature babies being born after five months pregnancy. At seven months most children born prematurely survive, with proper care. But if you give birth at two months this child will not survive.

I believe the same is true for the spiritual birth. If the spiritual baby is not around seven months old, awareness will return to the universe. God will call it back to the un-manifested awareness. But if the spiritual baby has completed the nine months of pregnancy and we should die before we have reach enlightenment, it is most likely we will survive anyway on one level. I don't believe that we need the body forever. When we go through and if we reach the nine months pregnancy, we can manifest a body any time we need and want, but to stay in the womb for millions of years seems boring to me. Why not go through the spiritual birth and see what is. I have a strange relationship with physical immortality. For me there is a big part of fear involved here, a desire to have guarantees. In my opinion life is very beautiful and if we honestly go through transformation, we inherit eternal life. But when it comes to individual awareness I can't see the difference in what form it will take. Why do we need a particular form if our father has promised us eternal life anyway?

These issues have been dealt with in different books and teachings. Gurdjieff, for instance talks about it in a very precise way when he says that we have both a chance to form the soul and not to form it and for those who do not form their soul before they die it is bad luck. In other, both eastern and western books we are presented with the idea that there is a certain form or entity that needs to reach a certain development. If we don't reach this level of development God will take us back to the un-manifested. In some cases this picture involves the concept of incarnation which is too complex to look into here.

The three main steps I have mentioned do not necessarily have to be done in sequence. Usually they overlap but are always present on any transformatory path. Once we deal with personal transformation we need to deal with ego, with the archetypal level. We need to open our birth canal and to go through the oneness in order to finally restore this lost paradise, which we in reality never lost, but merely lost the awareness of. It is not a question about being in paradise or not. We already are there. It is a question of becoming aware of the fact that we already are in paradise, which we are not aware of yet. And whatever technique we use, whatever particular step we take on our path Breathwork, and Rebirthing in particular, is a magic tool - a light that helps us go through these three steps.

How I use Breathwork with Clients in my Work as a Psychologist

INGRID WALLIN

Ingrid Wallin has worked as a family therapist in a children's psychiatric ward over 20 years and now has a private practice as a psychologist. Over the years Ingrid has been able to integrate Breathwork very successfully into her work. For several years she has worked with both psychotic and schizophrenic patients. Her work has been highly praised and she had built up extensive experience in her field. At the first Global Inspiration in Sweden, 1994, she gave an informal presentation of her work.

When I was asked to attend this conference I said yes almost immediately. Not until later, did I start asking myself what I could contribute - what I could share with you. My conclusion was that I should simply talk a bit about myself and how I work.

I am a psychologist and for many years I worked as a family therapist in a children's psychiatric ward, in a Swedish hospital. Part of my job there was to assess the needs of children with psychiatric problems and to record their case stories.

On the personal level, my interest has always been to seek alternatives. For a long time I subscribed to *Sökaren*. [1] It was there that I first read about Rebirthing in Sweden, in an article illustrated with a Rebirthing session in a wooden hot-tub. At around the same time, in 1982 or 83, a friend of mine met Lena Kristina Tuulse [2] and told me about her first experience of Rebirthing. Having heard about my friend's experiences I decided that I should get a first hand experience and went down to Gothenburg and attended my first Breathwork training with Lena Kristina. My main impression from this training, that I brought back home with me, was that it was something really important I had just experienced. I really felt as if I had got in touch with myself on a very deep level.

Already at the training I decided that I wanted my colleagues at the hospital to hear what Lena Kristina had to say. When I returned to work after the course, I found, to my satisfaction,

1 a well known Swedish alternative magazine called the Seeker

2 one of the head teachers of the main Swedish Breathwork School and co-organiser of the first Global Inspiration conference.

that the hospital had enough money set aside for education to pay for Lena Kristina to come and give us a lecture. To me it was a very positive outcome that all my colleagues were informed about Breathwork this way. And even if they did not try it themselves, my colleagues at the hospital clinic were positive to my new found method.

Later, I did the main Swedish nine-month Breathwork training programme. I got my education paid for by the county council [3]. As part of the county council's work development funding, I had to stay with the hospital for another two years. After that I felt a need to move away from the institutionalised world. At that time I had already started to work part time to have time to build up my private Breathwork clinic. I left the hospital in 1988.

During my time at the hospital I frequently used Breathwork both with the children and entire families. I also used to work with just the parents privately. My main way of assisting the parents was to help them learn to trust their own ability as parents. In this work, I felt safe using the Breathwork method in combination with my work with traditional counselling.

When I was preparing this presentation I had to ask myself what I am best at. My answer was that my main strength is probably that I am able to meet all my clients without fear. I work with people with severe psychological problems. This means that their behaviour can be very unpredictable. Breathwork has helped me to stay focused and present in my work. It does not matter if my client has psychotic tendencies or is under the influence of drugs, or has other similar reactions. I am still able to work with them without feeling afraid of them. It is my observation that when a person takes drugs i.e. psychopharmaceuticals, the breath can still penetrate the effects of this. That is, if the person is willing to allow this to happen. The block is not caused by the drugs but rather depends on whether the person is open to receive or not.

Part of my work with clients is to encourage them to talk about themselves and their personal life history, so that I can get a full picture of the whole family background. When a client tells me about their background I can often 'sense' where the problems are. I very rarely introduce Breathwork at my first meeting with a client, mainly due to lack of time. I see each client for one and half-hours and much of this time is spent on getting background material and case history. On the other hand, if I hear or sense during this process that my client has come

3 In Sweden they are in charge of the Swedish national health system. The Breathwork Training is recognised by the Swedish authorities and regularly funded as part of their new-career-schemes.

across some inner difficulty or blockage I ask him/her to take a deep breath and close the eyes right then and there, where s/he is sitting in the chair. I guide them to the place where I think the blockage is located. Mostly this creates a very strong reaction and leads to the client getting some sort of insight as to what they have been trying to escape. This is often their first contact with their inner selves and sometimes it can be enough to have this one contact for a client to move on in their personal process.

When a person has more severe problems or more fear inside, it will of course take much longer. I have worked with some clients for five or six years every week and they are still not fully recovered, despite the fact that their problems were identified at the very first session. In such a situation Breathwork does not work as a releasing factor for the client to get in touch with their inner power and strength. Sometimes it takes years of work for a person to actually trust the process of getting in touch with his or her own emotions. One can of course question if it really is necessary for a person to spend so much time on their personal process. All I am saying is that some people need a lot of time to get in touch with their emotions.

Some of my clients see me privately but I also work together with my local county council's school department and the local social services' special youth group, targeted at 16-17 year olds. The longer treatments are usually paid for by the national health system. Clients who see me privately often come once a month.

I find it rather difficult to describe the way I use Breathwork in my practise, since it varies so much. In certain situations it can be more effective for my client to sit in a chair and take some deep breaths, than to lie down in the conventional type of Breathwork session. The way I decide if my client should remain sitting and simply take a few breaths or to lie down for a full Breathwork session is entirely based on my intuitive feeling at that particular moment.

I accept that my treatment can take time since I know that regardless of the time it may take there is always a certain progress for the client. This is true even before the process has reached such an advanced stage that the client has developed their own ability sufficiently to handle their own situation.

To my knowledge not many of my colleagues use alternative therapies in their work the same way that I do. Of course I never tell any of my colleagues how they should work and I would never try to talk them into using my methods. If asked I will describe to them how I work, but that is all. If someone at the social service department should question if what I do is psychotherapy - my reply is always yes. To work as a psychotherapist is what I am here to do and what I get paid for. I firmly argue that what I do is psychotherapy even if my relationship with the client can be a lot closer and more interactive than in traditional psychotherapy, where you are supposed to maintain a certain distance. Although I have never been criticised by anyone I have at times wondered how my kind of work is really perceived by the Association of Psychotherapists, which is the ultimate supervisor of the work that I do. Still, this was more of a concern earlier on in my career. These days I don't think it would matter even if I were to lose my licence. I am confident enough about my work to know that even if they were to criticise me I would be able to deal with this.

To give you a bit more information about how I work, I'd like to share one case in particular with you. At the moment I have one client who I would not take through an ordinary Breathwork session lying down although I have used Breathwork with him sitting in a chair. The reason for this is that he has a very poor sense of boundaries and is unable to interpret signals from the environment correctly. If I were to ask him to lie down and do a conventional Breathwork session lying on his back, he would probably assume that I was inviting him to have a love affair with me. Despite all else, this would not be helpful for his recovery. For me such a misunderstanding may not be a big issue but to have to inform him about his mistake could damage him. His boundaries are too weak to handle the situation correctly. But even with a client like him, with such a severe problem, I am able to use the breath. Come to think of it, I don't think I have ever had a client where I haven't been able to involve a certain amount of Breathwork in my treatment.

In addition to counselling and Breathwork I use psychodrama in my work. I also use gestalt techniques even if I don't use it in the same way as a gestalt therapist would do. I am open to combining all kinds of techniques even if counselling and Breathwork have a dominant part. To talk to my clients can open them up and allow them to approach a certain experience from their past. There is no difference in the way I use Breathwork for clients who are on medication. The medication usually does not effect how they breathe. At the same time it is of course very important that the client informs me about any medication so that I am aware that the client has substantial underlying problems. I never tell my clients to stop their medication. It is important that they make this decision together with their doctor when they are ready for it. The medical doctors that I have contact with trust the work that I do and we never have any conflict about my clients.

I also work with people with diagnosed schizophrenia. For me seeing psychotic or schizophrenic clients simply means that I have to meet them on their level. Several years ago, when I had only been using Breathwork for some years, I decided to take one client through Breathwork sessions. It was a man in his 30's who was a patient in adult psychiatry. He had actually approached me himself and asked for a Breathwork session. During the session he got in touch with a lot of anger inside himself. He stood up and shouted at me: "You realise how dangerous I can be, don't you? I could kill you, you know!" My reaction was simply to say "Yes I know, but please lie down again".

To me this is really the key to it all. To trust that everything will pass. Again and again I have experienced that when I am in touch with my inner self, which is what Breathwork helps me to achieve, everything will work well in the end. This is my personal experience of Breathwork. This is what I bring into my work with clients. To be able to really be in touch with myself is in my view is the most important part of my work. This gives me the energy and motivation that makes it possible for me to work with clients all day long, and to work with clients and supervision to the extent that I do, which is some cases is eight to ten hours a day.

The way I look after myself in relation to my work is to do my own Breathwork sessions on a regular basis. I have developed my own technique that I use especially when I am out in the forest with my dog. Whatever takes place inside me at a particular moment, I manage to breathe through and let go with my breathing technique. Sometimes it can be a painful process. But that is all right and I still manage to let go.

Sometimes I breathe together with my clients, for a part of the sessions, but not always. Normally I only explain the Breathwork technique in detail when I prepare a client for a full Breathwork session. Breathwork works differently with different clients depending on their personal defences. The way I would define it is that it is more a question of different personalities than different problems for which Breathwork has a positive effect. It works better with people whose defences are not so rigid, regardless of their problem. Trust is an essential element in my work. It is trust that determines when a client is prepared to take the risk of getting closer to me. Some people do so immediately, others need more time.

I like my clients very much and I think this is another important element in my work. Still it can happen, especially when I have seen a client for a long time, that I feel a lot of anger inside and resistance inside me. When this occurs I simply allow it to happen and breathe in to the feeling. From experience I know that this feeling most certainly is there because I can sense what my client is going through and when I breathe into this thought the anger usually vanishes. Alternatively I express my anger in words; I may say out loud in the room "there is anger in the room right now". I don't specify who feels the anger, only that it is present. Although I take responsibility for the anger I experience I leave it at that, knowing that it most certainly belongs to my client. My client is projecting his or her feelings towards me, and instead of projecting my feelings back to my client I simply put it out in the room. Since I have no other relationship with my client outside the therapy room I can be fairly sure that the feeling belongs to my client. I allow my feelings to be present in order not to create confusion for my client. This is important especially in cases where the client may have experienced double messages as a child. I base this approach on the trust that my client knows that I am not out to judge rightly or wrongly. It depends on the client's personal history and at what stage we are in our relationship, exactly how I express my feelings. If it is in the beginning, I will not say anything. As I see it, there is no difference in a client who feels anger or is very pleasing and adaptive. If the latter happens in a session I deal with this the same way too. A meeting with a client is never just an observation. There is always a certain element of feelings involved. I always have to make sure that I never abuse the situation.

My contact with a client ranges from simply sitting opposite the client talking, to having the client breathing on my couch and even pushing the client really hard on the chest to stimulate the breathing. If there is a blockage I will find it this way. This means that sometime I can be very 'brutal' until the client is ready to let go of their blocked feeling.

The breathing has helped some of my clients who have been psychotic and made it possible for them to function well in society without medication. Sometimes a psychotic person finds it difficult to breathe deeper than normal more that a couple of minutes at the time. In such a case I let my client sit up and talk to me and only breathe deeper occasionally when they get in contact with a feeling. By sitting up they are not as inclined to regress, which is helpful in this particular situation.

I encourage my clients to use the breathing themselves. Many of my clients learn to use the breathing on their own when they have completed their therapy with me. Some come back on a regular basis, once a year, or once every second year, just to re-connect and to get some additional support for their personal development work. My advice to them is to keep breathing through their emotions and feel the contact with the earth under their feet while they do so.

I never bring up the subject of spirituality with my clients unless they bring it up, but if they do I am very happy to talk about it. I believe that my spiritual interest shines through my work anyway, even if I never bring up the subject.

When I work with children it is mainly because the parents bring their children to see me. I may use Breathwork for parents with psychotic children but never with psychotic children themselves. When I worked in the children's psychiatric ward I met children diagnosed with a variety of psychological problems. Still my personal interest has always been to work with the parents andto look at how they handle the problems they have with the children. I find it much more informative to see how the parents deal with their situation. It has never felt right to work just with the children. It seems more logical to focus on the parents and their relationship with their child. I never use Breathwork in this work, although I often encourage my clients to take deep and connected breaths. If I work with a parent and the child is present it is all right for the child to lie next to the parent. It works very well. Although I obviously focus on the parent during the session, it will inevitably involve the child too if he or she is present during the session. Usually the child will fall asleep. It is as if they think to themselves that finally somebody else is taking care of my mother so I get a break and relax.

In all work with children the main factor is to be very present. You need to be very present to detect the child's need. Then the child will get the space it needs. The most important in a relationship is to give space. The rest will follow by itself. You don't have to be too ambitious and try to find an appropriate pedagogical solution.

To illustrate further what I am talking about I'd like to share another case story with you. This is a woman aged 35 who has been sexually abused by her father. She has several sisters and brothers. From very early on in her life her mother is unable to be there for her and care for her needs. She is physically present but not psychologically, which means that the girl relates more to her father. She suppresses totally that her father is abusing her sexually. My client had been with me over a year when the abuse was revealed. She had first come to see me because her life was simply not functioning. At the time she first came to see me her whole family was very dysfunctional with several incidents of extreme violence. All her life, this woman had tried find a new mother.

Since I often use dream-work she once told me that she had been dreaming about my husband, my family and me. She had dreamt that she was our child. She expressed this kind of dependency several times and it got stronger and stronger until it erupted one day when she could not get hold of me on the telephone. Her brother had committed suicide and she needed to talk to me. She left several messages on my answer machine but for various practical reasons I did not phone her until after one week. She then told me about her disappointment with me and my way of handling the situation or as she described it, 'my nonchalance towards her'. Everything came out. All I could do was to acknowledge the fact that I indeed had not contacted her earlier.

After this incident we had a break for the summer and re-started our session in the autumn. At that time I went to great lengths to give very clear boundaries for our relationship. I explained very carefully who I was and who she was and our relationship together. Now that she herself had realised her problem with boundaries, that I had been aware of all along, she was able to start making real progress in her work with it. My way to handle her dependency of me was that rather than making myself popular by letting her "own me" I dealt with the angry reaction I had caused. In the long run this made our relationship healthier. This in turn had an affect on her other relationships - at work and with her friends and family.

As a principle I am very open and have a very close relationship with my clients during the treatment period. But outside the client-therapist situation I draw a clear line. I am here and they are there. I will talk to my clients on the phone, but I would never invite anyone to come to my home and I would never invite any of my clients to meet my family.

To leave the children's psychiatric ward and set up my

private practice was not an altogether easy decision. First of all it meant leaving a secure job and a regular income. This was a great decision for me. The fact that the level of my income would be directly linked with my own personal ability as a psychologist was a great issue for me. That fear was so great that I developed eczema in both hands in the process. When I really got in touch with my fear of handling my own situation, the eczema disappeared again.

Since starting my own practice I have never advertised or done any promotion of my work. All my clients have been referred to me by word of mouth. It has grown to such an extent that I now work full time and more. Up until now I have allowed my work to take up all my time. Now I am waiting to see if it will adjust itself to a more agreeable level. I think this will happen. I always believe that we all get exactly what we want in the end if we are prepared to wait for it.

The main increase of my workload is related to my work for four different social service departments. I also work for the city council assisting school children with various problems and I work as a supervisor for certain projects and with a sport rehabilitation centre that deals with psychosomatic problems. All these projects are paid for through the national health insurance. My work is still on a steady increase. Giving it a bit more thought, I am actually not that sure that my workload ever will decrease by itself unless I make the conscious decision to actually say no to work.

Thank you for listening.

Cluster Theory of Integration

This zone got the name of the distorted world,
though it is not distorted and isn't the world as it is.
R. Shakley

MICHAEL SCHERBAKOV

Michael Scherbakov, MA Physics, BA Arts and PhD Psychology, is director of the Institute for Personal Development and member of the International Academy of Psychological Sciences. Michael has developed several group and individual methods of psychotherapy and systems of personal development. His interests include research and advancement of personality and spiritual development, and Oriental and Slavonic spiritual practices. In his practical work, he combines modern psychotherapeutic methods and ancient spiritual practices. His work focuses on research and teaching the different ASC methods including Rebirthing, Shamanic and ancient Slavic practices. His scientific writing explores the structure of mind and develops its resources. Cluster Theory of Integration sets forth novel approaches to group and individual therapy. His work is covered in his book '7 trips to the structure of consciousness' and a number of articles in magazines as well as on TV.

Introduction
With the development of computer technology during the last 20 years, immediate aircraft modelling has become possible. When we draw up an aeroplane design in a computer we can calculate forces affecting a wing, load distribution etc. and thus, on the basis of the data, design a plane. But how were aircrafts built before the appearance of supercomputers in the early eighties? First, common intuitive knowledge was used, based on observations and simple experiment. Then new approximate theories and empirical equations appeared (Stokes equations). Coefficients were chosen with the help of special experiments. Although these models couldn't give the exact calculation of the aerodynamic processes, they described the true essence of all the sequences of events and, what is more important; they could

be used for aircraft construction. But how on earth is all this related to psychology?

Psychology nowadays has basically become a phenomenological science. The work of a psychologist resembles, to a certain extent the work of a computer operator, who has a vague understanding of all that is happening inside the 'box'. If something is wrong, he presses certain buttons, having remembered a case when it really worked. Sometimes it works, sometimes it doesn't.

If we could make a model of the neurone structure of the mind and take into consideration all interactions with the environment, we would have a universal key to investigate the mind, which would work in all spheres of psychology, from psychiatry to the various methods of personal development. But for the next 100 - 200 years this will hardly be possible. The Cluster Theory of Integration (CTI) is an attempt to map such considerations. It is an approximate model, based on common knowledge of how the mind is structured, which uses the apparatus of the solid state physics, quantum mechanics and the mathematical apparatus of topology. But unfortunately, due to the restricted timeframe, this presentation will be rather schematic and should be seen more as a thought-provoking introduction than a complete overview.

Integration and dissociation
Different therapeutic schools use models, based on the assumption that separate fields of consciousness, are responsible for certain functions. Examples of such dissociation could be 'parent' and 'adult' in transactional analysis, sub-personalities in NLP, gestalts in gestalt therapy and the Holotropic 'matrices'. Patterns and complexes are also examples of such dissociation approaches. As a rule, the numbers of observed patterns should not exceed ten, otherwise both client and therapist[1] will be completely confused. In all named models, conflicts between different parts of the personality have been investigated and a method for their integration has been suggested. In the CTI model, consciousness is presented in the form of large numbers of elementary patterns (EP). Such patterns reflect a definite structure of neurones. EP does not necessarily have a complete function, like the 'innerchild' in transaction analysis. Thus, EP is a certain elementary personal structure, not necessarily clearly dissociated. In the CTI model we mean the existence of a large number (tens of thousands - millions) of EP. Any union of EP

---

1 In Russia there are uncompromising views on what to call the leaders and the participants in different group and individual sessions. Here we call a person, who takes part in individual therapy or participates in a seminar or training a 'client' and a person, who carries out the consultations or therapy a 'therapist'. Though this terminology is not ideal, it will help us to keep the uniformity during the analysis of the different methods.

will name cluster and the process of such structure formation - the integration. Thus, according to our terminology both sub-personalities in NLP, the inner child in TA and gestalts are clusters[2].

2-D CTI model
Let's consider a simple 2-D model of consciousness (*Fig. 1*).

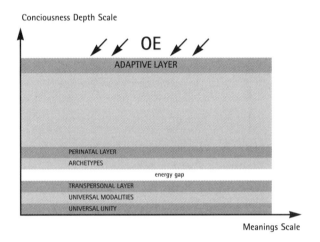

Fig. 1

The axis of ordinates describe the 'layer depth' of consciousness connected with the frequency of the minds electric activity (alpha rhythm, beta rhythm, etc.)[3]. The upper layer we call motivational or adaptive is the part of the consciousness responsible for behaviour, motivation and social adaptation. The lower layer is archetypal or transpersonal. It contains congenital archetypes and is inaccessible for understanding in ordinary conditions. Just above, there is a layer of consciousness connected with perinatal information [1][4]. It is obvious, that all layers, except for the upper layer, are inaccessible for immediate awareness and investigation. We can only interact with information placed in the middle layers in our dreams or in altered states of consciousness (ASC) [2], and with information from the deep layers, only during the specific conditions created by meditation, clinical death or immediately before death [3]. The lowest layer is the universal unity - a united integrated structure without any sense division. It is very important to note that although there is no direct approach to the deep layers of consciousness in

2 The notion of cluster exists in crystals and amorphous states physics. The use of the cluster analogy helps the analysis of the cluster interaction. To verify the correctness in using this terminology, from the physics position, goes beyond the scope of this article. We will just note that any neuronic structure can be observed as EP and an association of such structures - as a cluster.

3 In the simplified two-dimensional model given here, this co-ordination is not complete.

4 Note that the basic perinatal matrices in Grof's model can be observed as layers in the perinatal structures.

ordinary conditions, they still affect the personal structure, including behaviour, or the surface adaptive layer.

CTI uses a solid state physics model of consciousness structure in which the 'consciousness media' is represented in the form of an amorphous structure with short-range order [4]. In order to describe the processes in such structures, we will consider electrostatic, and importantly, electrodynamic interactions and also outer dynamic energo-informational fields.

The use of the dynamic model means that each element has its own characteristic wave-frequency and can be observed as a wave packet, interacting with the fields of other elements and outer electrodynamic fields. During all this, EP plays the role of 'building material'. The growth and interaction of clusters can be described with the help of amorphous state physics and quantum mechanics.

The important feature of the development of personality is interaction with the environment (social communication, personal perception, energy interaction, etc.). In the CTI model we will call the source of such interaction *'outer energy'* (OE). According to *Fig. 1* OE basically comes from the 'above', i. e. through the adaptive layer. Coming through deep seated layers and interacting with them, OE is gradually dampening, 'screening', with increasing strength when there are more structures in its way. It should be noted that direct influence on deep layers is also possible, but that it might occur in rather specific and rare situations in our western culture.

Psychotherapy in the CTI model.
From the CTI position main conflicts of a person are:
a) between surface structures and outer energy, the existence of *'non-resonant'*, not tuned to OE clusters.
b) between clusters
    In fact clusters appear in different ways and are not necessarily 'resonant', or tuned to each other. Conflicts between near clusters lead to the creation of tension in a system and possibly to the constant spontaneous change of structure under OE influence. In other words, a system with strong tension is unstable to outer influence. On the 'outer reaction' level this can be expressed as emotional instability and discomfort, and also in the form of functional and somatic disorders.

Behaviour therapy's aim is to identify problems of the first range or, so to say, the build up of surface structures on the OE. In such methods society, specific communication skills, and improved social adaptation on the rational level will teach the client behaviour mode and strategy. Here, in fact, therapy affects the deeper levels through the transformation of the surface levels. Sometimes such techniques work, sometimes not. Actually, if a strong deep cluster is near a surface structure, which has been treated, (*Fig. 2*), the change will not be stable. Sometimes when a deep cluster destroys a new, non built-up structure in its field, the system returns to the same condition, or better, to the intermediate one.

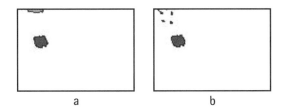

Fig. 2   a   b

Consequently, after a number of positive sessions, a client might suddenly declare that nothing has happened and everything is the same. In some cases, the deep clusters are so strong that they prevent the change of neighbouring adaptive structures. Thus, as a rule, phobias are not easily treated on a rational level. The different psychological schools have solved these problems in different ways. In the behaviour approaches, the methods of de-sensitisation for instance, have a long, systematic influence on the upper adaptive layer, which gradually rebuilds deeper layers through the upper layer's fields. It is important to note that such processes demand a constant strong boosting of the surface structure. In J. Wolp's example, he treated for phobia with the help of de-sensitisation 5 times a week for 7 months [5]. Treatment through emotional-rational therapy took Ellis 47 sessions over a 2 year period. Surface clusters formed by such methods can be rather insensitive to outer influence. As a whole, behaviour therapy is criticised for its unstable results. Other therapeutic methods aim at providing immediate access to the deep layers. These are first of all methods, based on the use of altered state of consciousness (ASC), such as directive and non-directive hypnosis, meditation and breathing techniques, etc. Here we will focus on such transpersonal breathing techniques as Holotropic Breathwork, Rebirthing and Vivation.

    All these techniques aim at immediate access to clusters in the deep layers. In classic Rebirthing a client passes through emotional, perinatal and natal experience [7]. During the process, integration and transformation of the deep cluster structures take place. Those who work with or have had personal experience of this technique will have noted the strong and brightly expressed catharsis integration; feelings are completely changed, the client may feel much younger, sometimes with a new understanding of life etc.

Sometimes such experiences are integrated into life, sometimes not. I know of cases where the client has passed through tens of such 'birth processes', without visible positive results. Let's observe the integration process of deep clusters in the CTI model (*Fig. 3*). This process can be initiated by a breathing session, transpersonal or energetic work.

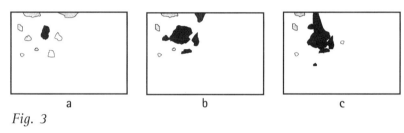

a   b   c

Fig. 3

1 grade - the formation of a new cluster structure. It can consist of a few, already existing clusters or a group of something new, developed from a point of greatest tension.

2 grade - Destruction or transformation of the nearest structures, non-resonant to a new strong cluster. If the nearest structure was responsible for an illness or a personal problem, the client might suddenly be cured. Thus, during one of our programs, on the day after a transpersonal process, a strong somatic illness suddenly disappeared in one client, without any outer connection with the session's context. But there is also another possible scenario - the not completely integrated process, when a newly born cluster has been destroyed by old non-resonant structures.

3 grade - build up of a deep cluster to a surface adaptive layer - the formation of a *'channel cluster'* (CC). Here the surface structures are changing. This involves changes in the behaviour and social adaptation. It must be noted that this grade does not always occur. The effectiveness of such CC formations depends on how the client and therapist do their follow up work - with discussions, additional exercises, further consultations etc. Psychoanalytical dream-work can be described as a typical CC formation in a definite sense-field.

It would be interesting to investigate the outcome if there

were no third grade and a simple formation of a strong deep-seated cluster occurred. Most likely this cluster would destroy the already formed adaptive structures in its field (Fig. 2b). After some time new ones would of course form but not as fast and it is impossible to predict the kind of structures that would occur. After such therapy the client might appear less adaptive and more frustrated than before. After a Reiki initiation one of the seminar participants, a schoolteacher ran around town naked and did not return to his normal self until the next day.

Similar examples can be seen after Holotropic Breathwork sessions. Of course, such examples are not typical. Often, under the influence of deep clusters, adaptive structures are reorganised in a 'positive direction' though the teacher will have to solve problems related to the temporal destruction of adaptive structures. In some cases the existence of a deep isolated cluster can force a person to take actions (coordinative to electrody-namic layering on an adaptive field), which s/he barely under-stands. A number of methods such as psycho-fascism, the devil's banishment in religious and esoteric traditions, hard shamanic initiations, some methods of military psychology contain a special destruction of adaptive layers' structures with the aim to replace them with new, more suitable ones. But provided that the third grade was successful the client will still return home with the channel cluster properly developed. Now the cluster structure is no longer in the resonant field of the therapist or the seminar group, but in the outer energy field of an inhabited area, which is mainly non-resonant.

4 grade. OE has influenced the upper layer of channel clusters. In this case OE can be manifested in the form of communication with colleagues and family, the common energy of a city, a flat or the environment. In many cases it leads to complete or partial destruction of an upper part of the consciousness (*Fig. 3*).

Deep-seated parts, less liable to the OE influence, are as a rule the strongest and the most stable. Such a process can be describes as the 'slipping roof' of a cluster (*Fig. 4*). Unfortunately this process is rather typical both for individual therapy with neurotic patients and for many personal development seminars.

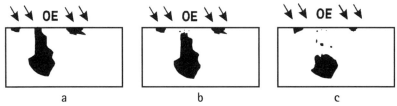

a   b   c

Fig. 4

After some time the client will note that the achieved results have vanished and old patterns have been restored. Such clients are inclined to solve their problems by attending seminars and 'collect' therapists who foster the formation of new specific cluster structures. Constant cluster destruction and rebuilding in the same zone can lead to a near-range structural change in a local part, a so-called softening of media. Most seminars and therapeutic methods will raise the temperature of the media by increasing EP mobility and facilitate clusters transformation. If a person with a 'softened' cluster structure attends a seminar, the therapists may be pleased to note an almost sudden integration. Nevertheless, since the neurones have learnt how to change character of the connections, the structure will rather quickly return to its former condition. In one seminar an American instructor was delighted by the progress of a woman who according to her own words, became aware of her self. As a consequence she became determined to change her nightmarish life. He was very surprised to hear that this phenomenon had repeated itself 4 or 5 times during the last six months. We can therefore conclude that the formation of the upper adaptive structure is very important.

It's advisable to either tune the structure to the OE, where the client will be, or suggest ways to create a new, more 'friendly' OE. Both approaches have been tested in practice. The first approach supposes a discussion of the client's subjective emotional experience. It's very important to base the work on the use of new experience in everyday life. It may be very effective to use visualisation for this. In the second approach the client takes responsibility for making his or her own living conditions the best possible. After our seminars people often change job, marital position or personal friends. It is very important to communicate with people who have 'resonant' energy. Close interaction with nature is also important. The energy in nature has more deep, archetypal clusters, than the energy in a city. Often after a seminar people feel the need to interact with nature [8]. It is necessary to use 'direct' access to deep clusters. This corresponds to the use of anchors in NLP, passing through the reminiscences in Ericsonian hypnosis, the reconstruction of our life story in NLP etc. This allows us to enter and completely recollect old experiences and re-establish a connection with them.

Resume
1. From the CTI position, the purpose of psychotherapy and personal development methods is to create strong, stable channel cluster with maximum depth.
2. The stability of a cluster is provided by:
   a) its dimension - the bigger a cluster, the more stable it is. It is to integrate clusters into the common structure in different purpose fields.
   b) the density of its structure. It is advisable to complete the process through extensive integration before the beginning of a new.
   c) its depth. It is advisable to work with different layers of consciousness, the perinatal and archetypal layer, in the same sense field.
   d) the capacity of its adaptive 'roof' - mostly exposed to the outer energy influence. Attention should be given to the work with adaptive layers, to line-up the resonance between them and the outer energy, including changes in OE.
3. Cluster formation can be made from any layer of consciousness, both from 'upwards down' and from 'downwards up'. The first way usually takes much longer but is more stable and secure. A combination of these ways probably leads to the formation of a common cluster structure of some resonant germs in the closely related sense fields.
4. Transformation of cluster structures and their integration often happen discretely, at the expense of the quantum 'tunnel' effect [9].

Cluster theory of enlightenment
Without discussing the formal description of enlightenment we would like to note, that from the CTI position, a structure with a global, closely packed cluster is responsible for the condition known as enlightenment. The enlightenment structure is not a set of local clusters, but one very big channel of super-cluster, embracing almost all spheres of meaning and all layers of consciousness. In the individual case 'local enlightenment' is possible. It means a big channel cluster, embracing all layers of consciousness, but with a limited field of meaning. It is the task of religions and spiritual practice to create such a structure.

Let's make a brief analysis of the different religions and spiritual systems; Christianity, the Russian Orthodox Church and

Catholicism. Here the clusters grow 'upwards down'. Much attention is given to the formalisation of a resonant OE - the ritual space, chanting in church, singing - multiple audio-visual and kinaesthetic anchors. One way to align resonance and create deep cluster germs is soft energetic initiations - baptism, Eucharist, the marriage ceremony and other sacraments. In such situations OE and surface clusters structures must be resonant, otherwise the surface layer will screen the OE, which sometimes happens. This is why much attention is given to the standardis-ation and monotony of rituals, initiations and to the details of ideological statements. In the history of Christianity even insignificant changes in rituals often led to dissidence and wars, after which each group formed their own narrow-resonant ritual space. It was not by chance that all other esoteric techniques were forbidden. These techniques could be good, but not resonant.

In Christianity great attention is given to OE of the uninhabited area. Don't be deluded, bad associations corrupt morals and manners - says the Scriptures (1 Cor. 15. 53). People who decide to devote themselves to spiritual development live near churches, in monasteries, or became hermits. In the latter case there is a spontaneous development of a deep cluster and a rebuilding of motivation, that strives to close off from the OE for the time being, to form a rather big and stable cluster structure. (To be in the OE of nature, resonates to deep and archetypal cluster so to say). The Orthodox Church used different a different approach to work with deep clusters in its esoteric techniques. Here the OE is partially screened with the help of special meditations (Jesus' prayer for instance)[5]. Christianity also suggested changing the OE in inhabited areas, i.e. to sanctify homes, joint prayers among family members, icons (anchors and the source of resonant energy), etc.

Buddhism
All that has been said about the creation of OE resonant fields in Christianity can also be referred to Buddhism. One of the Buddhist treasures is the Buddhist community ('sangha'). Still their model for cluster-growth is rather specific. Special attention is given to meditative practice, which means that the growth of deep clusters is conducted gradually on the adaptive layer. To achieve better effectiveness of such system they have special methods to expand their perceptibility, (Sattipatihana, Vipassana

---

5 Complications caused by interaction with people, who have non-transparent layers are noted in the Scriptures. 'It's worth speaking about, but difficult to interpret, because you are not capable to listen to' /J 5.11./

[3, 10] etc.) aimed at perceiving the world as it is. They aim is to achieve clarity in the adaptive structures of their perception, to block and destroy the non-resonant adaptive clusters and to liberate them from affections. Let's note that this 'direct way' practice solely work with deep clusters. Laymen combine their work to form subsurface clusters with practices on the adaptive level. Here monotony and ritual details are not as important, since the main work has been completed on the subsurface and deep levels. Buddhism is ready to assimilate other religions. Their technique for cluster growth make all religious wars senseless.

Apparently it is the difference between the main mechanisms of cluster structure formation in the different religions that stipulates the difference between western and Oriental cultures. In one culture, attention is given to the work with deep and subsurface layers, while build-up of the adaptive layer turns them off. In another - the focus is on the formation of good adaptive structure, resonant with OE and capable to effectively serve it, while the deep structures of a few people may be transformed according to their possibilities.

Islam
As a much younger religion, Islam uses both approaches. Strict limits and rituals combined with constant, though not so deep, meditations. Frequent prayers - 6 times a day - and multiple rigidly structured rituals substitute the monasteries. As a whole, Islam is a religion that works on the adaptive and subsurface layers. This is why group processes and monotony are so important. Since this religion switches on the straight action on the subsurface layer it is more stable towards outer influences, including other ideologies or territorial capture. Partial screening of the archetypal structures and the surface structures helps develop an indifference towards death in the name of great aims, which is realised on the adaptive level. On the whole, the inclusion of direct influence on subsurface layers stipulated by Islam, has the advantage of quick dissemination of its ideology, at the same time as it is rather conservative because of the subsurface screening.

Sufism, Zen Buddhism and methods of Direct Transmission
The Sufi and Zen Buddhist schools have developed very interesting techniques for global cluster growth. The outer energy is reduced to a minimum and activities constantly have to take place near a guru. During all this there is a permanent

formation of resonant cluster in the whole range of layers and sense, which can be strengthened by soft energetic initiations. It is important to note that the possibility to form resonant clusters is provided by the powerful outer field, mainly by the presence of a guru. When the cluster concentration is fairly good, the guru gives the disciple the last stimulation, either in the form of an initiation or by a simple blow to the head by a shoe. Following the principles of quantum mechanical effects - a sudden cluster then merges into one gigantic structure, which can also be expressed as the phenomena known as enlightenment (*Fig. 5*).

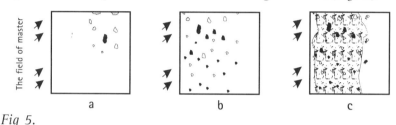

Fig 5.

Similar techniques are known to use straight transmission. Common in all cases is the constant presence of a guru and different forms of energetic initiations. In Japan Reiki was formed according to this principle. In Europe the permanent contacts with a master (teacher) has been reduced sharply or completely abandoned. In early Christianity the ceremony of baptism had a two-graded initiation after which the Holy Spirit descended on the christened person and gave him the ability to heal and to expand the perception of the world through the formation of a global and rather big channel cluster. At a later stage this capability was lost, although in some cases energetic initiation (Reiki, baptism, etc.) clusters of integration might occur without the teacher's (priest) constant presence. This is possible if a resonant system of near clusters already exists. This means that a person is spiritually ready for the given ideology and completely trusts the system and the priest (master), who leads the initiation.

Shamanic techniques
Shamanism is not a spiritual development technique suited for all people. It is more of a specialist training of a professional technique. As a shaman first of all needs supersensitive abilities and skills, including of course, foreseeing and healing abilities, this method leads to the formation of very strong clusters in the

archetypal zone. In order to restrict outer influences and strengthen the stability of the deep clusters, the adaptive layer is partially destroyed and turned into bipolar screening (some kind of p-n transition [4]). Such a shaman lives outside society, alone or with a disciple, and is badly adapted socially, sometimes even obviously 'abnormal'. The community in which he lives provides him with everything he needs.

The formation of the described structure, takes place with the help of hard initiations and direct influence on the deep layers, often with the help of narcotics or other natural compounds, which block the adaptive structures of consciousness. When dealing with such oriental techniques, especially Sufi and Shamanic in western seminars, it is very important to take these models into consideration.

In conclusion we note that on the one hand CTI is a structural meta-analysis of the existing approaches to work with consciousness. On the other hand it is also a model which helps to create and improve (and in the future computer simulation) different methods of working with consciousness. CTI has shown its effectiveness during the development of group and individual techniques for personal development. This theory was used in the design and creation of the trainings of 'Discovery', 'Inner Discovery' [8], methods of individual therapy - IBT (Integral Body therapy) [17], DLT (Deep levels therapy) [18].

The author thanks Mr. Girshon for the precious discussions, which has been a great help in the development of CTI.

Appendix.
Questions regarding the article.

How to describe the personal self-identification within the limits of the CTI model?
Personal self-identification is reflected by the common peculiarities of the structure and is the topological variable.

How does the creation of the foetus take place from the point of view of CTI?
During the first stage of creation it is a rather clear and transparent structure in the adaptive field with small clusters in the deep archetypal and perinatal layers. This is why children are more intuitive. The reactions during the first weeks of life are based on the information in the deep clusters [12, 13]. Then there

is a gradual growth of both the deep and adaptive structures. In western cultures these processes occur almost independently, but eventually a conflict occurs between the powerful clusters in these layers. Such conflicts are well described in psychoanalysis and in the Jungian approach, etc.

What is the difference between human and animals?
From birth animals have well-structured clusters in their deep layers, but fewer possibilities to form under-surface and middle structures. That is why animals have a much sharper perception in the archetypal and supersensitive fields than human beings. The weaker under-surface layer in animals makes the connection between the adaptive and archetypal layers easier, which means that the direct influence on deep layers immediately will transform the adaptive layers. My experiments to test the influence of the energetic force on guinea pigs' training, confirm this invisible CTI consequence. Because of the more straight connection between the layers, animals are been born more adaptive to life. They also develop faster in the first years of their lives. From the CTI position, a constant presence of domestic animals in the OE should have a favourable influence on people, precisely because of the much simpler and harmonious structure of their lower layers.

How can we describe an enlightened person's perception with the CTI model?
They have total perception, feeling and understanding on all layers and in all directions. This is possible due to the channel structure of the cluster. It is not that important to use speech or an adaptive layer as a mediator. All information resonates on all layers of their consciousness.

What is schizophrenia seen from the CTI position?
It is the presence of powerful non-resonant dissociated clusters in deep fields. In some cases, the formation of 'multiple' personality is possible under the influence of great dissociation. The great force of such clusters has influenced the adaptive layers until they are completely destroyed and reconstructed by the new fields of those clusters. During recession the adaptive structures can be rebuilt by the OE and therapist's presence, but under 'bad' OE, or an increase in temperature, they can be destroyed again. A person with very strong such cluster can influence other people, which increases the possibility of them

getting ill with schizophrenia.

What is neurosis and psychosis according to CTI?
Neurosis is a conflict between the adaptive and deep structures initiated most of all by non-resonant OE. Systematic, appropriate spiritual practice reduces the occurrence of neurosis. Psychosis is a conflict between surface structures and OE.

Which structures in the CTI model are responsible for our perception of the world and our behaviour?
All structures are responsible. The common consciousness structure in CTI represents the united holographic structure with a common dynamic field. In this case it is possible to interact with the Universal energy on the resonance level in any consciousness layer. Here CTI agrees with Pribram's holographic mind model [14]. In our culture the main and most studied interaction channel is through an adaptive layer.

How to access the archetypal structures?
It can be done in different ways with the help of deep meditative processes. For example, Holotropic Breathwork allows such access to a certain extent, but the process is badly controlled and the possibility to achieve integration with the adaptive layers can be hardened. Buddhist meditations on the World 'as it is' make the surface and under-surface structures more transparent and integrates deep clusters immediately, even if it is rather a long and laborious way. And lastly, the spontaneous emergence of a resonant channel is possible, conditioned by quantum effects (tunnel transition [9]), which causes sudden local enlightenment. This is the case for prophets, great gurus or creative people (artists, poets, scientists, etc.). Great energy is set free, contained in an archetypal layer, and opens access to informational fields in the Universe. This is because this layer contains clusters that are resonant to the energy of the Universe. They act as some kind of aerials or receivers.

What are the reasons for the division of the consciousness layers?
One of the reasons is the mind structure. The much older sections - ancient and frontal mind were formed during a billion years, while the cortex - during a few million. One result is the different specific frequencies, rhythms of the different sections of the mind. Such a structure hardens the immediate connection

between the archetypal and adaptive layers of our consciousness. At the same time CTI shows that consciousness is a united holographic space where connections can be fulfilled, not only through direct interaction, but also through quantum effects, if there are resonant structures. In terms of evolution man does not have guaranteed access from birth to some powerful resources of consciousness. Still it is completely possible that they will develop with the help of quantum effects.

What other dimensions do you use in the multidimensional CTI model?
One of the dimensions is the sense axis of the other brain hemisphere. The study of conflicts between archetypal projections gives precise and precious data of how our consciousness is structured. The work based on this approach, which takes quantum into account, is described elsewhere [20].

What are the structures in the deep levels of consciousness?
The deep level structures have been investigated elsewhere [19]. Here we can only note that CTI has a different approach than Jung's archetypal model or Stanislav Groff's approach. We introduce basic forms - global energetic structures and resonant to definite energetic modalities in the Universe. Water, fire, sex (sexual duality) can be related to these forms. A level's relative depth is bound with the duration of the evolutionary development of the given form. For instance, sex is higher than fire, but lower then the archetypal in Jung's model. The basic forms are resonant to large energy source in the Universe. Many religious, esoteric and magic techniques have been build around this principle.

BIBLIOGRAPY

1. Groff S. *Mind and beyond.*

2. Tart C., *Altered states of consciousness.*, NY, 1969.

3. Kapten U., *Meditation.*, 1991 see also. Moody R., *Life after life*, Kübler-Ross E., *Death as a last stage of life.*

4. Bushmanov N., *Solid States Physics.*, Moscow., 1971

5. Wolpe J., *Behaviour Therapy in complex neurotic states*, D. Goleman, R. R. Spith, *The essential Psychotherapy*, NY 1982

6. Ellis A., *From the essence of rational emotive therapy*, D. Goleman, R. R. Spith, *The essential Psychotherapy*, NY 1982

7. Kozlov V., *Free breathing.* 1993

8. Scherbakov M., *Adam's path to paradise*, Inward path 1-3, 1994

9. Blohintzev D., *Introduction to Quantum mechanics.*, Moscow., 1963

10. Thic Nhat Hanh, *Breath you are alive. Sutra on the full awareness of breathing,* Berkley, 1990
    New Scriptures.

11. Hayness., *White B. L, Held R., Visual accommodation in human infants.,* Science 148(65) p. 528-530

13. Gibson E. G., *Walk R. D., The visual cliff.,* Scientific American 202, p. 2-9

14. Pribram K., *Languages of the brain,* N. J., 1969

15. Sullivan D., *Geometric topology,* 1975

16. Scherbakov M. *7 trips to the structure of consciousness,* Moscow 1998

17. *Pozdnikov V., Scherbakov M., Integral Body therapy, in. Consciousness and breath,* Jaroslavl 1995

18. *Moscow journal of psychotherapy,* 3, 1993, p. 164-173

19 Scherbakov M., *Archetypes and beyond, Structures of consciousness.*

Scherbakov M. *Superscreen theory in. Consciousness and breath,* Jaroslavl 1995.

What is Rebirthing

Joy Manné

Joy Manné is founder and director of the School for Personal and Spiritual Development in Switzerland (closed in 1996) . She has a degree in Psychology and a PhD in Buddhist Psychology. She was trained in Spiritual Therapy by Hans Mensink and Tilke Platteel-Deur in Holland. Her teaching of Breathwork, energy and other new techniques is influenced by her knowledge of Buddhist methods.

I have learned here at the Global Inspiration conference in Sweden in 1994 that Rebirthing is practised and taught in 44 countries. Despite this great interest, as far as I have been able to ascertain, there is only a very limited type of literature on this subject, most of which can be designated "propaganda" or "hard-sell". Almost none of it is measured, questioning, well thought-out or constructively critical. The only two exceptions that I know are Nicholas Albery's *How to feel reborn : varieties of Rebirthing experience - an exploration of Rebirthing and associated primal therapies, the benefits and the dangers, the facts and the fictions,* written in 1985 and the more recent book by Gunnel Minett, *Breath and Spirit : Rebirthing as a healing technique.*

The lack of informative literature about Rebirthing coupled with the very large number of people interested in and practising Rebirthing makes it essential that we ask this question. People interested in Rebirthing have a right to intelligent, constructively critical information about it (as the people involved have the right to this kind of information about any other type of therapy or method for personal and spiritual growth). In this article I will make some propositions and observations regarding what Rebirthing is, and I will then make some suggestions for constructing a well-grounded process of personal and spiritual development using the Rebirthing method based upon the way I use it, which I call *Gentle Rebirthing.* I have a sentimental attachment to, as much as a professional, practical and theoretical interest in the question "What is Rebirthing?" This question and I have a shared history! I had the good fortune to take the *Three Year Training in Spiritual Therapy,* which was a training in Rebirthing and various other techniques with Hans Mensink and Tilke Platteel-Deur in Holland.[1] At the end of the training we were required to write a short paper whose subject was, *What is Rebirthing?* At that time I had no answer at all to this question and so I asked for more time. About seven years later, having created in my turn a school for personal and spiritual development, with a four year programme,[2] I have a rather full answer. My book, *Soul Therapy*[3] answers some aspects of this question, and I have other books and articles written or in preparation which will deal with the many and various other aspects of what I think Rebirthing is and how I use it and teach it as a technique for personal and spiritual development. Other Rebirthers and Breathworkers will have other ideas and I hope that my written communications will inspire them also to make their knowledge more widely available so that the quality of discussion that this important question is worth takes place.

What people say Rebirthing is
Rebirthing is interesting and I continue to discover new possibilities in using it, as do other Rebirthers. What is especially stimulating about Rebirthing is that there are many different ways of using it. If I look at the advertisements in the latest edition of in *Breathe International,*[4] the Rebirthing magazine, I see publicity for the "Foundation Training in Breathwork Psychotherapy", "The British College of Holistic Breath Therapy" and "The Professional Training". In a more detailed documentation that came with this latest edition, one training describes Rebirthing as a specific Yoga breathing technique. As I have my PhD in the Pali Buddhist texts[5] and my husband is a professor of Sanskrit (so that I have access to these texts in their own languages and access to a living-in expert when I need to consult one) I would like to know exactly which Yoga text includes information about Rebirthing-type breathing. It is fashionable, these days, to claim authenticity for modern practices in ancient Indian and other texts: Jung said that the East is the shadow of the West, and the opposite is also true. The

1 Hans Mensink and Tilke Platteel-Deur now train Rebirthers in Germany. 2 L'École d'Évolution Personnelle et Spirituelle, Directrice: Joy Manné, Ph.D. I ran this school from 1987 - 1995. 3 North Atlantic Books, Berkeley California, 1997.
4 October, November, December 1994 issue. 5 Pali is a language related to Sanskrit as Latin is to French, and the texts concerned provide the inspiration for the Buddhism practised in Sri Lanka, Burma and Thailand.

connection to ancient methods is interesting if proved - and I
will be quoting a Buddhist text below - but the value of a method
is dependent upon its present results and not upon its historical
origins, however interesting these may be.

As with all therapies, each practitioner uses a method
according to what worked for her or himself first of all, and what
works for her or his clients as learned through experience. My
own practice of Rebirthing is influenced by my knowledge of
Vipassana Meditation and of Buddhist psychology, especially the
exercises for development in the Pali Canon. I was taught
Vipassana by Dhiravamsa in 1965 and have been practising ever
since. The subject of my Ph.D. thesis was *Debates and Case
Histories in the Pali Canon.*

Some people think that Rebirthing is hyperventilation. This is
expressly asserted on the cover of Jacques de Panafieu's book, *Le
Rebirth Thérapie*[6] and a great deal of space in all of the books
that I know about Rebirthing is devoted to discussing what
hyperventilation and why it happens. Many people think that
Rebirthing is conscious connected breathing. That is in all the
books too. I was taught Rebirthing as strong short connected
breathing in the upper chest. This way in my first session I
relived my birth trauma and in my second all my chakras opened
up and the universe was making love with me. Both experiences
were overwhelming and I was not prepared for either.

Typical Rebirthing experiences
We can say more about what Rebirthing is if we consider the
kind of experiences people have through Rebirthing based upon
the existing literature.[7] The most famous - even notorious -
experiences connected with Rebirthing are the reliving of the
birth trauma in its many aspects, hyperventilation and tetany,
and discovering one's negative thoughts and how they create the
way we experience and interpret the events of our lives. Other
experiences typical of Rebirthing are regressions to painful
events in this life or in other lives - these experiences are often
emotional and frightening and may also be physically painful;
becoming aware of ones behaviour patterns - these experiences
are often emotionally painful; tingling sensations in the body -
based on how people feel after such an experience, I think this is
the energy in the body coming back into alignment and
harmony; experiences that bring up archetypal energies; sublime
and extraordinary altered states of consciousness. This is not
an exhaustive list. Nevertheless it is a very large variety of

6 Paris : Edition Retz, 1989 7 See e.g. the first Rebirthing books: Orr, Leonard and Sondra Ray (1977), Rebirthing for the New
Age (revised edition 1983). California : Trinity Publications and Leonard, Jim and Phil Laut (1983), Rebirthing : the science of
enjoying all of your life. Berkeley, California : Celestial Arts.

experiences and they are almost all very strong experiences.

So, as a first step, in answer to the question, "What is Rebirthing", we can say that Rebirthing is a breathing method that leads to these kinds of experiences.

Now, if this is all that Rebirthing does, then Rebirthing is just another of the many contemporary ways of stirring up the unconscious to better or worse effect, like a drug that induces an altered state of consciousness. After all, other techniques lead to the reliving of our birth trauma (hypnosis, Voice Dialogue, Bio-energetics, LSD, even Freudian analysis - D. W. Winnicott, a Freudian analyst, has described a case[8]), to regressions (almost all therapies), to tingling sensations in the body (meditation, Bio-energetics) to experiences that bring up archetypal energies (Jungian analysis), etc. The fundamental question is what comes after these experiences? If Rebirthing stirs up the experiences just mentioned, then we have to wonder, as we do with the use of consciousness altering drugs, what happens afterwards. What happens to people who have been brought to these experiences? How do they understand them? How do they cope with them? How do they integrate them? How do they live with them so that these experiences improve their lives?

What happens when people do Rebirthing? [9]
I think it is fair to call strong conscious connected breathing Traditional Rebirthing. When people are asked to do strong connected breathing - Traditional Rebirthing - there are three possible outcomes:

> (1) People can just do strong connected breathing
> - Traditional Rebirthing.

> (2) People protect themselves, or the unconscious protects itself, with tetany.

> (3) People cannot do Traditional Rebirthing because it is or seems dangerous for them.

(1) People can just do strong connected breathing
- Traditional Rebirthing.
Traditional Rebirthing works for these people. They can handle the strong experiences that this kind of breathing work induces.

They learn a lot about themselves, stay stable, integrate what happens and make progress. These people experience a good out-come. Many people fall into this category. I consider myself to be among them, at least partially, as I learned such a great deal

8 Winnicott, 1958. 9 A brief version of this section appeared in Breathe International, July, August, September 1994.

from my Traditional Rebirthing experiences.

Nevertheless, I know no-one for whom Rebirthing is a complete technique. Even people who thrive on Traditional Rebirthing are likely to use other techniques to go further. It is also true that very many people who are trained in Freudian or Jungian analysis, BioEnergy, Reincarnation Therapy, etc., add to their knowledge training and experience in other disciplines - many of them learn how to do Rebirthing!

(2) People who protect themselves with tetany.
This category brings us to one of those grand old myths of Traditional Rebirthing : hyperventilation and the resulting tetany.

Many people suffer painful paralysis of their hands and sometimes of their mouth during Traditional Rebirthing sessions and this is called tetany. It is said to be brought about by hyperventilation.[10] Sometimes some Rebirthers, when gathered together around a beer talk a lot about these experiences very proudly in a macho fashion, especially the men who have suffered 10 - 15 sessions like that. Although they do ask themselves good questions like "Why does this happen?" and "What is the good of it this?" and "What is the purpose of this suffering?" and try to explain it, their answers, like the explanations in the Rebirthing books, tend to justify the tetany. Their purpose is to prove that it is a good thing and further to prove that Rebirthing is in fact a cure for hyperventilation and that what doctors say about hyperventilation is wrong.[11] Why? Because hyperventilation and tetany are part of the mythology of Rebirthing.

Possibly all that has been written about hyperventilation is right, but in my view these are all secondary explanations, justifications for a phenomenon.

What does tetany, which can be the result of hyperventilation, do? What is its primary effect? What is its function?

Every technique that works with the breath is powerful. By powerful I mean that these techniques tend to give rather rapid access to unconscious material. But unconscious material can be dangerous to our stability and to our survival unless we are able to integrate it. The primary effect of the tetany that arises in reaction to hyperventilation is to stop dangerous material, material that the person could not handle and integrate, from coming up from the unconscious into consciousness because the pain that the tetany produces takes up all the energy and

10 See Albery, How to Feel Reborn, pp.84 - 120; Karl Raab, Die Bedeuting des Hyperventilations-Syndroms im Rebirthing-Atemprozess, in Rebirthing - Integrative Atemarbeit in theorie und praxis : vorträge und Seminare des 2. Deutscher Rebirthing-Kongress, Dusseldorf, Öktober 1992, pp.155-167.
11 See Orr and Ray, Leonard and Laut. See Albery for a more critical approach.

awareness available. It is a way our unconscious has of protecting us: it closes down to protect us from having experiences that
will be too strong or too painful to integrate. When there is a
good base and foundation, and a strong well-grounded Ego in
the Jungian sense where the strong, grounded Ego is a good and
a necessary thing there is no tetany, not even in the strongest
breathing rhythms.

*(3) People who cannot do Traditional Rebirthing because it is or
seems dangerous for them.*
Traditional Rebirthing can induce strong and overwhelming
emotional and ecstatic experiences.

Examples of Traditional Rebirthing inducing an overwhelming emotional experience are fortunately very rare - or perhaps
we do not talk about these cases enough? I know of cases of
people who have ended up in mental hospitals because they
could not integrate the memories of painful and traumatic events
brought about by Traditional Rebirthing done in groups. We
know that group work tends to bring on stronger experiences.

There are many people also who have problems with the
strong and overwhelming ecstatic experiences that Traditional
Rebirthing can induce. These very advanced altered states of
consciousness are often similar to those that are attained
normally only after many years of practise in the traditional
methods like yoga[12] or meditation. This means that these states
are attained only after the disciple has been prepared over a long
period of time to be able to contain and integrate them. These
altered states of consciousness have sometimes overwhelmed
people who could not integrate this very high quality experience
offered by - or torn from - their unconscious, and this has caused
them various problems.

An example of an overwhelming ecstatic experience is the
case of a strong man of about thirty, an Aikido teacher. He
experienced a Kundalini awakening in his first Traditional
Rebirthing session. Unfortunately, he had no basis into which to
integrate this experience which terrified him so much that he
stopped Rebirthing, judging it to be too dangerous. In my judgement that was a pity as Rebirthing would have been an
appropriate therapy for releasing his serious emotional problems
and enabling him to discover his vulnerability and his
sensitivity.

In still other cases the strong ecstatic experiences that came
up caused people to become "flippy" in the particular way that

12 In some forms of yoga the teacher induces an opening of the heart chakra or arouses the kundalini energy. Some western
people survive these experiences, and a lot of them don't and become seriously mentally destabilised.

seems associated with people who practise strong breathing techniques. In Jungian terms this 'flippiness' might be called
'inflation'. This 'flippiness' manifests in three extreme forms:

(1) various types of rather odd religious beliefs or
    other unrealistic beliefs or magical thought[13] and

(2) following all sorts of gurus. According to Nicholas
    Albery, Rebirthers are particularly associated with
    following the Indian teacher Babaji.[14]

(3) declaring oneself a guru.[15]

Leonard Orr, who is often attributed with founding
Rebirthing, and who now calls himself "Young Len Orr Raja" has
even gone so far as to proclaim himself a guru. He explains, "The
guru game when played consciously by both the guru and the
devotee is a beautiful game," and he invites us to become his
disciples on condition that, "(we) have to maintain economic self
sufficiency and tithe to him."[16]

Another teacher of breathing and other energy methods
permits his students - or are they, too, disciples - to refer to him
as "Buddha".

With regard to my first point here, the oddest religious type
of belief current among many Rebirthers is that of Physical
Immortality which they also subscribe to as a goal for themselves. This belief can be a prerequisite if one wishes to become
a member of some of the Rebirthing groups. It makes no sense to
me that Rebirthers - people who are supposed to have healed
their birth trauma, which is one of the prime claims of
Traditional Rebirthing - should be so afraid of re-incarnating
that they wish for physical immortality. If we really have healed
our birth trauma would we not rather have a great joy re-
incarnating, an enthusiasm for it and a vision of it as an
adventure?

With regard to my second and third points above, genuinely
applying oneself to one's personal and spiritual development
cannot be criticised. Sometimes following a guru is a form of
spiritual materialism: "my guru as opposed to anyone else's" for
example. In can also be a false way of seeking self-esteem,
authority and autonomy: "I follow such and such a guru so I am

13 See Albery, How to Feel Reborn, p.68f and elsewhere. 14 See Albery, How to Feel Reborn, p.72 and elsewhere. Many fol
lowers of Babaji think that the Rebirthing books do not do justice to their experience of him and are uncomfortable with
the way he is presented in them. I am not a follower of Babaji but I do think it is most important to respect the profound
experiences that he has been able to evoke in various people. If you are interested in an inspiring book on this subject, I
refer you to Babaji : Shri Haidakhan Wale Baba, by Gunnel Minnett, Stockholm, Sweden, 1986.
15 Mark Matousek's article, Plaster Saints?, in Common Boundary, January/February 1994, pp. 63,64 has written amusingly
about people who claim to be gurus. The article has as subtitle, Too many of our spiritual leaders don't live what they teach.
Why do we let them get away with it? 16 His expression is in Breathe international, Issue No. 58.

wise, etc. like he is." Giving up one's personal and spiritual development and trying to make another person responsible for it - which is one way in which some people follow gurus - does not lead to evolution and development. I will be talking later about aspects of the Buddhist teachings and their relationship to Rebirthing, and its relationship to them. The Buddha refused to place a senior monk in charge when he was dying, saying instead that his disciples should take the Teaching as their light, as their teacher. Essential to his teaching was the balance between faith and doubt. Basic to his method was awareness of the breathing.

Working with the breath
For me, Rebirthing is working with the breath. Working with the breath leads to personal and spiritual development. It facilitates any type of therapy. In the earliest Indian poetry, the Rigveda, the word for soul and for breath is the same - *atman*. Buddhist methods of meditation, yoga, tantra, as well as many methods of entering shamanic trances, are based on the breath. Whenever we become conscious of our breathing, we are doing something very powerful. The traditional Vipassana exercise of putting our attention on the breath is described like this in the Pali Buddhist sutras. The Buddha says,

"There is one *dhamma*, Monks, which when developed and practised frequently is very fruitful and deserves great praise. What is this one *dhamma*? It is mindfulness of breathing. And how, Monks, is mindfulness of breathing developed? How does it become very fruitful and deserving of great praise when practised frequently?

This is how. A monk goes into the forest or to the foot of a tree or to an uninhabited place and sits with his legs crossed, and with his body erect he generates mindfulness and being mindful he breathes out and being mindful he breathes in.

As he breathes out a long breath he recognises that he is breathing out a long breath; as he breathes in a long breath, he recognises that he is breathing in a long breath. As he breathes out a short breath he recognises that he is breathing out a short breath; as he breathes in a short breath, he recognises that he is breathing in a short breath.

He trains himself to breathe out experiencing his whole body and to breathe in experiencing his whole body. He trains himself to breathe out calming bodily activity and to breathe in calming bodily activity.

He trains himself to breathe out experiencing joy and to breathe in experiencing joy; to breathe out experiencing happiness and to breathe in experiencing happiness.

He trains himself to breathe out experiencing mental activity and to breathe in experiencing mental activity; to breathe out calming mental activity and to breathe in calming mental activity; to breathe out experiencing mind and to breathe in experiencing mind.[17]

He trains himself to breathe out pleasing the mind, and to breathe in pleasing the mind; to breathe out concentrating the mind and to breathe in concentrating the mind; to breathe out releasing the mind and to breathe in releasing the mind.

He trains himself to breathe out observing impermanence and to breathe in observing permanence; to breathe out observing freedom from passion and to breathe in observing freedom from passion; to breathe out observing cessation and to breathe in observing cessation; to breathe out observing renunciation and to breathe in observing renunciation."[18]

I have emphasised certain words and I know that every experienced Rebirther has had, at some point in reading this passage, an instant "I know what that is" experience, a recognition of something that has happened during a Rebirthing session.

This passage influences my way of practising Rebirthing, most especially the importance I place upon awareness or mindfulness of the breathing and of everything else that goes on in the body. I teach personal and spiritual development. At all times and in all cultures such a teaching has existed and it has always been founded on the discipline of creating a sound foundation. It has never been a slot-machine behaviour: never until the last 30 years have people been able to take a pill and induce a strong opening of the psyche with no pre-training. Respect for the psyche and for what happens when it opens has always been too strong - until recently. In order for the strong experiences that come up in Rebirthing to be integrated, I have developed a way of working with the breath which I call *Gentle Rebirthing.*

Gentle Rebirthing

Another way of describing "Gentle Rebirthing" is *Trusting the Process.* I use Gentle Rebirthing to construct a foundation for personal and physical development. This foundation is constructed in four stages. The first is the teaching of awareness. The second is an introduction to independent breath work. The third is beginning trance work. The fourth is Advanced Breath

17 Experiencing mind only experienced Rebirthers can do, who can watch the contents of their mind go past without being disturbed emotionally or physically or with regard to their concentration.
1 8 Majjhima-Nik?y? III. pp.82f. London : Pali Text Society, 1977.

Work. These stages are not necessarily discrete and may overlap.

Stage I. Awareness
What I noticed with many people who came to me for Rebirthing sessions is that they were not very good at awareness. These clients are often also quite dependent. They do not know what is going on inside them - they have little objective access to their thought processes, their feelings and emotions or their body sensations - and they have to be taught to be aware. I have to teach them this. This led me to my theory, or thoughts about *how to construct a process in therapy*. This is a very important question for all of us who work with personal and spiritual development and with the new methods that lead to this. How do we ensure that the process of development is grounded from the start and stays grounded?

The first thing I do with my clients is teaching them awareness. I use the breath as an anchor or means of grounding for self-exploration. I give this very simple instruction: *"Put your attention on your breathing and tell me what happens"*.

As I said, many people do not know what they feel. They do not know what emotions they are experiencing nor are they aware of what is going on in their body. They are often unaware of what thoughts are passing through their heads or how to use these for advancing in their development. Through starting in this way, clients learn where their attention is and how to work with what is coming up. In the beginning clients often need help. I observe changes in expression, in breathing rhythm, in their bodily position or in their gestures and I ask regularly, "What is happening?"

Another way of describing this part of my work is analytical Breathwork. Working in this way with the breath is analytical. I often think that it would have excited Freud and Jung. The relationship between awareness and analysis is very strong. First we become aware of what is happening, then we try to understand it.

Stage II. Introduction to independent breath work and beginning trance work.
At this point the client is introduced to independent Breathwork.

Let me go back to the Buddhist texts that I love so much and that I find so wise. In these texts there are two types of exercises: those that are based on awareness and those which are based on concentration and which lead to trance states. Now, once again, isn't that familiar from our practice of Rebirthing? There are sessions where we are aware, emotional and disturbed, perhaps, but aware, or sometimes simply peacefully aware. There are other sessions when the breathing breathes us. We are caught up into an experience which we cannot pull ourselves out of. The breathing breathes us and we have our experience - one could almost say, "our experience has us". This is a trance state. I think there are many different kinds of Rebirthing trance; I have not yet analysed them or compared them to the Buddhist states. Many different kinds of experiences come up in a Rebirthing trance from the emotionally and physically painful experience of reliving our birth trauma to ecstatic experiences.

Stage two in the way I practise Rebirthing is an introduction to independent breath work which is also the beginning of trance work. When the client has developed a good level of awareness and knows what is happening in her or his mind and body, I give the instruction, *"Put your attention on your breathing and let your body provide the rhythm, and tell me what is happening."*

This was one of my best discoveries in the development of my work with the breath. What happens is that the body of its own provides the breathing rhythm necessary to lead the client into the next step of her or his development. That means that either an awareness session or a trance session may take place. Everything is possible, and no pushing of the process has taken place.

Stage III. Inducing trance
A client who is now well-grounded and who is developing a strong and stable Ego, capable of integrating both traumatic and ecstatic experiences[19] can now be given the instruction *"Put your attention on your breathing, let your body provide the rhythm, and then make your breathing connected."*

This instruction will tend to lead to trance work, if that is what the client needs in a particular session. Trance work means that less control on the part of the client is possible, thus more ability to integrate difficult experiences without flipping is required.

Stage IV : Advanced breath work
At this stage, the client and I can begin to play.

An advanced client is well and truly grounded and has a strong Ego capable of integrating large-scale experiences, whether the trauma involved is large-scale or the ecstatic state is large-scale. At this point in a person's development, when a client is established well at this level, I feel free to offer them that they try to induce such a state. The client has been prepared for this work and in the discussion before the session we have discussed the various possibilities available: whether the client will follow the rhythm offered by her or his body or whether the client will really work the breath, physically, like an exercise - and if so, how? - or whether I will help the client by inducing such a state through various instructions or through guiding her or his breathing.

It is at this point that I do *Traditional Rebirthing*. I give the client the following instruction: *"Put your attention on your breathing and make your breathing connected."*

Advanced breath work will always induce in the prepared client experiences such as strong regressions to the birth trauma or to other traumas, including those from past lives, experiences of shamanic energies such as healing energy or archetypal energy, archetypal emotional states such as abandonment, sorrow and loneliness, or advanced ecstatic trance states.

That is how I practise Rebirthing and that is how I like to construct a process of personal and spiritual development. The stages are not water-tight but overlapping. The client with a strong foundation is never constrained; the client who does not have a strong foundation is obliged to develop one. When the breath is worked with, gently and respectively - no forcing, no pushing - then what needs to come up will come up and the client will be able to integrate it.

Now you know what I think Rebirthing is. I have one more thing to say: WHO SHOULD NOT DO REBIRTHING?

This is a important and fundamental question. My ability to answer it is limited, as I have no formal training in working with severely mentally disturbed people.

People who are capable of being aware of what is happening in their mind and body, and who are willing to take the responsibility to be aware of that and to take the responsibility to learn what they do and how they influence their life and their relationships can do awareness work with the breath. Anything further than this - even the most Gentle Rebirthing - is dangerous for people who do not have good grounding and a strong enough Ego. When the Ego is not strong, unconscious material can burst forth and be overwhelming. People whose Ego is not strong and grounded have identity problems. Any kind of work with the breath is powerful. Even the most gentle

19 These require education to integrate. This should be remembered as we do not have esoteric schools which used to look after the educational side, as once was the case.

Rebirthing can bring us into past-life experiences, for example, or to full regressions into past traumas such as sexual abuse or accidents or operations, and of course our birth and conception traumas. Full regression means more than just remembering: it means reliving in detail on the mental, emotional and physical level everything that happened during the trauma. The Ego, or the sense of personal identity, has to be strong enough to integrate what comes up.

People who have serious mental illnesses do not have strong enough Egos and so cannot handle this material.

If we are aware of what Rebirthing is, and how powerful it is, we will be careful not to use it where it is inappropriate. People want to run before they can walk, and when it comes to personal and spiritual development, are spiritual materialists. They are unrewarding clients and run genuine risks with regard to their own psyche.

What is Rebirthing?
To conclude, let me come back to my Buddhist texts. In these texts, the importance of a good base was fundamental, including a good base in ethics. This time I want to talk about REBIRTHING AND ETHICS.
The Buddha taught the Four Noble Truths. These are:

(1) The Truth of Suffering;
(2) the Truth of the Origin of Suffering;
(3) the Truth of the Cessation of Suffering; and
(4) the Path to the Cessation of Suffering, which is the *Noble Eightfold Path* of Right View, Right Thought, Right Speech, Right Bodily Action, Right Livelihood, Right Effort, Right Mindfulness and Right Concentration.

One of the many things that drew me to Rebirthing and continues to keep my commitment to Rebirthing is its honesty as a technique. When I was writing this lecture and wondering which among the many relevant teachings in the Buddhist texts to include, the *Noble Eightfold Path* came to mind: Right view, right thought, right speech, right action, right way of living, right exertion, right mindfulness and right concentration. I then became aware of something I had up till then taken for granted. The unqualified acceptance of and commitment to an ethical way of life that exists in most Rebirthers. Sometimes Rebirthers use the expression *Going for the Highest Truth.*

The Buddhists teach that the energy that we put into the world will come back to us. They call this *karma*. A commitment to ethics ensures that we put good energy into the world. I think that Rebirthers do that, spontaneously, because that is part of what happens when we work with the breath.

BIBLIOGRAPY

1. Albery, Nicholas (1985), *How to feel reborn : varieties of Rebirthing experience - an exploration of Rebirthing and associated primal therapies, the benefits and the dangers, the facts and the fictions.* London: Regeneration Press.

2. Manné, Joy (1997) *Soul Therapy.* Berkeley, California: North Atlantic Books.

3. Minett, Gunnel (1994), *Breath and Spirit: Rebirthing as a healing technique.* London: The Aquarian Press.

4. Winnicott, D.W. (1958), *Birth Memories, Birth Trauma and Anxiety* 1949-54. London: Collected Papers, 1958.

Chapter 2
Celebrate the Synergy

The Concept of an Integral Therapeutic Approach

WOJCIECH EICHELBERGER

Wojciech Eichelberger is a prominent Polish psychotherapist, trained in Gestalt Therapy at the Institute of Gestalt Therapy in Los Angeles, USA, influenced by Albert Peso, Jack Rosenberg, Roberto Assaglioli. A Zen practitioner since 1976. Co-founder of the Laboratory for Psychoeducation therapy and training centre, well know for its professional and ethical standards. His interest in Breathwork is deeply rooted in his integral approach to the issue of human suffering.

First of all what I am going to say may be very revealing to you. I am actually not as critical towards Breathwork as you may have expected. I have just learnt that I have been expected and even invited to be a critic of Breathwork. I will of course have some critical remarks to make, so maybe I will not disappoint you all together. What I will talk about mainly is to compare different types of psychotherapy - if you consider psycho-therapy in this context as a discipline.

I would like to start by drawing a figure, which may be known to many of you, and which is not my own invention, even if I no longer can remember where I got it from and I may also have added something to it myself.

If we look at the whole spectrum of psychotherapeutic intervention it can be described as a triangle with the mind aspect, in its more narrow sense, as one leg of the triangle, the body aspect as another leg and the substance, or the nourishment that we bring into our body as the third leg. This is of course not the full picture, but even now we can see that all three aspects are interrelated and any intervention could be applied to any of them. What effects one certainly effects the other two as well.

Fig 1.

If we look at the **Body** aspect we have many body oriented therapies. *Bioenergetics* is one. *Rolfing* is another, which in my view is one of the better therapies, since it does not involve any psychological perspective, just the body aspect. There are of course many other schools, but for now I will only mention these two since they are among the more well-known therapies in this area.

In the psychological aspect, which I refer to as **Mind** here, the schools that only consider the mind are called *Psychoanalytical therapy*. They only involve the psychological aspect, nothing else whatsoever. The same way as Rolfing focuses only on the body the psychological analytical therapies focus only on the psychological aspect. It is very clear and very one-sided.

Then we have the **Substance** aspect, which I think requires some explanation. Substance in this context refers to the substance within the human organism or human body, its building blocks so to say. It can be represented by *Macrobiotics* for instance, which concentrates on a dietary intervention. We try to influence the whole system by a more or less subtle dietary intervention.

Of course, as we can see all aspects are interrelated and we could say that approaching any of them would evenly influence the other two. But this is not the case. When we approach the body, like in Rolfing and we ignore the other two, we will sooner or later get to the impasse, we have no way to get any further. The change in the whole system is very temporary and not longstanding. We find out sooner or later that when we want to work through the body to ensure a change that would be long lasting and very penetrating, we have to include the psychological and the substance aspect as well. Like you do in

Hatha Yoga for example. When we do Hatha Yoga without including the dietary intervention we will be stuck sooner or later. We will not make sufficient progress.

The same applies to the substance aspect. When we use only Macrobiotics, i.e. we only use dietary intervention, we will not change the whole system, although Macrobiotics claim that it is able to do so. Maybe, who knows, but intervention in this aspect has a certain quality. It takes a lot of time. So maybe what Macrobiotics claims to be true would take at least 50 years or more. Because with substance intervention the substance changes very slowly and the change on the substance level will get its echo, so to say, in a very long time. So if we want to work on the substance level and start with the substance level, we also have to include the psychological and body aspects.

The same is of course also true for the psychological aspect. But this is not quite as certain. There are psychological or psychotherapeutic schools that claim, and they are right too, that they can change the human being, just by applying intervention on the psychological level. It is of course logical to, because when we look at it we can say that the mind comes first, followed by body and substance. There is a saying that the body will follow the mind. There is nothing you can do with the body if the mind is not involved or changed. So the mind has a superior position in this respect.

But now to the big question - where does Breathwork fit in to this? The answer is a real compliment to you, because Breathwork comes into the middle. Although in this context I would prefer to call it the **Energy** aspect. And of course the energy aspect touches on all the three other aspects that we have talked about before. But it is not just all the different Breathwork techniques that come into the energy aspect. Acupuncture also belongs here. It is a very subtle intervention in the body's energy flow. So in the middle we can put Breathwork and Acupuncture. We can also say that Breathwork or any other intervention in this aspect is a core intervention, which of course can be very effective for this very reason. From its position in the middle it touches upon all other aspects, which makes it a core intervention. It influences all other aspects at the same time. It changes the substance, the psychological aspect as well as the body aspect and can therefore be very effective, which indeed you all know already. At the same time it can be very dangerous, for the very same reason that it is a core intervention.

I will come back to this a little bit later, but before I do, I want to draw another circle in my illustration; a circle that goes around all other aspects and encompasses all. It embraces all other aspects at the same time, energy, body, mind and substance. This circle illustrates the Spiritual aspect.

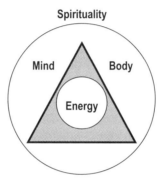

Fig 2.

Energy and Spirituality are very similar. You can say that they are of the same family but not identical. We often mistake one for the other. A person gets lots of energy and we say - "Oh, he is very spiritual". But this is not necessarily the case. In fact, you don't need to have a lot of energy to be spiritual although you will have a different type of energy of course. You can work a lot with the energy as in acupuncture but the person will not automatically get spiritual as a result. To become spiritual takes a special kind of training. But of course the really important issue here is that in order to get spiritual we have to put the three basic aspects as well as the energy aspect into some kind of harmony. If it is not in harmony the spiritual aspect is very dangerous. What can happen in effect is that you develop what is often known as spiritual materialism. Then the so-called spirituality works as a surrogate or compensation. If the psychological aspects, the body aspect, the substance aspects and the energy aspect are not in harmony, the spiritual aspect can be used as compensation. It will be used against its own goal or meaning and simply build up the ego. If your ego is very weak, you have no energy, a lot of psychological problems, lots of blocks in the body, the substance is not in harmony, and spirituality can be used as compensation. We are not spiritual. Instead we dress ourselves in it and use it as a sort of extra clothing against the world. And here is where I will finally come to my critical remarks about Breathwork.

I have met quite a few people involved in Rebirthing, who I would say, to my psychotherapeutic eye, are quite keen - and I base this on my 25 years of experience - who were not in harmony in all these aspects. They had a lot of energy going but the energy was not really flowing nicely and evenly and not in an open and gentle way. The energy was also used as a compensation for shortcomings that were present in all the other aspects. So we must be really careful when we use Breathwork. It is so easy to get carried away with energy and get ideas about ourselves that we are free, wise and able to do anything we want. But I will say we are not, unless there is some harmony in the three basic aspects. Therefore I am delighted to notice that the development in Breathwork means that you now take all of this into consideration in a very solid and professional way. If the ego is not strong and the body is not relaxed and flexible it can of course be dangerous with a lot of energy. You may have heard of the Yoga teacher, who writes about Yogic breathing exercises that if you do a lot of breathing exercises when your body is weak and rigid the body will eventually be destroyed. The breathing will work like a pneumatic drill that will hammer away at a very hard surface. It can be dangerous to the body as well as the ego. So if we have energy instead of ego, we will get hooked on energy the same way as we can get hooked on anything else if our ego is unbalanced or too weak. If we get hooked on energy this is just another addiction. So this is a danger to be aware of.

As I have already mentioned there is a danger of mistaking energy for spirituality. But in reality these two have nothing in common. Of course if we want to be spiritual we need some energy. But it requires energy that flows by itself, so to say. If your inner system is open and in balance it is fine. Then you will almost automatically have a lot of energy. But if your system is not open you will not have much energy flowing at all. It is of

course my experience as a psychotherapist that when you work
on the psychological level and the body level the energy will
start flowing. Your breathing will change by itself. You don't
have to make any direct intervention. On the other hand if you
do this intervention it is alright. You can teach conscious breathing and body therapy, which is quite often done. But on the other
hand it is dangerous to manipulate the breathing as a habit
because the breathing is a reflection of the body, mind and
spirit. So when you manipulate the breathing you manipulate
your whole self. It is all a very subtle process.

In fact I have met people that would breathe in a way that
was not 'themselves' so to say. They would do this artificial
breathing all the time. No matter what the situation was, whether
they were expressing love, tenderness, anger or whether they did
something different altogether, they kept breathing in an
artificial way that was not natural. They were manipulating
themselves and consequently also their minds and bodies. It is of
course possible to do this as a regular procedure, which in itself
can be right. But when the procedure ends you have to tell yourself to forget it. Just do your thing and be yourself. When the
time is right you can do your next breathing exercise, but you
mustn't manipulate yourself on an ongoing basis. It is the same
type of manipulation as you do with your psychological defences
or your body's defences. You can defend yourself against ongoing life; just by manipulating the breathing you are cutting
off yourself.

This is my comment regarding the energy aspect. I would
also like to make some final remarks regarding spirituality. As I
already have said, spirituality can also be used as a compensation for the weak ego. As my illustration shows the spirituality
is attached to the other aspects in some contact points at each
corner of the triangle. When the whole organism grows and
expands and is in harmony and it touches upon the contact
points, spirituality will happen automatically. You don't need to
push people into spirituality if they are really ready in all other
aspects. If they have no psychological problems, if the body is in
harmony, if the substance is balanced and the energy flows
freely, spirituality will be there. It is a natural state in your development. You can't avoid it. There is no need to 'make' yourself

spiritual. If should come by itself. If you make yourself spiritual, you are merely practising spiritual materialism.

Thank you for your attention.

Rebirthing – an Orphan Therapy or a Part of the Family of Psychotherapies?

JOY MANNÉ

Joy Manné is founder and director of the School for Personal and Spiritual Development in Switzerland (closed in 1995). She has a degree in Psychology and a PhD in Buddhist Psychology. She was trained in Spiritual Therapy by Hans Mensink and Tilke Platteel-Deur in Holland. Her teaching of Breathwork, energy and other new techniques is influenced by her knowledge of Buddhist methods.

"To lose one parent, Mr Worthing, may be regarded as a misfortune; to lose both looks like carelessness." (Oscar Wilde, The importance of being Earnest, Act I)

The first book published about Rebirthing is called *Rebirthing for the New Age* and was written by Leonard Orr and Sondra Ray and published in 1977 (revised edition 1983). The second is called *Rebirthing : the science of enjoying all of your life* and was published in 1983 by Jim Leonard and Phil Laut, who now call the type of Rebirthing they do *Vivation*. In Orr & Ray, Leonard Orr is acknowledged as the founder of Rebirthing. There are no other acknowledgements in that book with regard to influences upon Rebirthing,[1] although a relationship with psychoanalysis and psychotherapy is alluded to in the following comparison which is written with reference to the trauma of painful memories which frequently come back through Rebirthing:

"Rebirthing is focussed on releasing rather than on re-experiencing the trauma. ... If psychoanalysis and psychotherapy are like diligently picking through your psychological garbage in an attempt to understand it, then Rebirthing (in most cases) is like carrying out your garbage in one fell swoop." [2]

"In most cases". Is this in fact an acknowledgement that in the remaining cases Rebirthing is like psychoanalysis and psychotherapy, so that these are among its parents and ancestors?

---

1 Leboyer's Birth without Violence is mentioned and Janov's Primal Scream is mentioned, but neither is acknowledged as a source or as an inspiration for Rebirthing.
2 Orr and Ray, p. 88.

The influence of Babaji, their spiritual master, on Leonard Orr and Sondra Ray is acknowledged in many places in this book.

In Leonard & Laut, Leonard Orr is once again acknowledged as the founder of Rebirthing. I have found no reference to other therapies in this book.

Is Rebirthing really an orphan therapy as these books seem to indicate? Has it really no roots in the development of psychotherapy, which, James Hillman and Michael Ventura tell us, has gone on for 100 years "- and the world is getting worse".[3]

Nicholas Albery, in his book *How to feel reborn : varieties of Rebirthing experience - an exploration of Rebirthing and associated primal therapies, the benefits and the dangers, the facts and the fictions*, comments that "New therapies and new techniques often emphasise their newness by not fully acknowledging their indebtedness to their predecessors."[4] Albery discusses some of the roots of Rebirthing. So does Irène Abbondio in her excellent monograph, *Traumatisme de la naissance et souffle dans la psychologie occidentale : manual de référence à l'usage des Thérapeutes du Souffle.*[5]

The first book, Orr & Ray, already claimed that approximately half a million people[6] had been rebirthed. The second book, in which 'Rebirthing' was awarded its capital letter claims that Rebirthing "has been used successfully by millions of people throughout the world."[7] These numbers are certainly exaggerated and may be taken to designate 'a lot' in American culture, just as in the Buddhist texts certain numbers like 1250 or 500 designate simply 'a lot' and are not to be taken literally.[8] Certainly there are enough people who practice Rebirthing, i.e. who receive Rebirthing sessions, give Rebirthing sessions and teach Rebirthing, for it to warrant taking seriously. The Rebirthers took themselves seriously, and together with other breathworkers, at a conference in Sweden in July-August 1994 founded The International Breathwork Foundation which has among its goals making Rebirthing more widely known, research, documentation, professionalism and international co-operation.

Perhaps, if the 'orphan therapy' that Rebirthing seems to be can find its parent therapies, and thus its roots, it will be able to grow in the way that I myself, many other Rebirthers and the International Breathwork Foundation would like it to. Its interests in research require roots in other theories, therapies and practices. Its connection to other theories, therapies and practices requires recognition so that they, in return, can become more

3 Hillman, James and Michael Ventura, 1993. 4 Albery. 5 Abbondio, 1994. This can be obtained directly from her at Irène Abbondio, Cité Derrière 4, CH - 1005 Lausanne. 6 Orr and Ray, 173. 7 Leonard and Laut. 8 Manné, 1990. These numbers frequently designate the size of the Buddha's following, especially during debates with members of other religions.

effective through adopting some of its methods.

For the purposes of this paper I will take several prominent aspects of Rebirthing and show that they have in fact respectable roots - as Jack Worthing turned out to have in Oscar Wilde's play The Importance of Being Earnest - in psychoanalysis, psychotherapy and in the mystical traditions of many religions.

Rebirthing not only has ancestors but it has descendants. By placing Rebirthing in the family of therapies to which it belongs its contribution can better be recognised, and we can better develop the training of Rebirthers and thus the way Rebirthing is practised. We can also suggest those other methods which could usefully incorporate Rebirthing techniques.

WHAT IS REBIRTHING?

This question cannot be answered in full in one article. I have written about it in the article on my school[9] that appeared in *Breathe*[10] and in my book, *Soul Therapy*[11] on this subject in preparation: this is not a simple question to answer and my purpose here is only to establish some aspects of the parentage and the heritage of Rebirthing. What I will say is that it is a very powerful, interesting and important method of psychotherapy and of personal and spiritual development based upon Breathwork, whose potential and effects have barely begun to be seriously described

Rebirthing is particularly identified with being a breathing technique which brings about regression so that memories of the Rebirthee's[12] birth trauma and of other traumas previously unconscious become accessible to consciousness. Rebirthing recognises that people repeat unproductive behaviour patterns and works with these through the breath, through relationship trainings and through affirmations. The repetition of unproductive behaviour patterns is known technically in psychoanalysis as the Repetition Compulsion. Rebirthing leads to a large variety of altered states of consciousness, to what Maslow called peak experiences,[13] to transpersonal states and to ecstatic experiences. It is these aspects of Rebirthing and their roots in other therapies and practices that I will write about in this paper under the following headings:

  (1) Rebirthing and breathing methods,

9 L'École d'Évolution Personnelle et Spirituelle a four year training in Rebirthing, Voice Dialogue, and other methods for accompanying people in their personal and spiritual development. 10 Manné, 1994. 11 Berkeley, California: North Atlantic Books, 1997. 12 This is the usual term for the person receiving the Rebirthing session. 13 Maslow, 1968.

(2) Rebirthing and the birth trauma,

(3) Rebirthing and regression,

(4) Rebirthing and the Repetition Compulsion, and

(5) Rebirthing and spiritual development.

I am purposefully avoiding what Albery calls 'the Wilder Fringes'[14] of Rebirthing, such as Orr & Ray's ideas about Physical Immortality (although I suspect that someone with enthusiasm for this subject will be able to relate it to Freud's concepts of the Death Urge and the Pleasure Principle) and the first 42 pages of Leonard & Laut which purport to explain all of life and which I find unreadable. These first books about Rebirthing are not easy to read because of their 'wilder fringes'. Nevertheless they contain a considerable amount of interesting and useful material. I hope that through my training in philology I will be able to reveal some of this in what follows.

1. Rebirthing and breathing methods

Rebirthing is also called 'conscious breathing' or 'energy breathing' or "a relaxed, continuous breathing rhythm".[15]

The potential parent of this aspect of Rebirthing might be Arthur Janov who is known for having invented Primal Scream therapy or Primal therapy.

Janov gives the impression that he would like to have been the father of Rebirthing. In fact, in the 1970's he came near to inventing it with his Primal Scream Therapy and his birth trauma work.[16] Chapter 9 of his book *The Primal Scream* could almost be about Rebirthing:

"The technique of deep breathing is used during Primal Therapy to get the patient closer to his feelings... patients reported the differences in their breathing after therapy; only after they had begun to breathe deeply did they understand how shallow their breathing had been previously... Proper breathing should be instinctual.. forcing the Primal patient to breath deeply often helps lift the lid of repression. The result is the emission of explosive force, .. Primal breathing techniques become the via regia to the Pain, unblocking memories along the way... they are the pathway to the unconscious.

It is tempting to minimise the Primal experience as simply a result of the hyperventilation syndrome ..

14 Albery, 1985, pp. 67-83. 15 Orr in Orr and Ray, xvii. 16 See Albery, Chapter 2, pp. 19-66 for a full and interesting discussion of the relationship between Primal Scream therapy and Rebirthing. Pp.41-66 contain a discussion between Albery and Janov, commented upon by Leonard Orr, Eve Jones and Avoda Judith Collignon. The two latter are prominent practitioners of Rebirthing.

In the majority of cases, breathing techniques are either not necessary or rarely used after the first few days of therapy. It must be remembered that it is the Pain we are after and that breathing is one of many devices we use to arrive at it."[17]

The indispensable element in a Rebirthing session is the breathing technique. Janov came near, but did not quite invent Rebirthing, as his last paragraph clearly shows. This makes him very cross, and he blames others for misinforming him:

"When I started out we were told that it was impossible for a person to relive his birth because the nervous system was not sufficiently mature at the time to record usable memories. I discounted the event of birth for years due to that misinformation. We know now that the birth trauma is indeed coded and stored in the nervous system. A whole cottage industry of rebirthers has grown up around my discoveries, leading to the most dangerous kind of charlatanism."[18]

Here Janov tries to claim Rebirthing as his offspring. The fact that he is so very angry about not being recognised as the inventor of Rebirthing tells us how important and how powerful a therapy he thinks Rebirthing is.

For various reasons the Rebirthing method of breathing has become identified with hyperventilation. Orr & Ray claims its importance,[19] yet, not all of the case histories in their book relate the results of Rebirthing to hyperventilation.[20] Leonard & Laut dismiss it as unnecessary in just one paragraph.[21] There are also many passages like the following in both Orr & Ray and Leonard & Laut:

"Rebirthing is primarily a relaxed, continuous breathing rhythm in which the inhale is connected to the exhale in a continuous circle. This rhythm has to be intuitive, because the purpose of the breathing is to breathe life energy as well as air. Breathing life energy cannot be done with a mechanical breathing technique. Energy is the source of the physical body and the universe. The breathing mechanism is a vehicle to reach aliveness, but it is not automatic. spiritual breathing is intuitive, it is an inspiration, not a discipline. The key to success at conscious breathing is softness and gentleness."[22]

I have argued against the use of hyperventilation, which I see

17 Janov, 1973, p.125f. 18 Janov, 1991, p. xii. 19 Orr and Ray, p. 20, 173-179; Albery, Chapter 4, pp.84-120.
20 E.g. Sondra's does (Orr and Ray, xxiif) while Rick's (Orr and Ray, pp.115-123) and Gary's (Orr and Ray, pp.123-138) do not, etc. 21 Leonard and Laut, 51. 22 Orr, in Orr and Ray, xvii.

as a way of raping the unconscious, in my article in Breathe Magazine and in my book.

Perhaps this identification with hyperventilation is the Janov element in Rebirthing's heritage: its Janov gene!

Of course neither Janov nor anyone else invented working with the breath. As long ago as ancient India, Buddhism and Yoga and other disciplines recognised the importance of the breath, and based their methods and techniques for spiritual development upon it.[23]

Many people who have done Rebirthing will recognise some of the experiences described in this passage, such as recognising the type of breathing, breathing in such a way as to experience the whole body and breathing in such a way as to experience joy, etc.

With regard to other ancient methods of using the breath, Gunnel Minett has written about Chinese breathing methods and about Kundalini in her book, *Breath and Spirit : Rebirthing as a healing technique*.[24]

Janov is one potential ancestor of Rebirthing. In the history of psychoanalyis, the importance of the breath as a tool for the release of tension was recognised already by Wilhelm Reich, once an orthodox Freudian,[25] and by his student Alexander Lowen who created Bio-Energetics. Reich and Lowen are also potential ancestors of Rebirthing, at least with regard to the use of the breath in therapy, as are Georg Groddeck, Fritz Perls and other Gestaltists.[26] The ancient Indian methods for spiritual development based upon the breath, which were becoming increasingly widely known in America at the time that Rebirthing was invented are other potential ancestors. Thus, with regard to the use of the breath in therapy, we may conclude that Rebirthing has a very respectable pedigree.

2. Rebirthing and the birth trauma
Rebirthing is particularly connected with recovering memories of the birth trauma.

"The word Rebirthing was originally used because we used redwood hot tubs to stimulate birth memories and people literally rewrote their birth scripts in the subconscious. A hot tub is a simulated womb."[27]

23 See further the Buddhist breathing exercise described in Joy Manné's lecture in chapter one. 24 Pp. 37–49. 25 Brown, 1964, p. 100. 26 See Abbondio, Chapter Les Psychothérapies centrées sur le corps, pp. 9 - 15. 27 Orr in Orr and Ray, xvii, xx–xxiv.

Rebirthing recognises the importance of the birth trauma in the formation of character and in its influence over the way people live their lives.

"The purpose of Rebirthing is to remember and re-experience one's birth; to relive it physiologically, psychologically, and spiritually the moment of one's first breath and release the trauma of it. The process begins the transformation of the subconscious impression of birth from one of primal pain to one of pleasure. the effects on life are immediate. Negative energy patterns held in the mind and body start to dissolve. 'Youthing' replaces aging and life becomes more fun. It is learning how to fill the physical body with divine energy on a practical daily basis."[28]

The potential parent of birth trauma psychology is Wilhelm Rank, one of Freud's early followers, who had the theory that all neurosis originates in the trauma of birth.[29] Orr himself admits admiration for Nandor Fodor, a New York analyst influenced by Rank,[30] whose book, The Search for the Beloved, he describes as "the best book written so far about birth trauma".[31] D. W. Winnicott also took seriously the influence of the type of birth a baby has upon her or his future life and problems.[32] During the last fifteen or twenty years, research into the life, functioning and capacities of the baby from conception onwards has increased[33] and goes on increasing.[34] I do not know how it is possible for anyone who has read this research to have any doubt at all that conception, gestation and birth influence the life of the human being. On the subject of birth trauma psychology, Rebirthing has a respectable pedigree, and many brothers and sisters.

As among the practitioners of all therapies, there are black sheep in the family. These should not be the excuse to execute the whole family, nor - if you will forgive me - to throw the very promising, healthy baby away with the bath water! When Yapko refers to "a therapy called Rebirthing and reparenting .. which involved guiding the individual back in time in order to relive the process of being born"[35] or to "a therapeutic process commonly called Rebirthing in which a therapist tells the client she "must have (had) a traumatic birth", he is scape-goating or gossiping and this is disappointing in an otherwise remarkably

28 Orr and Ray, 71. 29 Rank (1924), see Brown, 1964, p.52-54. 30 Brown, 1964, p.54. 31 Albery, 1985 p. 64. 32 Winnicott, 1958, cited in Abbondio, 1994, p.7. 33 See Albery, 1985, pp. 121-148. Abbondio, 1994, pp. 34-41. 34 See e.g. Pre- and Perinatal Psychology Journal and Primal Health Research among others. 35 Yapko, 1994 : 62.

sensitive, intelligent and well-balanced book. All therapies that work with the birth trauma, or which 'guide' clients back to their birth trauma or to anything else are not Rebirthing, or hypnosis, or Voice Dialogue, or Freudian analysis, etc., nor does every qualified Rebirther necessarily or invariably use Rebirthing to 'guide' the client back to her/his birth trauma, or anywhere else for that matter.

3. Rebirthing and regression
Regression, not only to the birth trauma but also to other childhood traumas is a fundamental part of the Rebirthing experience.

"If people experience their birth in Rebirthing, they may go on to re-experience various periods of infancy which are wrought with feelings of helplessness and hopelessness. These periods can last for weeks and are sometimes accompanied by symptoms ..." [36]

Regression is known to take place during psychoanalysis and during almost every other psychotherapy. Regression means going back to a painful event that took place in the past and that has been forgotten or repressed so that it comes back into consciousness on all levels and in full detail. The remembering can involve re-experiencing the event in detail including physical pain and other symptoms, hearing again the sounds that are part of the memory, etc. Regression can also mean going back to an infantile way of functioning. Regression is an essential part of therapies that believe that painful experiences that are unconscious need to become conscious so that their influence can be integrated and the individual become free of it. Some therapies take a positive attitude towards regression and find it empowering. Others take a negative view and find it dis-empowering. One may deduce from this that judgements about the usefulness of regression as a psychotherapeutic experience depend upon the theories, the school and, above all, upon the competence of the practitioner to work with this phenomenon and the efficiency of the technique for dealing with it, rather than upon a solid theoretical basis.

There are therapies today which are abusing the capacity for regression by inducing it under unreliable conditions. The book

36 Orr and Ray, 95.

True Stories of False Memories by Eleanor Goldstein,and Kevin Farmer cites examples of people being persuaded that they had been sexually abused during hypnotherapy or under the influence of a supposed 'truth drug'. The memories that these particular forms of induced regression are supposed to give access to are increasingly considered unreliable due to their vulnerability to influence by the therapist.[37]

The ubiquity of the phenomenon of regression in therapy is one further element that puts the erstwhile orphan, Rebirthing, into a family of therapies, a family which, in the case of this subject too seems to include several black sheep![38]

With regard to regression in therapy, the Rebirthing method has something important to offer.

Historically, birth memories were induced in Rebirthing, either through the use of sleeping bags to stimulate the womb experience[39] or through reading Leboyer[40] or through strong, connected breathing with a snorkel in a hot tub. This is quite unnecessary.[41] In fact, all the client has to do is to put her or his attention on their breathing, in the neutral manner described in the Buddhist text.

As he breathes in a long breath he recognises that he is breathing in a long breath; as he breathes out a long breath, he recognises that he is breathing out a long breath. As he breathes in a short breath he recognises that he is breathing in a short breath; as he breathes out a short breath, he recognises that he is breathing out a short breath, and feelings in the body, memories and thoughts will become conscious. They will become conscious of their own accord without the use of suggestion. Without any suggestion or coercion, the body will find the breathing rhythm that is most conducive to the integration of the experience that is coming into consciousness.

I have called this minimal method of working with the breath Gentle Rebirthing to distinguish it from Traditional Rebirthing, which is how I describe the Rebirthing that is based on strong connected breathing and hyperventilation.[42] Some clients have to be taught to be aware of what is going on in their mind and body, in the same way as people have to be taught to meditate. In these cases regressions do not take place until the client has competence in self-awareness. This makes this way of working

37 There has been a discussion of this in The Therapist, Volume 2, Nos. 1 and 2, 1994. See also New Scientist, 23 July 1994.
38 See Yapko, 1994. 39 E.G. Orr and Ray, xxi. 40 E.g. Orr and Ray, 124. 41 Manné, 1994; Manné, 1997, Part VII.
42 See Manné, 1994 and Manné, forthcoming, Part VII.

very safe. When we trust the unconscious and do not try to manipulate or to coerce it, it will open up and reveal its secrets in a balanced and healthy way so that the integration that the client is capable of can occur.[43]

In the context of regression, Rebirthing, especially Gentle Rebirthing[44] is solidly part of the family of therapies that work well with this phenomenon.

4. Rebirthing and the repetition compulsion

I have said[45] that those of Freud's ideas that are good and useful are now so much a part of our way of thinking that they have become part of our psychological common sense. This is certainly true of aspects of his observation of the compulsion to repeat.

Freud noticed a compulsion to repeat in normal people,

"all of whose relationships have the same outcome: such as the benefactor who is abandoned in anger after a time by each of his protégés, however much they may otherwise differ from one another, and who thus seems doomed to taste all the bitterness of ingratitude; or the man whose friendships all end in betrayal by his friend; or the man who time after time in the course of his life raises someone else into a position of great private or public authority and then, after a certain interval, himself upsets that authority and replaces him by a new one; or, again, the lover each of whose love affairs with a woman passes through the same phases and reaches the same conclusion."[46]

In these cases the compulsion to repeat is related to active behaviour, but Freud noticed that it also occurs as a passive experience, over which a person has no influence. He cites the case of "the woman who married three successive husbands each of whom fell ill soon afterwards and had to be nursed by her on their death-beds."[47]

The compulsion to repeat occurs in the transference.[48] This means - and I do not know whether Freud said this or not, but enough analysts of all descriptions have observed this[49] - that it will also occur in the counter-transference except in those rare practitioners who have gone beyond projection.[50]

We now know that the compulsion to repeat causes family

43 "The unconscious - that is to say, the repressed - offers no resistance whatever to the efforts of the treatment. Indeed, it itself has no other endeavour than to break through the pressure weighing down on it and force its way either to consciousness or to a discharge through some real action." Freud, 1920, p.189. 44 See Manné, 1994, 1997. 45 Manné, 1997.
46 Freud, 1920, p.292. Freud discusses the compulsion to repeat in terms of the pleasure principle. 47 Op.cit. p.293.
48 Op.cit. p. 291. 49 Myers, 1992; Siegel and Lowe, 1993. 50 See the section on Projection in Manné, forthcoming.

problems such as sexual and other abuse to repeat over generations, just as genes cause families to be predisposed to certain illnesses.

Rebirthing recognises the compulsion to repeat and takes a practical approach to it through the breathing method, through relationship work and through exercises. The way the theory is presented can be very clear, if simplistic, or it can belong to what Albery politely calls The Wilder Fringes.[51]

The compulsion to repeat is explained in the Rebirthing maxim 'Thought is Creative'. What this means in Rebirthing terms is that "Your thoughts always produce results! .. Your positive thoughts produce positive results for you, and your negative thoughts produce negative results."[52] The compulsion to repeat is treated first of all through becoming aware of the negative thoughts that are causing the unproductive situations and events to repeat and then through the use of autosuggestion in the form of Affirmations:

"An affirmation is a positive thought that you choose to immerse in your consciousness to produce a desired result."[53]

"An affirmation is basically a good thought to hold in your mind."[54]

So, for example, Sondra Ray had a tendency to smash up her car once a month, a pattern which she was unable to stop. Leonard Orr gave her the affirmation: "I now have a safe driving consciousness" to work on. Sondra stopped smashing up her car.[55] Both of the early books contain abundant information on how to use affirmations.[56] Affirmations do not have to be used in a superficial or simplistic manner, although they often are. Well used, they are a way of gently and finely performing archaeology on the unconscious and can productively reveal thoughts and beliefs that have been very deeply hidden.[57]

The compulsion to repeat unproductive behaviour patterns that regularly spoil relationships is treated in Sondra Ray's book, *Loving Relationships*. This book contains a great deal of useful information, good advice and exercises, and not too much wilder fringe material.

That what and how we think has a great deal of influence over our lives and causes us to repeat unproductive behaviour patterns has become common knowledge in the almost twenty

51 Albery, 1985, pp. 67-83. 52 Orr and Ray, p.53. 53 Orr and Ray, 65. Their italics. 54 Leonard and Laut, 76. 55 Orr and Ray, 2f. 56 Orr and Ray, 65-69, etc.; Leonard and Laut, 76f, 115-143. 57 See Manné, forthcoming.

years since the first Rebirthing book was published and it was not new then.[58] Combined with techniques like creative visualisation, affirmations are now used in almost all of the new therapies and also in medical circumstances: for example, to fight cancer.[59] In its recognition of the compulsion to repeat, Rebirthing has respectable ancestors and, in its way of dealing with it, many siblings.

5. Rebirthing and spiritual development

Rebirthing has from the beginning been connected with spiritual development. Leonard Orr is described by Sondra Ray as someone who read metaphysical books, and who from the beginning gave his students books like *Life and Teaching of the Masters of the Far East* to read.[60]

The energy release is one among very many examples of moving spiritual experiences that happen through Rebirthing. It is described in this way,

"At some point in Rebirthing there is a reconnection to Divine Energy and as a result you may experience vibrating and tingling in your body. It starts in different places in different people and, before Rebirthing is complete, it usually is felt throughout the whole body. This energy reconnects your body to the universal energy by vibrating out tension which is the manifestation of negative mental mass. Negative mental mass can be permanently dissolved by continuing to breathe in a regular rhythm while your body is vibrating and tingling - experiencing your reconnection to the Divine Energy."[61]

All religions and spiritual practices that use the breath in any way in order to attain altered states of consciousness share the parentage of this aspect of Rebirthing. I have quoted from a Theravada Buddhist texts above simply because I happen to know these texts well. Experts on other texts could have found interesting and relevant material from their study and discipline.[62] With regard to its recognition of the importance and indeed the necessity of spiritual experiences, Rebirthing has both ancestors and a pedigree in the literature of many religions and spiritual practices.

What about ancestors in psychology?

58 See Albery, p.19. Orr's exposition of the notion that thoughts are creative also contains similarities to Kelly's Personal Construct Theory. 59 Simonton et al, 1978. 60 Orr and Ray, 19. 61 Orr and Ray, 83; see further 83-87. 62 See e.g. Minett, pp. 37-49.

Historically, As Luckoff et al say, "psychiatry, in its diagnostic classification systems as well as its theory, research, and practice, has tended to either ignore or pathologies the religious and spiritual dimensions of life. ... From Freud's writings through the 1976 report on mysticism by the Group for the Advancement of Psychiatry (GAP), there has been a tendency to associate spiritual experiences with psycho-pathology."[63] Luckoff et al's article documents "the religiosity gap between clinicians and patients," and holds responsible "the inadequate training in religious and spiritual issues (of clinicians), and the role that biological primacy has played in creating insensitivity to these issues." This religiosity gap could be the reason why so many people have turned to the new therapies, and are still turning to the new therapies, that have sprung up during the last twenty or thirty years: the established therapies were not and still are not meeting their needs. Luckoff et al proposed that a new category of 'psycho-religious' or 'psycho-spiritual problems' be included in the DSM-IV[64] and this has now been done.[65] They also propose that professionals be adequately trained to deal with these problems. Rebirthing is an appropriate method for these people to learn and Rebirthers who have had a good training, which includes an adequate knowledge of psychology,[66] are competent to deal with many of these problems.

Despite a general incompetence on the part of psychiatry to deal with the spiritual aspect of human life, the *Journal of Humanistic Psychology* and the *Journal of Transpersonal Psychology* are now well established, and it is in this current that Rebirthing has its ancestors, siblings and descendants.

REBIRTHING'S PEDIGREE

It is actually quite dangerous to be an orphan, as we all know. There is no-one to protect an orphan, and anyone can lay claim to it at any time!

Leonard Orr and Sondra Ray are certainly the literary parents of Rebirthing.

I have shown in this article that, whether its literary parents acknowledge it or not, Rebirthing has a respectable pedigree: it has respectable grandparents and other ancestors in psycho-

63 Luckoff et al, 1992, p.673. 64 Diagnostic and Statistical Manual of Mental Disorders - IV. 65 DSM-IV, Section V62.89 Religious or Spiritual Problem. 66 See Manné, 1997, Part VI.

analysis and in psychotherapy and belongs fully to the family of psychotherapies. Furthermore, it has ancestors in various respectable spiritual disciplines. It has enough family to protect it and to help it to grow up!

Albery said, "There seems to be very little that is original in the main bits that make up the Rebirthing package."[67] I have presented here some of the conceptual ancestors of Rebirthing: psychotherapies and spiritual practices that realise the importance of the breath, that respect the importance of the birth trauma, that acknowledge the importance of regression in the healing of the psyche, that recognise the compulsion to repeat and that appreciate the importance of the development of the spiritual aspects of the human being. In this way I have shown that at least in these aspects Rebirthing has connections to other psychotherapies. To say that there is "very little that is original", as Albery has done, seems to me, however, to be an exaggeration.

Rebirthing makes an original contribution to psychotherapy through its way of working with the breath: not the notorious use of hyperventilation which I reject entirely - although I accept that strong and deep breathing techniques, when well-used and brought in at the appropriate moment in the development process, can lead to important transpersonal experiences[68] - but also, and particularly, its gentle uses.[69] I have argued that Rebirthing is an energy psychotherapy,[70] and it is as an energy psychotherapy that it deals with the phenomena described above in an original, constructive and important way. I will have more to say about how well Rebirthing deals with these phenomena, about Energy Psychotherapy, and about how the competent use of Breathwork, including Rebirthing, constructs an authentic process of psychotherapy which encompasses the full range of personal and spiritual development, from problems that we might call 'Freudian' through experiences that we might call 'Jungian', through the Humanistic to the Transpersonal.[71]

67 Albery, p.19. 68 Manné, 1994, 1997. 69 See the quote above; See also Manne, 1994, 1997. 70 Manne, 1997.
71 See Rowan, 1994, p.7.

BIBLIOGRAPHY

1. Abbondio, Irène (1994), Traumatisme de la naissance et souffle dans la psychologie occidentale : manual de référence à l'usage des Thérapeutes du Souffle. Irène Abbondio, Cité Derrière 4, CH - 1005 Lausanne.

2. Albery, Nicholas (1985), How to feel reborn : varieties of Rebirthing experience - an exploration of Rebirthing and associated primal therapies, the benefits and the dangers, the facts and the fictions. London : Regeneration Press.

3. Brown, J.A.C. (1964), Freud and the Post-Freudians. England : Penguin Books. [1974 ed.]

4. Freud, Sigmund (1920), Beyond the Pleasure Principle, in The Pelican Freud Library, Volume 11, On Metapsychology : the theory of Psychoanalysis. Pelican Books, 1984.

5. DSM IV. Diagnostic and Statistical Manual of Mental Disorders. (1994) American Psychiatric Association : Washington DC.

6. Goldstein, Eleanor and Kevin Farmer (1993), True Stories of False Memories. Florida : SIRS Books.

7. Hillman, James and Michael Ventura (1993), We've had a hundred years of psychotherapy - and the world's getting worse. Harper, San Francisco.

8. Janov, Arthur (1991), The New Primal Scream. London : Abacus. pp.xii.

9. Journal of Transpersonal Psychology, P.O.Box 4437 Stanford, California 94305. 1969-

10. Journal of Humanistic Psychology, Suite 205, 1314 Westwood Boulevard, Los Angeles, CA 90024, USA. 1961-

11. Kelly, George A. (1963), A Theory of Personality : the Psychology of Personal Constructs. New York : W:W: Norton & Company.

12. Leboyer, Frederick (1975), Birth without Violence. London : Wildwood House.

13. Leonard, Jim and Phil Laut (1983), Rebirthing : the science of enjoying all of your life. Berkeley, California : Celestial Arts.

14. Luckoff, David, Franis Lu and Robert Turner (1992), ?Towards a More Culturally Sensitive DSM-IV : Psychoreligious and Psychospiritual Problems. Journal of Nervous and Mental Disease, Vol.180, No.11, November 1992.

15. Manné, Joy (1990), Categories of Sutta in the Pali Nikiyas and their implications for our appreciation of the Buddhist teaching and literature.? Journal of the Pali Text Society, XV, 29-87. See pp. 45, ii; 49, c.

16. (1994), École D'Évolution Personnelle et Spirituelle', in Breathe Magazine, July, August September 1994.

17. (1997), Soul Therapy. Berkeley, California: North Atlantic Books.

18. Maslow, Abraham H. (1968), Towards a Psychology of Being. New York : D. Van Nostrand Company. [2nd ed.], (1971).

19. Minett, Gunnel (1994), Breath and Spirit : Rebirthing as a healing technique. London: The Aquarian Press.

20. Myers, Wayne A. (1992), Shrink Dreams : the secret longings, fantasies, and prejudices of therapists and how they affect their patients. New York : Simon and Schuster.

21. New Scientist, July 23 1994, pp.32-35.

22. Orr, Leonard and Sondra Ray (1977), Rebirthing for the New Age (revised edition 1983). California : Trinity Publications

23. Pre and Perinatal Psychology Journal, Human Sciences Press, Inc., 233 Spring Street, New York, N.Y. 10013 -1578.

24. Primal Health Research, Primal Health Research Centre, 59 Roderick Road, London NW3 2NP. The editor of this journal is Dr. Michel Odent, a leading influence with regard to gentle childbirth practices.

25. Rank, Otto (1924) The Trauma of Birth. : New York : Dover Publications, 1993 edition.

26. Rowan, John (1994), A Guide to Humanistic Psychology. Britain : the Association for Humanistic Psychology. [First edition 1987]

27. Siegel, Stanley & Ed Lowe, Jr. (1993), The Patient who cured his Therapist : and other tales of therapy. USA : Plume (Penguin).

28. Simonton, O. Carl, Stephanie Matthews-Simonton, and James Creighton, (1978), Getting Well Again : A step-by-step, self-help guide to overcoming cancer for patients and their families. Los Angeles : J. P. Tarcher.

29. The Therapist, Journal of the European Therapy Studies Institute, 1 Lovers Meadow, Chalvington, Hailsham, East Sussex, GB - BN27 3TE10.

30. Winnicott, D.W. (1958), Birth Memories, Birth Trauma and Anxiety 1949-54. London : Collected Papers, 1958.

31. Yapko, Michael D. (1994), Suggestions of Abuse : true and false memories of childhood sexual trauma. New York : Simon and Schuster, 1994.

The Role of Carbon Dioxide in a Rebirthing Session

SERGEI GORSKY

Sergei Gorsky is one of the key organisers in the Russian human potential movement. During the last years, Sergei and his colleagues have carried out extensive research on the medical, physiological and psychological aspects of various forms of Breathwork.

There is one very serious question that Rebirthers have asked and been asked all these years that they haven't had the adequate answer to. It is the question of hyperventilation and Rebirthing. Without false humility, I can now say that I think I may have an answer to that.

Let us start by taking a look at what happens with the carbon dioxide level during a Rebirthing session in terms of the dynamic of carbon dioxide percentage. To start with in a session it actually drops - for the first 10-15 minutes. Then it starts going up and at some point it reaches the initial level. Then it goes higher than the initial level and continues to go up during the session and for at least another half-hour after the actual session.

Altogether this is a very flattering result for Rebirthers, since it in effect means that Rebirthing does not cause a loss of carbon dioxide, which is something we have been blamed for frequently over a number of years. The carbon dioxide level only drops a little in the beginning. This may happen because the Rebirther is unprofessional or that the Rebirthee has a high resistance level or in special cases like Holotropic Breathwork that is designed to cause initial hyperventilation. But regardless of how much it drops in the beginning it very quickly resumes its initial level and finishes at the end of a session, usually around 20 to 30 percent higher than the initial value. This is very important. It is probably a key result within the body and I will spend the main part of this lecture to try to show you why this is important.

Why is carbon dioxide such a crucial function in the body?

And why do we get a 20 to 30 percent increase after a Rebirthing session?

To establish the real function of the carbon dioxide we really need to start from the very basics and look at the way the oxygen takes from the outside air into the cells in our body. It is a fairly complicated path. First of all the oxygen has two transfer stations on its way. The first is when we breathe in and the oxygen goes through the membranes in the lungs into the bloodstream, using the same method as your average water purifier - a method called osmosis. Because of the difference in the partial pressure in the inhaled air and the blood, the oxygen enters the bloodstream in the membranes of the lungs. In the bloodstream, the oxygen molecules get connected to haemoglobin molecules and form a nice unity. It then travels in the bloodstream together with the haemoglobin and enters every cell of the body.

Here we have the second transfer station. The haemoglobin disassociates and releases the oxygen to the cell at the same time as it takes away the waste products of the metabolism in the form of carbon dioxide. It is a fairly complicated process which has the end result that every cell will receive haemoglobin and liberated oxygen, both essential for the cell to function. In order for this reaction to take place it is necessary to have a certain level of carbon dioxide dissolved in the bloodstream. We need carbon dioxide as a catalyst for this reaction. If there is no carbon dioxide the haemoglobin will never release oxygen to the cell. This is why carbon monoxide is so dangerous. Carbon monoxide is the gas that people get poisoned by if for instance, their heating system does not work properly. It attaches itself to the haemoglobin so that the haemoglobin cannot deliver oxygen to the cells. The brain then dies because it does not get enough oxygen.

The disassociation of haemoglobin i.e. effectiveness of this reaction is directly proportional to the level of carbon dioxide. This process is called the carbon-oxygen exchange and it is one of the most basic chemical reactions in our body.

Who can guess the carbon dioxide level when we are born? At birth and in the womb we have a maximum level of carbon dioxide, which for the sake of argument, I will give the figure of nine. Nature gives us the most effective kick-start we could possibly wish for. We spend the first nine months in the womb, in an ideal biological situation. The carbon-oxygen exchange in the body functions in the most ideal way.

What is our normal level throughout life? It is around half of what we had at birth, or around five. When we die it drops to around three. Or rather the other way around - when the carbon dioxide level drops to below three - we die, we cannot function as a body anymore. We need at least 3 percent to have an adequate supply of oxygen. If not we have the same reaction as with carbon monoxide poisoning. We have all the oxygen we need but it never reaches the cells in our brain. The haemoglobin is unable to deliver it.

So this whole story about the healing breath is not a story about oxygen. All the nice legends about oxygenating the blood or oxygenating the brain are just that - legends. Rebirthing is not about oxygenation. Rebirthing is about increasing the effectiveness of using the oxygen. We have enough oxygen in our bloodstream. In fact we have more oxygen that we can use anyway. The problem is that if we don't have enough carbon dioxide we cannot use all this oxygen effectively. The cells simply do not receive all the oxygen that is available.

Now let's move on quickly from birth till around two or three years of age where we have lost about half of the carbon dioxide level. What we lose together with this is very interesting. Let's see where the chain of cause and effect will lead us.

Together with losing carbon dioxide we lose the acid-alkaline balance in the body. We become acid. We all know how important it is to eat a healthy diet in order to have a healthy alkaline balance in the body. But even more important than to eat healthily is to breathe healthily. In fact even if my diet is very healthy and my breathing pattern is not I will still be acidic. The acid shift suppresses the immune system. And when the immune system is suppressed we are open to disease. It may be psychosomatic disease or some kind if virus infection that the immune system cannot resist effectively.

By losing 50 percent of our carbon dioxide level we lose 50 percent of our immunity right away. And more interestingly - our life expectancy is directly proportional to the level of carbon dioxide. So when we lose half of our carbon dioxide we lose half of our life expectancy right away. We could live on average 150-160 years if we remain on our highest carbon dioxide. Certain research is being done that deals with the fact that the tissues of the body need a certain number of cycles of blood in the circulation and that the higher the percentage of carbon dioxide the slower or longer the cycle. We don't need to pump the same level of blood to supply the same amount of oxygen. Our heart and inner organs become more relaxed and we still get enough. In other words, during the first two or three years we literally lose a lot of vitality or life force from our body.

The next question is how we lose carbon dioxide? The answer is very simple. We breathe it out. We breathe out all the precious carbon dioxide. Which in itself is a paradox since we still are taught at school that we breathe out a lot of bad carbon dioxide. We exhale to get rid of this awful and bad carbon dioxide that we don't need for our body.

But the line here is very subtle and may in fact also be the start of our problem. This may in fact be why we start to build up tension in our exhale. In every exhale we breathe out a little bit more than we are supposed to and eventually the balance starts to shift from nine, which is the most effective level to four or five which is quite close to three. And we all know by now what that means. The World Health Organisation's standard is 5.5.

Research shows that we breathe too little. In order to breathe fully we need to have six or seven. But why do we exhale that much? Why do we breathe out all this carbon dioxide? The answer to this leads us to make a connection with our consciousness and the shape of our breathing pattern. This is a very interesting fact that, in my view, Rebirthers don't pay enough attention to. Human beings breathe in a way that no other beings on this earth do. People breathe in a totally different way than animals do. I am not talking about breathing through the mouth or nose, although this may be related. I am talking more about the shape of the breathing.

When a baby is born it breathes exactly like animals. You can observe how a baby breathes during the first two or three months and compare it with animals. The newborn baby breathes in a totally natural way. Then, as we grow up, the breathing pattern changes and moves gradually away from the natural breathing pattern. In the end the only time we return to our natural breathing pattern is when we sleep, when we die or when we do Rebirthing. The breathing is probably the system in our body that is the least protected from our emotional state of consciousness. No other system can be influenced by our emotions or our will the way the breathing can. We cannot change the temperature in our body. We have to work hard to learn to change the temperature of the body, if we ever will learn it. We cannot change the heartbeat much. We cannot change our basic metabolism. But with the breathing we can do whatever we want. We can slow it down and even stop it completely. It is very much affected by our conscious will and it is also very affected by our emotional will.

Breathing is a very vulnerable mechanism. It is very connected with our current state of consciousness. The higher the move in a freer flow, the higher the brain frequency and the more distorted the breathing pattern gets. The only time we breathe naturally is when we are in delta brainwaves. This is to say when we are born and during the first year of our lives, when we are in a very deep sleep, when we are in a very deep coma or when we die. The higher the frequency of the brain the more distorted the breathing pattern. The breathing pattern is influenced by all the tension and by all the conflicts we store in our subconscious and conscious mind.

As a comment here I could mention that very intense stress, of the kind that can be caused by an accident of some kind, may actually alter the breathing and restore a very natural breathing pattern. This happens quite frequently. But to find out why this happens we will have to look at each individual situation and how a person reacts to it.

What is this natural breathing pattern that we are talking about? If we watch a newborn baby or an animal we will notice that the inhale will happen with one steady muscle movement, which is not too tense and still quite strong. From the very beginning to the very end there is steady muscle tension, like a pump. Then at the very end at the peak, it is like a miracle takes place. There is no pause, no break, not even like the slightest stop. The baby or the animal completely relaxes the breathing muscles and the exhales takes place with different dynamics. The exhale is never caused by muscle tension. The exhale simply happens through gravity and difference in gas pressure inside the ribcage and outside. The exhale is slow and relaxed and almost stops at the end. It comes to almost a pause but it never breaks. It never stops completely. The very last moment when we think it will stop, there is another strong and steady inhale and then another totally relaxed exhale. That is the natural breathing pattern.

You may notice that this is very close to how you breathe in a Rebirthing session. This is the pattern that is natural for the deep archetypal and transpersonal areas of our consciousness. This is usually how we breathe when we go into trance or into extended consciousness. There are of course different instructions for the breathing in a Rebirthing session but in general this is how we breathe. I would also say that the Holotropic breathing session is slightly different and has the furthest deviation from the pattern I have described. This may also be why Holotropic Breathwork reaches the deepest decrease in carbon dioxide.

How do adults usually breathe? I say usually because I don't want to use the word normally here. Our inhale is not steady. There are all kinds of stops and pulls. It kind of consists of several attempts to breathe. This is actually an indication of stress and conflict. There are even certain devices that can estimate the level of stress by the constriction in the breathing pattern. The more disturbance in the breath, the higher the level of stress. It is also very difficult to shift from inhale to exhale. The animal just relaxes all the muscles to exhale. The paradox is that the human has to make an effort to start to exhale. Instead of relaxing we make an extra effort to turn inhale into exhale. We can never ever relax completely on the exhale. So the exhale also becomes stressed and distorted. The inhale becomes longer than in natural breathing and the exhale becomes shorter than natural. The natural breath is probably two to one i.e. the exhale is approximately twice as long as the inhale. Again when people are under stress they have a short and tensed exhale.

This is how we get rid of carbon dioxide. We produce it inside as a product of our metabolism and release it with the exhale. When we exhale more than we inhale we lose carbon dioxide. We need to keep more of it than we produce otherwise we disturb the carbon dioxide exchange in the body.

Now we reconstruct the whole chain of cause and effect. It starts with fragmentation of the consciousness or an increased conflict in our personality. This leads to distortion of the natural breathing pattern. The breathing corresponds with the fragmentation of consciousness, i.e. when we are getting in conflict with our consciousness in our personality.

There are two breathing centres in the brain. One is closer to the frontal lobe and is younger in evolutionary terms. It is more connected with our personality or the modern levels of consciousness. The other is very deep inside of what is called the limbic system of the brain. The very part of the brain which covers the pituitary, the hypothalamus and the pineal glands. The area of the brain that in the last century has been named the locus of consciousness and where the brain has most separation or fragmentation of consciousness.

There is a very important and beautiful book published by Ernest Lawrence Rossi, a friend and colleague of Milton Erikson.

It puts together research from the last fifteen years of the way various states of consciousness affect the body down to the genetic level. It is priceless for any Rebirther or Breathworker and even though it is written from the position of Ericsonian hypnosis it is very connected. The title of the book is "The Psychobiology of Mind-Body Healing - New concepts of therapeutic hypnosis."

It shows how the state of consciousness through the limbic system affects four major regulatory systems in our body. The immune system, the endocrine system, the autonomic nervous system and the neuro-peptides. When there is a conflict in such a deep level of our consciousness it affects the whole body immediately. And it affects the breathing first because the breathing centre is right near the centres in the limbic system that are responsible for our emotions and suppressed emotions. Every time we have tensions in our subconscious it directly affects the breathing pattern. On the other side, when we change the breathing pattern, when we make it more natural and more relaxed, it affects very deep structures of the brain and not only brings out old suppressed emotion or material but also integrates it. It allows us to relax and integrate suppressed emotions and material.

Since I am not trained in the medical profession I personally can't go much deeper into this but if you want to go deeper into this subject there are many good books that will describe how these centres function and interact in more detail. There is also some new research in Russia, which I have only had a chance to glance through so far, that shows the changes in the biochemistry of the brain during a breathing session. These are changes that actually can transform the brain and most likely be transferred through the genetic material to our children.

When we change the breathing pattern it effects the breathing centre within the limbic brain. The breathing centre is situated quite close to the emotional centre. The limbic system is where we store all the layers of emotional material. First of all a change in the breathing patterns helps to bring emotional material into our awareness and secondly it creates delta and theta brain waves which makes our integrative ability much higher than in everyday life. This way it gives us access to early childhood traumas but also our early childhood ability to integrate oneness.

But let us now return to the breathing pattern. The first part in this sequence is that carbon dioxide goes down. Once the breathing pattern is distorted we start to breathe out carbon dioxide.

The fourth step in our chain is distortion of the carbon-oxygen exchange. It is a very basic reaction for our body. It becomes less and less affected. Our cells start receiving less oxygen and the whole system needs to work harder to supply the body and in particular the brain with the oxygen it needs.

The fifth step is a shift towards being acidic. The homeostasis of the human body gets distorted and we gradually become acidic. That in turn suppresses the immunity, which goes down.

So there is a direct connection between the state of our consciousness and the state of our body and that connection goes through the breathing. That is the major importance of the breath. The breath is literally a way to connect spirit and body. Soul and body. The breath is one of the channels connecting the state of our consciousness with the state of our body. In the chain I am presenting here we can also take a look at the remedies that human being have come up with over thousands of years, how they work and at what level.

Unfortunately we will detect that most of modern medicine works with the very end of the chain. Even if we replace one or heal one symptom or do something at the end of the chain without changing the rest the body, we will simply develop another symptom, and another, and another and so on. To deal with the immunity or the acidic shift through diet, exercise or other activities is a little bit better. Still we only deal with the steps 5, 6 and 7 in our chain. Even if it is a bit better it is still not the answer. The only answer is to transform the consciousness. That is the radical answer.

There are a lot of therapies, techniques and methods aimed at changing our consciousness but most of them don't use the breath. They use it only in some kind of processes and very few put one and two together. Rebirthing is unique in that way that it focuses on the two steps in the beginning of the chain. Not only does it use the natural breathing pattern which is healing in itself, it uses our natural breathing pattern to integrate consciousness. A lot of the additional work in Rebirthing is also immediately directed to integrate fragments of our consciousness, or of our sub-personalities.

This is why Rebirthers continuously adopt achievements in humanistic and transpersonal psychology. There are a lot of great methods in Psycho-synthesis, Psychodrama and Gestalt that falls into this category but they don't use breathing. Once we combine them with breathing they become ten or a hundred times more effective.

I have already told you that the Russian research into Rebirthing has established that carbon dioxide goes up after a session. This is a very good indication of when a session is completed or integrated. I can even show you a very simple way to check how long we can make the pause in our breathing after a session. What you do is simply to measure the time you can hold your breath comfortably after a complete exhale. Not after the inhale, but after the exhale.

In the beginning you can usually hold your breath for about ten to fifteen seconds. It is said that when you can hold it for a minute you are a totally healthy person. This pause is directly proportional to the level of carbon dioxide. You check before and after a session. After the session it will usually be 20 or 30 % higher. If it is not it means that your client has not completed the session and may need to breathe a little bit longer. If it does not increase after the session or if it decreases it means that we still are in the process of integration. This increase obviously doesn't stay for a long time. We know that it goes up for at least half an hour after the session. We also know that people who do Rebirthing sessions on a continuous basis, that is to say at least once a week, start to improve their carbon dioxide level. This will improve their immunity system.

It is also possible through psychological tests to directly check the level of conflict or fragmentation. People who do Rebirthing on a continuous basis show improvement in all seven steps. Their consciousness becomes more integrated. The breathing pattern becomes more natural. People who do Rebirthing start to breathe differently. This is one result of Rebirthing. It is also one reason why we call Rebirthing Free Breathing in Russia. You are liberated from the dictatorship of the ego. The ego is not a totalitarian controller anymore and the breathing returns back to natural breathing and becomes liberated. So 'liberated breath' as Rebirthing is called in Swedish is a very precise term for it.

This also provides answers for our most common questions. One question is why Rebirthing has such an unspecific influence on the body. There are hundreds of documented cases of healing from all forms of psychological and physical illness even to severe forms such as cancer. So Rebirthing has a very unspecific general effect on the body. It does not just affect the liver, lungs or immunity. It affects the whole body. Here we can start to see answers to why this is the case when we note that the efforts of Rebirthing go beyond or precede every specific disorder by going into the carbon-oxygen exchange which is the basic physiological reaction in the body. It also goes to integration of consciousness.

The chain I have tried to illustrate also answers another of our questions, namely, why Rebirthing sometimes is a strain on the body and why it sometimes isn't. At the end of the chain - the physical disease - the body has a certain level of inertia. Here even a certain increase of the immunity would not be able to compensate the physical changes that take place in severe illnesses such as cancer.

Sometimes Rebirthing does not bring enough increase in order to heal a specific physical condition. Because the influence of Rebirthing is so unspecific it cannot be measured in a certain increase in liver, lung or heart activity. Often the increase in immunity is not enough to heal the far stages of the disease. But fortunately enough the efforts of Rebirthing can be noticed not only on the body level but also the mental and emotional level.

It is not a big problem to lose some carbon dioxide at the beginning of a session. What happens when we start to lose carbon dioxide is that our consciousness starts to mobilise itself and the deeper levels of our consciousness start to think that this stupid ego is again putting everything through a dangerous experience. This is one reason why people in Holotropic breathing go through transpersonal experiences. They start to exhale vigorously and something inside them soon realises that this is a dangerous occupation. We cannot allow the ego to blow away all the carbon dioxide and allow the body to die prematurely. So it decides to take over and make the body realise how the world really is. This is how we get extended experiences.

A lot of Shamanic and Sufi technologies are using this breathing with extensive exhale simply to activate the deep primal survival mechanisms. This mechanism is activated when deep levels of consciousness take over and want to become enlightened. Then the breathing pattern changes and the carbon dioxide start to raise. It is like a pendulum. If we push the pendulum towards one side it automatically also goes towards the other. So let's remember that the reason the level drops in the beginning is the exhale and the exhale can be done consciously as a tool to reach the three percent level or as a tool to activate deeper levels of consciousness or it can be done unconsciously because of resistance in the client, or in the therapist or in both.

Since it is very difficult to relax the exhale completely, if you are unfamiliar with Rebirthing emotional material starts to surface. It usually creates a certain level of tension and this tension in turn starts to bring down the level of carbon dioxide. In a very gentle session there is almost no decrease but then again not much is happening.

If we finally return to hyperventilation, which I started out this lecture by mentioning, it takes place during a breathing session - and this is something that both Rebirthers and the unprepared client have to face.

Yet at the same time it has to be mentioned that the visible effect of hyperventilation - the cramps that may occur during a session - can be changed dramatically in a split second. The reason for this is that the chemical reaction that takes place in the body is very quick. When consciousness shifts, the hypothalamus and pituitary glands can effect the blood stream and the big portions of endorphins and neuro-peptides and other chemical reactions of which I hardly remember the name can shift very quickly and change the chemistry of the body within a split second.

But let's be very precise here. Hyperventilation happens often in a Rebirthing session but Rebirthing does not cause hypocapnia. Hyperventilation is the process that make us lose carbon dioxide and during a Rebirthing session there is a certain loss in the short term but not in the long term. Hypocapnia on the other hand is losing carbon dioxide over a long period of time which is a disease caused by people who over a period of time constantly force the exhale and as a consequence get depleted of carbon dioxide. In the long run this leads to a run down of the bodily functions and can lead to very serious illness because the immune system gets very damaged. Nicholas Albery talks about this in his book and claims that Rebirthing may actually lead to chronic hyperventilation syndrome. And he is right about this that it is not short term hyperventilation that is the problem but rather long term chronic hyperventilation whereas he is wrong assuming that Rebirthing leads to long term hyperventilation and makes people breathe in short forced exhales both in and between sessions.

My argument is that we can respond to his claim by saying no, this is not the case. The level of carbon dioxide goes up over a period of time and the five or ten minutes of hyperventilation that may occur in the beginning of a session does not make much difference unless you are a suffering from epilepsy or another similar illness in which case we have to be very careful of the breathing pattern.

In a Holotropic breathing session for instance it starts with a very long preparation before a session with very deep relaxation. This is very important because the relaxation in the body prepares the breathing centres to handle the decrease of carbon dioxide without affecting the body too much. So the best way to do a Rebirthing session, and especially if you intend to do an intense breathing session is to have a long nice and gentle relaxation period before you start the actual session. That will make your breath become more effective.

But let's move over and talk a little bit about the mental side of things. To estimate the change of attitude the best way is to work with the context we have through life. What I mean here is for instance that we all have a certain idea of how warm or cold this room is. This is the type of context I refer to here. So taking your average person on the street, the way they deal with their contexts will express two key qualities. Their context will usually be one dimensional or dualistic. They will perceive the world as good/bad, right/wrong, pleasant/unpleasant, black/ white and so on in a linear context.

Another quality will be that this context will be within reach - I'd rather be right than happy. This is usually a starting point for the average client. They prefer to be right more than they prefer to be happy.

So this is how our clients start. It may seem unimportant but we can look at world history and notice that suffering, pain and even wars happen, not because of money, land or natural resources. The largest cause of world suffering is difference in contexts or beliefs. People who believe in Jesus have felt completely justified to kill people who believe in Allah. All religious, national and cultural wars occur simply because of a linear difference in context. Still most of the problems on earth derive from difference in beliefs. This is a very important fact which actually is really easy to check in a psychological test. The good news for Breathwork is that it actually helps to shift the linear to be more multidimensional. Instead of perceiving the world as good, bad, right or wrong, in terms of linear perception, people start to develop multidimensional perception. They start to perceive different aspects of oneness at the same time. They don't judge the world the same way anymore. This happens not only on their conscious level, which is easy, but also on a deep subconscious level, which can be established in psychological tests. They also develop a flexibility in their contexts.

The context is like a frame for the picture and usually we walk around carrying four or five favourite frames with us, where we try to fit in everything that happens to us. Instead we start to customise our frame to fit every single event. The context also starts to have less and less importance and the content of each experience starts to become more important than the context. People start to perceive life directly without the mediator of the belief system. It is still there but its role is diminished. That in turn will decrease pain and suffering. You probably all know that the carriers of most pain are religious fundamentalists, communists and fascists. People with the most rigid belief systems. Rebirthing dissolves the rigidity of our belief systems.

BIBLIOGRAPY

1. Rossi, Ernest Lawrence: *The Psychobiology of Mind-Body Healing - New concepts of therapeutic hypnosis*, Norton, New York, 1986

2. Albery, Nicholas (1985), *How to feel reborn: varieties of Rebirthing experience - an exploration of Rebirthing and associated primal therapies, the benefits and the dangers, the facts and the fictions.* London: Regeneration Press.

Chapter 3

Breathwork and Spirituality

Transference and Counter-Transference in Spiritual and Transpersonal Work

KYLEA TAYLOR

Kylea Taylor MS, MFT has written numerous articles and given presentations, both in the U.S. and abroad, on her unique model of ethics for caregivers. She is a staff trainer for the Grof Transpersonal Training and author of "The Ethics of Caring: Honoring the Web of Life in Our Professional Healing Relationships" and "The Breathwork Experience: Exploration and Healing in Nonordinary States of Consciousness". Since 1991 she has been Editor of The Inner Door, the newsletter for the Association for Holotropic Breathwork International. She has been counselling in the addictions recovery field since 1970. She is a licensed Marriage and Family Therapist and consultant/ trainer in a private practice in Santa Cruz, CA

As I grow older family becomes more important. This feels like another branch of a family that I didn't know I had. A work family where we all share the same values, that share the same kind of techniques and are working in the same way with people. So I am really delighted to be here. The work family that I came from is about five hundred Holotropic Breathwork certified people[1] that have taken a training with Stanislav Grof and are doing workshops all over the world. I am an officer of the Board and editor of the newsletter of the Association of Holotropic Breathwork International. Because I came here, I can get information from you and take it back to that community. I think one of the questions we get a lot in our workshops from people is "what is Rebirthing?" Is Holotropic Breathwork anything like Rebirthing? Most of us really do not know the answer to that question first-hand. That is one of the reasons I wanted to come to the conference and find out about Rebirthing and other techniques.

This topic I am going to cover tonight is not really about Breathwork *per se*. It is about the profound relationship we have

---

1 In the year 2000 there are about 700 Holotropic Breathwork facilitators worldwide who have been certified by the Grof Transpersonal Training following nine weeks of residential training, 10 consultations, and several apprenticeships, over a period of not less than two years.

with our clients in any therapeutic situation. My belief is that ethics is really at the heart of any therapeutic relationship. A lot of us have had ethics courses added on to our courses at school. At the end of a counselling course in school we get taught about the law, about professional codes, and it is all about what not to do wrong so that we do not get sued by clients.

This is not the kind of ethics that I want to talk about tonight. I really believe that ethics is about having a right relationship with clients in the Buddhist sense of that word right livelihood, right relationship. When we get into trouble in our relationship with clients it is when we get off track with that right relationship and each of those examples are examples of an ethical problem.

The core issues in ethics are money, sex, and power. This is what all the professional codes have been written about, and they are issues that resonate at the very core of our being. Sex, money, and power are the things that we greatly desire and most are afraid of. But there is also, what I have identified, spiritual longings that are even more at the core of our inner being and that can also cause problems and get us off track because of our own fears and desires. Spiritual longing often arises in the transpersonal work that we do, working with clients in what Stanislav Grof calls *nonordinary states of consciousness*, otherwise known as altered states of consciousness. These states bring up, as you know, very powerful and intense core issues. Not only in the client, but also in the person who is working with the clients.

The approach that I am writing about and teaching about is kind of a new/old approach. It is a more spiritual approach. It involves right relationship and doing no harm, which is the first principle of medical or any therapeutic practise, and doing one's own deep work, which all of you know the importance of very well. Thus by doing our own work and by doing no harm, and by using a little bit of technique, we can assist clients. We do not need much technique, but we need to have done our own work to communicate right relationship. It is the right relationship, rather than technique, that is most therapeutic.

I think ethics could also be called spiritual *sadhana* because it is about looking at our own reactions. Making sure that our fears and desires and our own spiritual longings and spiritual fears do not get in the way of the client's best interests. It could also be called deep ecology because it is really about connection to other people and maintaining that connection in a right way.

My colleague, Dr Katherine Ziegler, in the United States says that, "ethics is really true compassion for one's client and one's self together".

There are a lot of other reasons why, when working with nonordinary states, the ethical pitfalls are much more subtle, confusing, and complicated. I will give you a couple of examples. Bartering, for example, when we exchange massage with a client, or where we have some kind of other barter arrangement. When we barter, the professional boundaries are becoming less clear, and one has to be very, very clear with one's self. The client has to be clear also to have that kind of arrangement work.

Also when there is a merging experience. Has anybody had a merging experience with a client where they really felt that they went into the nonordinary state also and had a spiritual experience along with the client? I can see some nodding in the audience. What happens when you leave that nonordinary state with the client? Is it easy to go back to your professional relationship? Does the client feel that now you are connected with them in a different way? How do we manage this transition from the nonordinary state to the ordinary state and vice versa? It can be difficult.

Kundalini brings in a lot of energy. In a kundalini opening experience there is often a lot of energy in the second chakra. People in kundalini opening are much more attractive, not just sexually attractive but also spiritually attractive. This can present a problem for the caregiver who is attracted to that spiritual energy. Maybe they do not even know that they are attracted to the spiritual energy and not the person. At any rate the caregiver is doing the client a disservice if the caregiver acts on that sexual part, does not recognise the spiritual part, and does not help the energy proceed undistracted up through the chakras.

Spiritual mentoring is another example. When a client transfers the spiritual part of them, their highest spiritual part onto the caregiver or the therapist and sees that person as Shiva, for example, or as someone who can help them or initiate them through sex, then the transference might be tempting to the therapist. Maybe the client becomes willing to do anything for the caregiver, just because they have transferred that highest part of themselves to this person. So how do we handle that? How do we put a client's interest first and make sure that we are protecting our clients?

A quality of timelessness sometimes contributes to ethical

problems. When you go into a nonordinary state it is a timeless state. We often feel that what happens in that state does not apply to ordinary life. This is another rationalisation, but it is very subtle. What happens in a nonordinary state both does and does not apply to ordinary life. What we do in nonordinary states may effect others in our ordinary lives even if it does not feel as if it will at the time. In nonordinary states we get a lot of shadow surprises with ourselves and with our clients. If a "demon" is released in the client, what then is released in us? Maybe our sexual desire that we have been pushing down or maybe our desire for power or knowledge over the client and the client's spiritual path. The power of rationalisation, as I said before, is even greater in nonordinary states.

Let me give you a definition of ethics that I like a lot.

"An ethic of care involves a morality grounded in relationship and response. In responding we do not appeal to abstract principles that we may appeal to rules of thumb rather we pay attention to the concrete other in his or her real situation. You also pay attention to the effect of response on the network of care that sustain us both." [2]

I really like that last part. *We pay attention to the effect of our response on the network of care that sustains us both.* In other words how does what we do in therapy effect the relationship of this person? How does it effect our own relationships? How does it effect the higher good of that person? So again, ethics is really the heart of therapy. It is really the core of right relationship, which in turn is really the healing that goes on in therapy.

I want to show you the model that I talk about in my book. The model is in three parts. There is a short list of vulnerabilities to unethical behaviour. Then there is a chart that you can refer to when you have that kind of awkward feeling in your stomach as if something is not quite right in this relationship. There might be a problem here, but you do not know what it is, because it is subtle and confusing and complicated. You can go back to this chart to look at how you might be off track in the relationship and look at what might be happening with the client that is leading you off track. Both things. The third part is just a very short list of keys to professional ethical behaviour.

I would like to go over this with the help of some visual aids.

2 Manning, R. (1992). Speaking from the heart: A feminist perspective on ethics. Lanham, MD: Rowman & Littlefield Publishers, Inc.

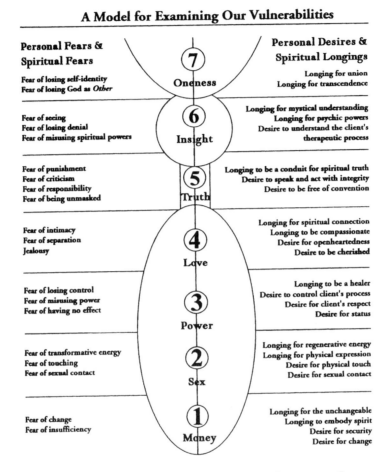

A Model for Examining Our Vulnerabilities

Personal Fears & Spiritual Fears		Personal Desires & Spiritual Longings
Fear of losing self-identity Fear of losing God as *Other*	**7** Oneness	Longing for union Longing for transcendence
Fear of seeing Fear of losing denial Fear of misusing spiritual powers	**6** Insight	Longing for mystical understanding Longing for psychic powers Desire to understand the client's therapeutic process
Fear of punishment Fear of criticism Fear of responsibility Fear of being unmasked	**5** Truth	Longing to be a conduit for spiritual truth Desire to speak and act with integrity Desire to be free of convention
Fear of intimacy Fear of separation Jealousy	**4** Love	Longing for spiritual connection Longing to be compassionate Desire for openheartedness Desire to be cherished
Fear of losing control Fear of misusing power Fear of having no effect	**3** Power	Longing to be a healer Desire to control client's process Desire for client's respect Desire for status
Fear of transformative energy Fear of touching Fear of sexual contact	**2** Sex	Longing for regenerative energy Longing for physical expression Desire for physical touch Desire for sexual contact
Fear of change Fear of insufficiency	**1** Money	Longing for the unchangeable Longing to embody spirit Desire for security Desire for change

Caregiver Vulnerabilities to Ethical Misconduct

Fig 1.

These are the vulnerabilities to unethical behaviour. Disregard for the client most of us who have got this far in working with clients in non-ordinary states do not have this one. But I think some people do. Most of us have good intent, otherwise we would not be doing what we are doing. The impulse to heal people is good. But we can be susceptible to caregiver

3 Published with permission from the author and Hanford Mead Publishers.

burn-out, and we can also be ignorant of some of the subtle complicated pitfalls that we might get into. Often we also under-estimate the power of the non-ordinary state to effect us. This is particularly true with people who have not worked much with non-ordinary states. You never know until it really hits you what kind of powerful thing is going to happen between you and a client.

The last two are really the substance of the work with my chart that I will show you next. There are our own unexamined issues with money, sex, and power and our unacknowledged longings for love, truth, insight, and spiritual connection.

This chart represents the human body and the seven chakras. What I did was to put this together from Buddhism and Hinduism. These are the seven chakras from yoga in Hinduism which seem to match the ethical issues that people have when working with clients. And the outer columns are from Buddhism. Buddhism talks a lot about attachment and how our fears and desires pull us off our spiritual track. So I put the personal fears and the spiritual fears on one side; the spiritual desires and the spiritual longings on the other side. If you know your yoga, you will know that the shushumna runs through the centre of the chakras. This line in my chart represents right relationship. It represents right relationship to a client, to ourselves, to our spiritual past, and to God, as we understand God. It is a straight line, expressing an appropriate relationship to all the different areas of human thought, energy, action, and emotion.

What happens when we have our fears, or when our desires and our longings come into play? Sometimes we get pulled off track. So if this line were a rubber band the fears would pull it one way. Let me put in the names of the chakras or centres before we talk about them one by one. The first one I call Money. The second one I call Sex, which is a fairly common issue in ethical literature. The third I call Power, the fourth one I call Love, the fifth one I call Truth, the sixth one I call Insight and the seventh I call Oneness.

The first chakra I call Money, but it could also be called Change. In the yoga system, the longing for spiritual growth starts in the first chakra so there is a longing for change - a long-ing for union. But there is also fear. There is fear of insecurity, fear of insufficiency as a therapist. Maybe I will not be doing the person any good. If I feel fear about my inadequacy it can pull me off track from the right relationship. Or on the other side the desires and longings.

In the second chakra, Sex, I could fear transformative energy, or fear touch. Some therapists have a fear of touching their clients. Some people would love to over-nurture their clients. So we can have either desire for touching or fear of touching and either one can very subtly pull us off whatever *right relationship* is for a particular client at a particular time. We can also have desire for sexual contact or the desire of the longing for transformative energy. An example of this is if we have a kundalini client who is really expressing this transformative energy and sexual energy, and we really long to have that ourselves. We long for this either consciously or unconsciously. So we may want to co-opt it in some way. Acquire it or subvert it.

The third is Power. On one side are the fears, the fear of losing control, fear of misusing power, fear of perhaps having no effect at all. All of that takes us into ourselves and away from our presence with the client. On the other hand we can have a longing to be a healer in the power sense. People who would love to be shamans, magicians, gurus and so forth have this longing. This in itself it not a bad thing. It is coming from really good impulse. But when it gets involved with ego it takes us off the track of right relationship then it is time to pull ourselves back to the centre again.

In the fourth chakra, Love, there might be fear of intimacy. The fear of getting really intimate with a clients, because you are thinking, "What do I do at the end of the session? Can I really handle that change back into the ordinary roles again?" Fear of separation is another issue. Spiritual jealousy comes in here. What if the client is really having mystical experiences, or out-of-body experiences and we really want those experiences for ourselves. We are really into our jealousy instead of being supportive and encouraging the client in his or her experience. On the longings and desires side of the chart, there is our own desire to be cherished, our own desire or longing to be open-hearted. We want our eyes to always be happy and our hearts to always be open. That kind of longing. This takes us away from being authentic in the fourth chakra.

In the fifth chakra, there is Truth. Maybe you get into a fear of being unmasked. Have you ever noticed that when a client is in a non-ordinary state, they really tell you the truth. Sometimes it is not really what you want to hear. It is easy to go off the line of right relationship at that time by not owning and admitting that we are afraid.

In the sixth chakra, Insight, we can have a longing for mystical understanding. A longing for psychic power is one instance of this, or another is a desire to understand a client's process. I do not think any of us would be in this job if we did not have a longing to understand the client's process. Here we have to let go of answers and trust the process. We can also have a fear of loosing denial. In other words a fear of really seeing what is so.

The seventh chakra is Oneness. This one is quite interesting. People have all kinds of beliefs about duality -about God as *other* for example. Maybe a client is having an experience where he or she becomes God. Because of one's belief system the therapist cannot go along with that. This person has had a oneness experience and it is not been supported because of belief systems. With an experience of Oneness, it is really important to nurture the person and welcome them back. A rebirth experience *per se* is like that, like a unity experience.

These are the keys to professional ethical behaviour. They include one authentic caring and three willingnesses. I do not think authentic caring needs any explanation. One willingness is the *willingness to examine one's own motivations* - to see what is bringing you off track with your clients. Another willingness is the *willingness to tell the truth* not only to oneself, but maybe to others and maybe to the client, depending on whether it is in the client's best interest or not. I think one of the reasons we have had so many problems with ethical pitfalls is that people are unwilling to tell other people where and how they fell into pits because of the shame involved. When we start talking to each other and we start helping each other giving each other feedback about where we are in trouble or where we might be in trouble I think it is going to get a lot better.

The last one is *willingness to ask for help and to learn.* Willingness to ask for consultation if we are feeling that uneasy feeling and we cannot get through it by ourselves. One thing I have in Santa Cruz, California that helps me is a little self-supervision group. It is really about case consultations about clients, but most of what we talk about are ethical issues, such as where I am doing something that is in my best interest and not in the client's best interest. This gets very, very subtle, and we need each other's help in order to really look at ourselves, do our own work and do our best to stay in right relationship to spirit, to ourselves, and to our clients.

Breathland

Sergei Gorsky

Sergei Gorsky is one of the key organisers in the Russian human potential movement. During the last years, Sergei and his colleagues have carried out extensive research on the medical, physiological and psychological aspects of various forms of Breathwork.

I would like to talk about the Breathway and Breathland and share some of the maps I have carefully collected over the years I have worked with Breathwork.

Because of my interest in the history of Breathwork I have noticed that there are certain similarities between the history of Breathwork and the people practising this discipline. Then we have individual stories from people who practice Breathwork on a continual basis. In other words the individual dynamics of the client or person who does Breathwork and the dynamics of the general Breathwork session.

To talk in metaphors, it looks like the global planetary Breathwork session started in the early seventies and that we are now coming to the moment of integration. It has taken us about twenty years or a little bit more to complete one session. When I realised this, it made me a little sad to see how long it has taken to reach completion, but then I thought it is just one session and there are more to come.

But before I develop this further, let us start with the micro cosmos in the breathing session and look at the breathway that leads us through the session. Then we will return to the macro cosmos and look at the way it is reflected as a drop of water in the individual session.

The breathing session can be described as a dance between two dancers - the dance between 'I breathe' and 'breathing happening'. This symbolism has a very deep physiological meaning connected with the fact that there are two breathing centres in the brain. One is younger than the other and is situated in the modern layers of the brain. This is the more personal level that allows us to say 'I breathe' and allows us to control the breathing consciously. The other we find very deep in the transpersonal level of the brain, in the so-called limbic system of the brain. This is the centre that allows 'breathing to happen' for us. Not only can we say that 'I breathe' but that 'the breath breathes me'. The second centre also has many neighbouring deep emotional centres. It is this neighbourhood that makes Breathwork so transformational and deep. It is when we activate this second breathing centre that so much is brought up to the surface and so much changes in our lives.

The Breathway looks like this. We start with 'I Breathe'. We make a conscious decision to lie down or to sit in front of a mirror. We may put on some music and start to breathe. Soon we start feeling something. We start to register various signals in the body - emotional signals, memories etc. In the first ten or fifteen minutes of the session we use the breathing to invite another pair of dancers into the dance. It is the sympathetic system, the autonomic nervous system, and the parasympathetic system. The sympathetic system is responsible for tensions in the body. Every time we feel pain, heaviness, tension or fear, it comes from the sympathetic system.

When we experience the characteristic beautiful flow of gentle energy or tingling in the session, it comes from the parasympathetic part of the system. There is a very deep connection between the sympathetic part and our personal level of consciousness and the parasympathetic and the transpersonal level of our consciousness. So our story starts on a very personal level. When we register all these signals, this is nothing more than the body level presentation of our body. The very structure of our personality or ego has a body level presentation.

In the beginning of the session all we do is simply to increase these signals. The conscious breathing, especially if it is intense breathing, shifts the chemistry of the body in a way that makes us more aware of the signals from the sympathetic system and also of the structure of our body. The points we notice the most are the areas where we identify with our ego.

Soon, after fifteen to thirty minutes, the picture changes. After going through certain feelings of pain and tension something shifts and we start to feel beautiful waves of energy, or visions or some other kind of sensation. In that moment the breathway leads us on to the more transpersonal part of our consciousness. We notice that the breath takes over and 'starts to happen' as if by itself. At the same time the tension and pain starts to subside in the body and is replaced by much more flow of energy, tingling and other signs that indicate that the parasympathetic system is activated. This is the stage of the breathing session where people have all kinds of archetypal and transpersonal experiences.

After that follows the third stage, the stage of integration, when the personal and transpersonal come together - as if the dance is concluding in a final embrace. At the end of a good session we feel that there is a very deep unity between who we are and what is taking place. This unity is represented on many levels - emotional, mental, behavioural, social relations - everything.

Most of this is true not only for the Breathwork session but also for other therapies. There are a number of therapies that can be described within the same metaphor of the personal and transpersonal. So in order not to limit ourselves only with theoretical concepts I'd also like to give you a direct experience of what I am trying to describe. I'd like us to do a very simple and short breathing process that will give you the feel of what it is like.

For this you need to sit comfortably and keep your spine straight and close your eyes. Start by taking full control of your breath. Make sure you control it one hundred percent. Every tiny little moment of the breathing you are in control. Notice how you can get your breathing to slow down or how you can make it shallower. Experiment with it to establish your control. Notice how the breathing totally surrenders to you. You can fully control it. Then slowly start to let go of the control and let the breath happen by itself. Notice how far you can let go of the control. Notice how the breath happens by itself, naturally. Now find the middle path between 'I breathe' and 'breathing happening'. Introduce just a little bit of 'I breathe' - of control of the breathing. Then observe the relationship between the personal and the transpersonal 'dancers' in your breathing. Are they having fun dancing? Is one trying to take over the other? Do they perhaps argue of who is in charge? Is it possible for you to feel both at the same time? Maybe you get identified with one of them? Try keeping this middle path of the breath and slowly return back to the room and open your eyes.

It is not very easy to feel both dancers - both aspects of the breathing - at once. Still it is crucially important in the long run because when they work together they open us on a very deep level. There is also a physiological reason behind this. This deep second centre works by collecting the signals from all the muscles in the body. It also reverses the signals from one particular muscle, which is the diaphragm. So in order to go really deep into the breathing during a session, the body should be as relaxed as possible at the same time as the diaphragm should be as active as possible, which is not very easy. It takes practice. But if you keep this balance, and follow the dance of these two dancers, you will follow the breathway in your breathing session and balance the personal and transpersonal in this part of your life.

What happens after that? Having observed many Breathworkers over a long period of time, I have noticed that after their initial period of euphoria - of real joy about Breathwork - many of them become very transpersonal and anti-social. They become very transcendent.

So it seems as if the same dynamics apply in our individual story. There are many reasons for this. Breathwork is a very intense and effective way of working with the self. When we start doing Breathwork we shake our total identity. If we were something before we started doing Breathwork, without realising that we identify ourselves with our behavioural patterns, we may become nothing, after about a year of doing Breathwork. But at least we are aware of this. Breathwork destroys attachments and identifications very quickly and for many this feels very painful. It is like opening doors and finding skeletons that come out to dance around you. You realise that you are like this or that and that you have this or that side to yourself. I am not this, but I have all of that - so who does that make me in the end? This is a pattern that many of you may already be familiar with.

My observation is that many of those who did Rebirthing in the seventies and eighties destroyed their identity too quickly without really knowing what to do with transcendence. This had a strong effect on our social environment. The divorce rate was high. Very pure Breathworker were basically unable to hold a normal job. People created sort of parallel, transcendent, social institutions and social structure that were almost illusionary. Still, for many this was fun.

About two or three years ago, I and many other Breathworkers began to notice that more and more 'normal' people came to the trainings. Once again we had normal people coming to our trainings. Many Breathworkers started to become normal people, albeit slowly and sometimes painfully, wearing three piece suites, using cellular phones or indeed earning money for a change. So the breathway has worked for a lot of individual Rebirthers. We started in the personal and we really went into the far end on the transpersonal. Many of us managed to survive and start bringing together the two. For many clients and therapists the transpersonal is something almost mystical - something they want so badly that they give up everything personal. But then they realise that there is nobody left to enjoy the transpersonal experience. More and more they realise that it is not about becoming transpersonal or moving in this direction but rather about integrating different aspects.

Given that we have started a discussion recently, to identify what Breathwork is - who we as therapists are and who we are not - I'd like to draw a map of the Breathland, to offer my understanding of who we are.

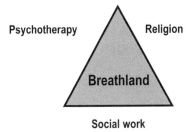

Our land - that I call Breathland - is a triangle with three neighbouring countries. The country of psychotherapy, the country of social work and the country of mystical or religious self-realisation, or whichever name we give this country. For thousands of years, and in particular for the last hundred years, this triangle was a war zone. It is a very rich and powerful land. Most of the new ideas in psychotherapy, a new understanding of mysticism and social technology came from the area within this triangle. Our neighbours represent the three principles that we balance - personal, transpersonal and social. We are reaching the point, and I am talking about IBF here, where we need to set up border treaties with the neighbouring countries and really define who are our clients and who are not.

In my view the client is a person who wants integration of the personal, transpersonal and social aspects of his or her life. If the person has a very wounded or deformed personality he or she needs to go to the psychotherapist or even psychiatrist. It is not a Breathwork client. If the person is not really interested in transformation, in social adaptation, in having a family but just interested in going into the transpersonal states in whatever form, through prayers, mediation or other forms of devotion. Then he or she is not a Breathwork client but needs to find a guru. The same applies for the social aspect. If the person has not yet become interested in the principles of transformation but simply has social problems, it is the social worker that will solve his or her problems. My interpretation of their search for help, and I have been involved in many psychological and social tests to confirm this, is that more and more people want all three. They are not satisfied with just one or two of the aspects. They want us, the Breathworkers, as professionals. In order to have a name for this area; I call it transformational work - an analogy of social work and transformational work.

We live in a world where forms are changing very quickly. All forms, economic, political, religious, change faster and faster. If we stay with our old personal forms and keep them rigid it will get more and more painful. If we dismantle our forms too quickly it will get even more painful because we get lost in the transpersonal ocean. There is a real need for the art and science of change - of transformation or changing forms. The word transformation also has another nice meaning - the analogy of the word transpersonal, namely beyond form. It means changing form and going beyond form into formlessness.

I see the transcendental challenge as a deep underlying reason for Breathwork and especially for Rebirthing in the seventies and eighties. Once we shake our personality - once we really get rid of our identity - we open up a Pandora's box and invite archetypal patterns of behaviour into our lives deep. This means that if we become too transcended, we start to behave like children; we invite archaic patterns; we start behaving like savages, like people who lived 20,000 years ago. We open a way to very strong forces, which have been controlled by the social structure of the last 2000 years. But in our personal lives and in organisations this control has been very weak and once the Pandora's box has been opened it is very difficult to contain this transpersonal power - to give it adequate social manifestation. So I want to propose a new breathway - instead of moving like a pendulum between the personal and transpersonal with obvious dangers on both sides, we start to learn to find the balance from the very beginning. There are very simple techniques that allow us to balance the personal and transpersonal through the breath. We need to emphasise that they can be expanded much further, through body movement such as the Feldenkreis technique and similar techniques that explore the connection between 'I move' and 'movement that happens'. There is a part in our attention that we can control - I perceive, I am aware - and there is a deeper transpersonal part that grabs everything. If we establish this balance, the relationship between the human and God, between the personality and the eternity from the very beginning, we would not need to go to extremes, or we will at least be prepared to go to extremes later if we would like to.

I want to touch one more aspect of the breathway that is connected with the relationship of male and female - the natural breathing pattern, the breathing pattern that occurs when we are born, or when we sleep, for example. In a breathing pattern that is not controlled by our ego or by our personality, we notice a strong active inhale and relaxed exhale. In such a natural breathing pattern, inhale is yang or the masculine. It is active - something that I do. The exhale on the other hand is something that happens. It is more yin or feminine - it surrenders, as it does in adults who are not asleep. Please notice that I am reluctant to use the word awake. It is totally different. It is a kind of mushy inhale that is much longer than it is supposed to be and much weaker. Then we have a forceful rather than a relaxed exhale. So in our breathing pattern yin and yang have changed place. For me this accounts for all the confusion of the feminine and masculine roles that we have experienced in the twentieth century. Because the breathway is such a deep underlying principle of our lives, even a minor distortion in the breath manifests itself as a distortion in our personal lives and as a major distortion in our social lives.

To finish I would like to discuss the roles of Breathwork in our consciousness, as I see it. The structure of consciousness can be described as consisting of the personal level with a lot of structure and a lot of separation. Here we have awareness but no oneness. Then we have a narrow archetypal level and a deeper transpersonal level. Here we have oneness but no awareness. Our major problem is that two of the most important elements are in different places of our consciousness.

This structure is also represented in the body. The upper or personal part is represented by the tensions in the sympathetic nervous system. The deeper archetypal or transpersonal parts are represented by the flowing parasympathetic signals. When we start a Breathwork session we increase the pressure in one part and start to feel it immediately in the different parts of our body and in different parts of our soul. So the first role of Breathwork is diagnostic - to notice our ego's needs. We also notice the areas of identification - so Breathwork diagnoses the problem areas of our personality.

The second role of the breath is disinfecting. It is as if the pressure takes away the rotten old cast that we have stuck on our wound - something that we may have suppressed for twenty or thirty years without noticing. It is like preparing the wound for healing. It becomes more painful but at least it is clean and it is open for healing. The moment we shift from these tensions to the parasympathetic vibrations, the personality starts to heal. It starts to dissolve. This is the third role of the breathing. It is like a balm that heals the wounds of the personality. When we have done some healing of the ego the whole dynamic shifts. You probably notice that after about a year of crying or smashing pillows or expressing rage with screaming and shouting you get a bit bored with it. It is not as much fun anymore. You want something deeper. That corresponds to the fact that the energy that now enters is no longer blown away through the holes in the ego but goes down and opens the archetypal areas of the consciousness. It opens the birth canal so that the birth can take place. I shared these figures last year and will do so again. In a breathing session the theta activity goes up fifty percent and the delta activity sometimes goes up 200 percent. So the shape of our consciousness changes. We gain more access to the deeper levels of our consciousness. This is the fourth role of Breathwork. After initial work on the personality it opens us up to the deeper essence of our consciousness. A good metaphor for the Breathwork session is that it is a rehearsal of enlightenment. We open the birth canal, look around into the transpersonal, check it out and then, at the end of the session, we go back and close the birth canal. Once we do this often enough we start to experience both parts of reality. We start to feel who we are and that everybody and everything that happens around us consists of two parts - two partners, dancers or co-creators, who are having a beautiful experience in the breath is the dance floor. It is the music and everything that connects our person with eternity. It is a middle path that allows us to feel human and as God at the same time.

Music Therapy and Breathwork:
a Path to Self-Realisation

ARTURO DE LUCA

Arturo de Luca is a psychologist and psychotherapist with a Jungian background. He is professor of Ethnic Medicine at the Jean Monnet University in Brussels and professor of Psychology at the University of Rome. He has worked for many years with music, Breathwork and Tibetan Medicine together with Transpersonal Psychology and has founded the International Centre for Psychology, Psychotherapy and Humanistic Sciences in Naples, Italy, where he conducts an intense research programme in the field of psychosomatic medicine and states of consciousness. He also teaches transpersonal psychology and is the author of the books, The New Age and Transpersonal Psychology.

The topic that I will discuss in this lecture is the result of twenty years of study and practice with Breathwork, music and psychotherapy. As a Jungian psychologist, I felt the need to broaden my knowledge of sound and breath, using different cultures and frameworks. All primitive myths consider sound and breath as the originating principles of the universe. Breath and sound are considered the primordial act from which creation began. In particular, in the Veda creation myths, the world is generated from a stream of fire whose essence is breath and sound. In the Greek myths, the order of the universe is music that follows the rhythm of the celestial bodies. These concepts have been confirmed in the paradigm of twentieth century science, a holistic world vision that supersedes the limited vision of Newtonian science. In this paradigm the reality of the universe is no longer made up of isolated particles of matter, but by a network of intertwined energies. This reality is believed to have an intelligence of its own. Furthermore, the structures are not linked according to the causality principle, but they follow an objective that Jung defined as 'the principle of synchronicity'.

In my psychotherapeutic work, I was led to acknowledge this energetic link or connection. Furthermore, the concepts of modern music therapy have shown the existence of an originating sound frequency. This ancestral sound is found as a wave of vibrations, which is just like the imprinting that exists before our birth as a foetus. Life in the embryo develops through these rhythms whose nature is both biological and emotional; in fact, the placenta acts as both a physiological and emotional resonating chamber, and through its contractions shapes the basic structure of the individual. As a result the embryo is composed of three biological layers of tissues which we will examine shortly to better illustrate how sound and breath function together.

Before addressing the topic, it is necessary to distinguish three dimensions in the breathing process: (1) a biological bodily dimension (2) a mental dimension which may be considered conscious or unconscious and (3) the deepest dimension which considers breath as a part of the vital energy of the universe. This concept has been developed in eastern psychological models and is still alive in some primitive cultures. In the course of my travels, I have been able to observe that in these cultures, dancing and singing form an essential part of healing and purification rituals.

The Use of Music in the Breathwork Process
I will give a brief outline of some of the categories of music that can be used in the Breathwork process.

(1) Music for Relaxation - includes sounds and harmonies that mainly affect the physiological structures of the body, releasing stress and anxiety while stimulating the "alpha" function in the brain.
(2) Evocative Music - refer to the past or the present and activates memories and feelings of longing or nostalgia, enabling the integration of negative emotions such as anguish, depression and excessive attachment to the past.
(3) Cathartic Music - produces catharsis and transformation. It can be mystical music or awe-inspiring or dramatic and includes music characterising archetypal and mythical themes of war which emphasise the emotional conflict to the point of producing an intense emotional discharge.
(4) Consciousness-expanding Music - music and sounds which awaken the self, as a unifying centre in preparation for the process of self-realisation. This music produces great benefits and encourages harmony on all three levels of the human being.

A key aspect of this method is the use of therapeutic and ancestral rhythms and sounds that act directly on the client's archetypal world.

This concept also has been shown to be valid in the field of modern embryology as applied to breathing. In fact, although the embryo appears from the first weeks of life as an organic whole, no matter how scarcely differentiated the embryonic disc may be, it is made up of three biological layers: (1) ectoderm (2) mesoderm and (3) endoderm. Now as we have already shown in our studies and research, although these three layers are inextricably connected, their roles become increasingly autonomous in the course of evolution, even if they are originally linked to three different energies, organs and perceptions.

An essential fact is that the conflict between these original structures, or the excessive autonomy of one of them, inevitably leads to uncomfortable situations, stress or pathologies. Music and sound can rectify this imbalance, re-establishing the correct degree of interaction between the three energies insofar as they act directly upon the fundamental biological rhythms of life in the period leading up to birth. The modern concepts of physics in the field of sound and music therapy show that the foetus develops in an environment full of vibrations, rhythms and resonance of varying frequencies: the mother's breathing rhythm, the rhythm of her heartbeat, the abdominal contractions, etc.

Sound Energy and the Archetypes
According to Jung, Archetypes are original biological and psychic models that govern the evolution of life. Archetypes are found in the collective unconscious and manifest themselves in dreams, in myths and in human fantasies from time immemorial. Many primeval shapes such as the circle, the star and the labyrinth, are archetypal images and because they also contain a vibratory frequency, consequently have a therapeutical value. This means that the most effective breathing rhythms and music are those that reach the latent healing power in our deepest, ancestral unconscious. In particular, the music that is used must address these archaic levels of our psyche. It tends to activate the subterranean world of personal and universal symbols that Fromm rightly defined as "the forgotten language". Re-experiencing the transpersonal energies of the archetypes is the true objective of this type of Breathwork. Some of these archetypes are those described by Jung in his work as the Great Mother, the Shadow, the Animus and the Anima. However, my

personal work with music has led me to adopt a very effective method based on the progressive evocation of seven fundamental archetypes linked to the seven chakras: the Inner Child, the Wanderer, the Seeker, the Warrior, the Winner, the Magician and the Sage.

The Choice of Music for the Therapy

This is the most important and delicate part of the whole procedure. This is the starting point for the "process of change" that is the pivotal point of the therapy. A basic rule is the following: "Every initiative of the therapist must always seek to respect the disposition and expectations of the subject; the music of the suggested exercise must reflect their state of mind." J.Jost's sentence still holds true: "the music therapist must be fully conscious of the effect of the available music resource."

During the Therapeutic Process

The following phase consists of the immersion into music, a music meditation or the execution of a technique (dance, drawing, vocalisation, etc.). In this phase, the therapist must have the know-how to reach a level of consciousness that can evoke the emergence of intense emotions, memories, etc, but mostly of 'archetypal images'. Only such images can lead the subject to face the most important and troublesome issues of their life. An essential part of the whole therapy depends upon the work of abreaction or emotional catharsis that only an expert can appropriately elicit.

The main emotions and transpersonal states

During the therapy, music or exercises are used to evoke these reactions working on duality or 'polarity'. Other music must then be employed to evoke transpersonal feelings and to enter into transpersonal states of consciousness to complete the process.

Simplicity and Immortality

NEMI NATH

Nemi Nath is the founder of Breath Connection, one of Australia's leading Rebirthing organisations. She is a Rebirther and Trainer, Yoga teacher and Spiritual Healer, She is establishing a community lifestyle with a small group of people who are also involved in the running of "Kaivalya Meru", a retreat centre at Lillian Rock in New South Wales, Australia.

Close Your Eyes and listen to your breath... breathe.... breathe. On your inbreath breathe up to and into your crown centre and on your outbreath breathe into and out through your heart.

Welcome, I would like to start by sharing a vow that I took last year during Robert Coon's workshop on immortality:

> *"I gratefully receive and radiate universal abundance.*
> *I live in the present moment in the spirit of everlasting Life.*
> *In Light, Love and Joy I hold sacred the gift of liberation*
> *of my body into its truest form in accordance and harmony*
> *with the highest and truest will, and for the benefit of all life forms.*
> *In loving service. So be it, it is done."*

The subject of physical immortality was difficult for me to get interested in at the beginning of my Rebirthing life, and for many years I totally avoided it. I met many immortalists whose integrity I questioned. At the same time, participants in my groups would constantly ask my view on physical immortality.

For a few years I managed to refer the answers to immortalists until, finally, I decided to take a look into the subject myself which has been linked with Rebirthing since its beginnings.

Breathwork for me is about simplicity amongst other things, and so is life. Immortality seemed very complicated at the time and far out of reach. I have had many experiences in life where I got stuck in complicated theories, until one day, through the practice of Agnihotra, I encountered a really beautiful lesson about simplicity and life. Here is the story.

Agnihotra is a sunrise and sunset fire ritual, which involves meditating with a fire lit in a small copper pyramid. Amongst other things the fire is fuelled with dried cow dung. When I first bought the kit for performing the ceremony it came with a supply of dried cow dung, enough to get started with and organise my own supply. Picking up the cow dung was very humbling and turned into a cosmic lesson about ordinariness. On the one hand picking up cow dung was very grounding and earthy and on the other hand the fire enhanced such a still, divine space for meditation - Cosmic ordinariness. The story speaks for itself, and it helped me to tackle the subject of immortality. If in the future we all attain mastery over our bodies, immortality would be the ordinary state of being.

The only thing that I can really call my own is my body. Two nights ago I had a dream where all my structures collapsed. I know this experience well from the past. I find myself in a place or in a state where nothing that existed before was still in existence. My life's lesson here was to be simple enough to have only a few structures and not be depending on them. Then the impact of a collapse is minimal. There is nothing on the planet that any of us own, except our bodies. That makes life really simple because, really it all goes on inside the body.

It is the last night of the conference and I have had a really beautiful experience here. I feel nourished and full and rich and I have made strong and deep connections. Things like this mean much more to me than materialism for example. Materialism is people believing that life occurs outside of the body, that the outside is more important then the inside, and that the body needs a huge building to keep it safe, lots of money to keep it entertained and extravagant foods to keep it happy.

A lot of people don't respect their body and some people believe that the body is not very important. I don't share that belief. I believe that the body is my temple. If I want to embody my spirit I need to have a sacred place for it here in the physical world. My Life is a journey of gently but surely caring about my body, my temple and our journey together towards union.

Breathing or Breathwork has been the most effective tool I know for learning to be in my body. Every breath I take takes me there, into what is mine. That is simplicity! Breath is the vehicle for spirit, and breathing is spirit in action.

I see two types of people, people who are conscious and people who are unconscious. That is simplified too. Everyone has access to spirit through the breath, whether they are conscious or not. Even if we are unconscious, spirit touches us. Being conscious means we are able to notice that we are being touched, and that we are able to learn to embody spirit. Our unconsciousness will lead us to death, because our body will only live until we have used it up so to speak, by living off its physical energy. Through conscious connection to spirit we increase our ability to live and our potential to become immortal.

The unconscious birth-death cycle is not a bad path. Many, many people live this path. There are many experiences to be had and learned on this path. We live on a planet of free will. Free will is the only way to awaken and to learn to embody spirit. Awakening is the bridge between unconsciousness and consciousness. You cannot really say that one person is more conscious than another. How would you measure consciousness? You would need a new scientific device for measuring consciousness. Someone asked me once how much power I want, and I could not answer the question because I could not find a measure for power.

The conscious path leads to life, simply because life force is pleasant and enjoyable and God-filled. Once we have had a taste of life force flowing plentifully we want more and more. My main focus of work over the past 15 years has been to assist people in their awakening to their own life force, how to use it and increase it to become more conscious and more alive.

During this journey of assisting people I found different stages into life. They are also very simple or at least the theory is simple and logical. Step by step people need to give up anything that assists their body to die. One of the stages is to give up substance addiction. Another to give up habits and patterns. Another stage is to set intentions for better experiences. When people first begin to work on themselves they cannot see where they are heading, and all they really know is what they don't want. At this stage, Breathwork with the intention to clear attachments is appropriate. Once people's heart chakras have opened, they begin to understand what they want in life externally as well as internally. Inner work takes on a more positive focus with positive intentions.

The concept of clearing something disappears. The focus shifts to integrating something new. The next stage is finding ones place in life. People wonder where they belong. People look for soul friends or like-minded people. They begin to look for purpose in life and question its meaning - Who are we and what are we here for? This gradually awakens the desire and the wish to find one's truth. The search for where we belong is not a spatial experience any more but becomes an internal experience and the discovery that there is really only ever one truth in every moment. That is another simple thing in life. The key to living life is to find just that one thing that is true from moment to moment. When you have achieved that you are enlightened.... how easy that sounds!

Breathwork is the science of life. Immortals, graduates of life, do not exactly come in crowds. At what age do we accept someone as immortal, and how does one become a practitioner of life if we are not immortal yet? None of us really classify as a real teacher of life. We have not integrated life, so how can we teach it? Who has the means to do so..... but life itself. Yes, Life is our teacher.

To become a teacher or a facilitator of life two things are important. One is accepting life as a teacher and the other is the commitment to life. Again this sounds very simple. I met a teacher once who had some very simple advice. He said: "There are no guidelines on the master path except that one's behaviour has to be impeccable and one needs to look back at one's footsteps." You are your own judge of whether you like your footprints or not."

When I first began work as a Rebirther I felt more like a student of life than a teacher. The method was new and there were not many proven guidelines, and I developed my own methodology. Intuition was my greatest reliance. Scientific methodologies for this new field of Breathwork did not exist so I invented my own primitive research method.

In meditation I was given a blueprint about how to work with relationships. Then, all I had to do was to start a group and totally rely on my intuition and it was all there. To evaluate what I had done I used repetition. I would record what I had done during a workshop and repeat it whilst observing the clients and observing myself.

For example, I would conduct the same workshop in the same sequence several times over. The people would always be different and so would I, because I also grew in the process. Even if the people came back, they would be different also and it was difficult to come to clear "scientific" results. Logic was also not applicable. What I did observe through my records was that after five to ten repetitions the essential ingredients of the course became visible. Everything that was unessential dropped away. Only life supporting processes remained. The essence that stood out was life. The only thing stable in all the chaos of Breathwork was life! By pursuing life I found a sense of stability and strength.

After some years I decided to find my own opinion on immortality. I decided to take the theme of immortality into some of my sessions. The first thing I found was that we all breathe the same air. What I breathe out you breathe in and what you breathe out I breathe in. My body is made out of your body and your body is made out of my body, because we exchange gaseous bodily substances. At first it was quite a frightening thought for me to realise that even on the physical level we are not really separate. My next insight was that, if there were no immortal masters to hold Light on the planet, we would just die away. We would not be knowledgeable enough to sustain our life. My appreciation for the spiritual support we receive multiplied by many thousand at that time. Since then I have been interested in meeting people who have attained degrees of body mastery.

The *breatharian*[1] movement is one of the groups I encountered. Here I found another pitfall of the path, attachment to phenomena. I am not saying that *breatharianism* is phenomena, it is very real and achievable.

It is the motive to become a breatharian or an immortal or anything else that turns the path into a pitfall. It is not about not eating, or not dying. It is only about being here now. That brings me back to the beginning where I started, the simplicity of living with spirit.

"I gratefully receive and radiate universal abundance.
I live in the present moment in the spirit of everlasting Life.
In Light, Love and Joy I hold sacred the gift of liberation of my body
into its truest form in accordance and harmony with the highest and
truest will, and for the benefit of all life forms.
In loving service. So be it, it is done."

---

1 The Breatharian movement or Breatharianism is a very extreme form of Breathwork practiced by an increasing number of people in the West, where you learn to live without food and learn to live on Prana (life energy) alone. (Editor's comment)

Chapter 4

Breathwork and Psychology

Breath is a Language

JOY MANNÉ

*Joy Manné is founder and director of the School for Personal and
Spiritual Development in Switzerland (closed in 1996). She has
a degree in Psychology and a PhD in Buddhist Psychology. She
was trained in Spiritual Therapy by Hans Mensink and Tilke
Platteel-Deur in Holland. Her teaching of Breathwork, energy
and other new techniques is influenced by her knowledge of
Buddhist methods.*

When we take our first breath we inform the world that we are
alive, and when we finally stop drawing breath, we inform the
world of our departure. Breath is a language.

Breath is a language with its own vocabulary. Among its
words are long breaths and short breaths, and more or less noisy
breaths: puffing, panting, yawning, gasps, snorts and sighs.

> Some gestures combine movement with sound effects. The bull snorts
> when he is angry. People who are furious usually take short breaths and
> expel the air through their nostrils in spurts similar to snorting. In a
> sorrowful situation, highly emotional people take deep breaths and expel
> the air slowly, making long, sighing sounds. Breathing also plays a
> prominent part in the communication of frustration and disgust.
> (Nierenberg & Calero, p. 78f)

Coughing, choking and suffocating, too, are part of the
vocabulary of breath language. This is what Georg Groddeck
says about coughs:

> A cough, any sort of cough, expresses the wish either to blow off
> something which is regarded as unpleasant, or to get rid of something
> already felt to be within the organism, whether as part of itself or as a
> foreign body, and whether of a mental or of a physical nature.
> (Groddeck, 1951, p. 133)

The way the words of a language are combined to make
meaningful utterances is its syntax. Breath is a language with its
own syntax and structure. Breath language is meaningful.

The part of the body in which the breath takes place is significant. When we are under stress we breathe at collarbone level. One component of the physical response to stress is a shift from the relative dominance of abdominal to thoracic breathing. When we are afraid our breathing moves from our belly to our chest. The contraction of abdominal muscles for protection of organs in that part of the body serves as a survival mechanism.

> In difficult situations - for example in marital quarrels or with the unexpected appearance of one's employer - we see that this gasping for breath and cramp in the diaphragm and stomach regions assumes frightening dimensions. Breathing stops, or a breath is hastily drawn, and the situation - which probably demands our greatest responsiveness - is hopelessly lost. (Elsa Gindler, 1986-7, p.9)

Breath is a language with its own expressions, symbols and metaphors: We wait *with bated breath. We catch our breath* in fear or anticipation; we *hold our breath* during moments of tension, pressure, strain, anxiety, danger and excitement; and when we are at ease again, *we breathe freely. We breathe freely* also in an atmosphere of intellectual freedom.

Breath is a language with its own rules. These may be obeyed or broken:

> A person should respond to an increase in excitement or charge by increasing his rate of breathing. Instead, many people are uncomfortable with the charge and they attempt to control their excitement so they can stay calm, cool, and collected.' They do this by curtailing their breathing. The reason that they do this is that breathing deeply and fully amplifies their awareness of feelings. Many of the feelings that emerge with the deep breathing are uncomfortable ones, so most people avoid awareness by restricting their breathing. Unfortunately, while restricting the breathing to repress uncomfortable feelings, they restrict feelings of pleasure as well. This is not just a reaction we see in therapy, but a common pattern of the average man-on-the-street. Most people breath with only a portion of their lung capacity during the normal day and then hold their breath when they get tense or frightened. (Rosenberg, 1985, 106f)

Breath language is especially rich in communicating emotion:

> Nearly all strong emotions, crying, anger, fear, and pleasure, involve increased breathing. So it is not surprising that if a person seeks to repress emotion, breathing reduction is a central dynamic. (Boadella, 1994, p.241)
> Just as we behave, move, act, according to our specific makeup and

express ourselves uniquely through gestures so does our breathing
pattern express our inner situation, varying in accordance with inner and
outer circumstances. The usually arrhythmic respiration goes with our
normal diffusion of attention, and changes with emotional states:
agitated in anger, stopped momentarily in fear, gasping with amazement,
choking with sadness, sighing with relief, etc. (Proskauer, 1994, p. 255)

In our vocabulary, expressions about the breath are
expressions about our emotional or physical state, or both
together. Further, disordered breathing shows stress and anxiety;
hesitation and mental conflict can trigger asthma attacks; fear
and sadness cause breathing changes. Our habitual rhythms of
breathing regulate our state of consciousness and our emotions
in daily life. A change in our rhythm of breathing induces a
change in our state of consciousness, as the elements of breath
language above show. Breath is a psychological language. It is
the language that describes our state of consciousness. If dreams
are the royal road to the unconscious, breath is the royal
expressway.

Breath, however, is not only a psychological language. In
health and physical illness, in psychotherapy and in personal
and spiritual development, breath can be used as a means of
diagnosis, with its own descriptive and prescriptive vocabulary.
And breath language has a transpersonal dimension. We are
energy beings, beings of psychological and physical energy.
Breath is our language of energy and harmony, as Robert Fried
says so poetically:

The physical world is made up of particles which are arranged spatially,
in three dimensions, in accordance with the interplay of attracting and
repelling forces which, in composite, we call 'energy.' Energy fluctuates
periodically. One of its properties is 'frequency.' The interplay of energy
changes is dynamic and, in the aggregate, gives all things physical a
continuous dynamic periodicity which we observe as rhythm. Most
aspects of physical matter have their own rhythm, a signature, as it were,
which interacts with other such rhythms to result in yet new rhythms for
the aggregate. When physical matter is combined into a life form, we
may observe it to have a complex interplay of these energy oscillations -
something like the score of a symphony - where, at any moment in time,
each component plays its characteristic 'note' as part of its own melody
and rhythm, and the aggregate creates a distinct new sound,
superimposed on yet a new rhythm. And so it is in psychophysiology
that we begin with an assessment of the rhythm of the energy in an
organ system, because we recognised dysrhythmia as dysfunction, and

we believe that we can, like turning the pegs on a violin, restore the
rhythm to the strings that will give the organ the proper pitch and
harmonic composition. ... We do it with the .. body organs .. And most
importantly, we do it with the breathing. (Fried, 1993, p. 305f)

BREATH IS A LANGUAGE OF ILLNESS

Breath is a language of illness. When we are ill, our
breathing is affected; when our breathing is inadequate, our
health is effected. Breathwork can heal some illnesses, while in
other illnesses inadequate breathing is a life-saver.

Hyperventilation [1]
Most frequently breath language speaks of illness through hyperventilation (HV).

What is hyperventilation? As usual the medical profession
does not agree, but at the moment it seems to be the bucket
diagnosis into which as many ailments as possible are put! HV is
not easily diagnosed. People with it have been misdiagnosed as
having cardiovascular, respiratory, neurological, psychological,
gastrointestinal, musculo-skeletal, endocrine and allergic
problems.

How, then, is hyperventilation defined? This is how Fried
describes its bio-chemistry:

> An increase in the periodicity of this [i.e. the normal] breathing cycle
> inconsistent with metabolic demand may result in an increase in the
> amount of CO_2 expelled from the lungs (hypocapnia), reducing the blood
> CO_2 content below that required for proper function (hypocarbia). This
> process is called hyperventilation and results in a momentary shift of the
> acid-base equilibrium of blood toward alkalosis. (Fried, 1993 : 302)

Clinicians often use the hyperventilation-challenge as a
means of diagnosis. "The HV-challenge (has) the person breathe
deeply and rapidly (perhaps twenty to thirty breaths per minute
[this is hyperpnea, over-breathing] for two to three minutes."[2] It
induces the symptoms from which the client is seeking relief, and
thus is supposed to validate their origin. These are the symptoms
induced by the HV-challenge:

(a) Very deep breathing at 12 breaths per minute in a normal person,
      produces tetany in 15 to 30 minutes;

(b) Initially there is a slight transient tremor of the eyelids and facial
      musculature - usually one side only (and typically the right side);

---

1 The information in this section comes primarily from Robert Fried's books.

(c) Tremors are replaced by muscular rigidity in the face and hands - the lips form a circle, close against the teeth, thumb and fingers are extended; the width of the hand is reduced to the 'obstetrician's hand' configuration;

(d) If hyperpnea is discontinued at this point no rigidity is noted in other parts of the body;

(e) Subjective sensation of slight dizziness and rigidity; numbness, and tingling in the affected parts are noted;

(f) Primary sensations of gross contact - pain, heat, and cold - are rendered more acute; reaction to stimuli is enhanced; on the other hand, the exercise of judgement is blunted, the power of attention is lessened, and consciousness is reduced. (Fried, 1993 : 194, quoting Rosett, 1924 : 332-333)

In fact, the HV-challenge produces an astonishing array of sensory, affective, and somatic symptoms, for example, faintness, apprehension, anxiety, depression, panic, and phobia, and a considerable constellation of somatic sensations including chest pain and muscle spasms. Fried, a leading authority on hyperventilation, does not recommend this procedure and considers it hazardous. The main danger, as he sees it, is that the client is relieved that, for example, the chest pain is not due to something more serious, whereas it may in fact be an important symptom.

Hyperventilation is a dangerous process that is both brought about by illness and that leads to illness. Anxiety causes primary HV, cardiovascular, heart and renal disease may cause secondary HV, while HV itself can bring about organic and psychological symptoms. Chronic HV is a physiological disorder of the acid-base balance of the blood. Chronic hyperventilation may upset cardiac electrolyte balance. Chest symptoms and ECG-trace abnormalities are common. Hyperventilation may cause kidney problems. It may lead to vasoconstriction that also effects the brain. It will affect on the lymph and immune systems. It affects mental health,

> Hyperventilation is repeatedly causally implicated in stress syndromes, and in most mental disorders, including depression, anxiety, panic and phobias. Its symptoms span those encountered in most such complaints, including anxiety, dizziness, faintness, apprehension, a feeling of unreality, vertigo, and often the fear of going crazy, or of dying. The numerous studies which link these disorders and symptoms, while by no means in unanimous agreement as to aetiology, overwhelmingly point to

2 Fried, 1993, p. 42.

respiratory patterns, and the physiological ventilatory response to CO_2 .
(Fried, 1993, p. 302)

Anxiety and hysteria have been called respiratory neuroses. Fried says, "Anxiety neurotics seem to have the lion's share of HV....They are the mainstay of clinical practice. They are numerous, condition readily, adjust poorly, and have disordered breathing of a type that heightens their symptoms."[3]
Breathing is affected in neurosis, and in psychosis, schizophrenia and panic attacks, which Fried points out, have the same symptoms as hyperventilation.
People with psychopathological conditions have particular breathing patterns,

> Sighing; increased respiration rate (tachypnea); irregularity of respiration
> (inhalation and exhalation) disturbances of co-ordination; sharp
> transition between inhalation and exhalation; curtailed expiration and
> prolonged inspiration; respiration wholly or mainly thoracic; shallow
> respiration; inspiratory shift of median position. (Fried, 1993, p. 199,
> citing other research)

Breathing can be affected by nutrition which can also cause hyperventilation:

Is hyperventilation a myth?
Is hyperventilation a myth, an explain-all medical category, or a cure?
Fried knows all there is to know about breathing - except for what can be done *psycho*therapeutically through Breathwork. Ley, too, is ignorant of the psychotherapeutic potential of hyperventilation,

> The links that connect breathing with cognition and emotion have
> important implications for theory and practice. If hyperventilation
> accompanies strong emotions (i.e. fear, frustration, anger, and sadness),
> then some of the irrational and bizarre behaviours and cognitions
> associated with these emotions (e.g. hysteria) may, in part, be a
> consequence of an underlying cerebral hypoxia produced by
> hyperventilation. (Ley, 1994, p. 89)

This way of thinking reduces all feelings to chemistry, and eliminates the essential quality of humanness in human beings including feeling, experiencing and suffering. Maybe hyperventilation does not induce hysteria - that all-time favourite derogatory category used by psychiatrists and others

3 Fried, 1993, p. 230.

for what they cannot understand - but is, as Wilfried Ehrmann has proposed, "aquite sophisticated tool of the unconscious to trick the permanent manipulation and control of conscious-ness."[4] In other words, hyperventilation may be a way in which the unconscious moves towards healing and integration.

Hendricks, who knows how to work psychotherapeutically with the breath, understands this. He says this about hyperventilation,

> If you started to hyperventilate in a doctor's office, he or she would probably have you breathe into a paper bag, saturating your blood with carbon dioxide and restoring the balance. If you started to hyperventilate in my office, I would invite you to contact the emotion you were concealing and breathe into it. After a few deep belly-breaths into the fear, anger, or sadness, you would probably have a release of the emotion and feel better than you did before....There is an emotional trigger that starts the hyperventilation. If you can identify and deal with the emotion, the hyperventilation fades quickly. (Hendricks, p. 169)

Hyperventilation is a shamanic technique which induces trance and other altered states of consciousness. I prefer to call this phenomenon, i.e. the Breathwork that induces altered states of conscious '*augmented breathing.*' My position is that induced hyperventilation should never be used in therapy! Unless there is adequate preparation, it rapes the unconscious, precipitating the emergence of repressed traumatic material or other altered states of consciousness which the person does not have the means to deal with and integrate.[5] Hyperventilation was used by Reich; it was used extensively in early Rebirthing and is still used by some Rebirthers, and it is still used extensively by Janov in his Primal Therapy and by Stanislav Grof in his Holotropic Breathwork. Grof says,

> The practice of Holotropic Breathwork provides deep insights into the dynamics of the 'hyperventilation syndrome'....It shows that the richness of the response to *faster breathing* cannot be understood in simple physio logical terms, because it is a complex psychosomatic phenomenon that reflects the entire psycho-biological and even spiritual history of the individual. The symptoms induced by *rapid breathing* can appear in all areas of the body and in all possible combinations. Systematic study of these reactions shows that they represent intensification of pre-existing psychosomatic symptoms or exteriorisation of various latent symptoms. Continuation of *accelerated breathing* makes it possible to trace these symptoms to their sources in the unconscious - to memories of traumatic biographical events, biological birth, prenatal traumas, and even various

4 Manné, 1997 ii, p, 171. [5] Manné, 1994, p. 508; 1997 ii, Chapter 20. See also the Dialogue on Hyperventilation between Kylea Taylor and Joy Manné in The Healing Breath: a Journal of Breathwork Practice, Psychology and Spirituality at www.i-breathe.com/thb12/index.htm

transpersonal gestalts (e.g. phylogenetic memories, past life experiences, and archetypal motifs.) (Grof, 1997, p. 9, *my italics*)

Let us note that while Grof does use the term 'hyperventilation' to describe what he does in Holotropic Breathwork™, in this passage (and throughout his text) he also uses terms like 'faster breathing,' '**rapid breathing**,' and 'accelerated breathing.' Grof also asserts that hyperventilation can cure certain medical problems that others try to cure by slowing down the breathing.[6]
For Grof, it is almost a religious belief that hyperventilation produces his results, but the same results occur in Breathwork without hyperventilation or any other type of forced rapid breathing, as well as through a large variety of techniques that do not use the breath.

Rebirthing is criticised for its use of hyperventilation. Minett, however, sees it in this way,

> There is a precise distinction between the correct breathing pattern in a Rebirthing session and hyperventilation. There are, however, often situations during a Rebirthing session which may cause the person to fall into a hyperventilation pattern. This is certainly not intended and a good therapist will know how to prevent this. Breathing during Rebirthing should really be called 'super-breathing' - an optimal method of breathing. It will not cause hyperventilation, regardless of the speed and intensity of the breathing, as long as the relaxed exhale is maintained. The body may experience intense physical sensations, vibrations, or tingling during Rebirthing; this is, however, generally perceived as positive and pleasant. (Minett, p. 65, see also pp. 92, 117)

Minett calls this way of breathing 'super-breathing' and I call it 'augmented breathing.'[7] As so much disease and dis-ease is associated with hyperventilation, I prefer to have it as a specific medical category which describes a defined medical condition, namely, a physiological breathing ailment. 'Hyper' is not a healthy or attractive concept, while 'super' evokes the power of a good breathing session, and 'augmented' evokes music, adventure, and training to improve capacity. Spontaneous rapid, or faster, or accelerated, or augmented or super breathing will occur in breathing sessions, quite spontaneously and of itself, when it is useful for development and healing.

BREATH IS A LANGUAGE OF HEALTH

Breath is a language of health and harmony. Our breath is the

6 Grof, 1997, p. 8.   7 Manné, 1997 ii, p. 170.

language through which is revealed whether our body is inrhythm with itself or out of it, in other words, its state of health, energy-flow and well-being. Fried has pointed out that, "All body functions are breathing related,"[8] and therefore breathing is "the fulcrum for the balancing act we call health."[9] Carola Speads says, "The quality of our breathing determines the quality of our lives: Health, moods, energy, creativity, all depend on the oxygen supply provided by our breathing, and she warns us, that "the pressures of our modern-day life have created an almost literally breath-less culture."[10]

If breathing is so important for health, how should we breathe? Is there a correct way to breathe? Can we learn to avoid being part of the 'literally breathless culture'?

This is how breathing works:

> The mechanism of breathing involves the body from the shoulders and collarbone down to the bottom of the pelvis. Total breathing in should begin at the abdomen and in a flowing way come all the way up to the collar bone. Breathing out reverses this wave. Breathing in (inspiration) begins with the diaphragm, a large dome-shaped muscle under the lower ribs that divides the lungs and rib cage (thoracic cavity) from the abdominal cavity. As the diaphragm contracts, it pushes down on the abdominal viscera (stomach, liver, intestines), pushing them outward as far as the abdominal muscles will allow. At the same time, the contraction of the diaphragm forces the ribs upward and outward. They expand from side to side, front to back, up and down, and each rib turns upward like a Venetian blind. The movement of the ribs and diaphragm expands the two elastic lungs. When the lungs are expanded, a vacuum is created in the lungs and the air from outside rushes in. (Schutz, *Here comes Everybody*, p. 194, in Dychtwald, p. 140)

It is generally agreed that abdominal breathing is the correct way to breathe.

> In healthy breathing the stomach muscles are relaxed, allowing the breath to swell the abdomen with each breath. In upside-down breathing, the stomach muscles are tight and the breath inflates the chest....If the abdominal muscles are too tight, the diaphragm (the main muscle involved in breathing) cannot move through its full range of motion. (Hendricks, p. 39)

Some competent people, however, think there is no correct way to breathe:

> Because of the diversity of influences on our breathing, it is obvious that there cannot be one best way of breathing. I emphasise this because as

8 Fried, 1990, p. 60.   9 Fried, 1993, p. 304.   10 Speads, 1995, p. 36.

soon as people become aware of the inadequacy of their breathing
habits, they invariably ask, "Now, what is the best way of breathing?" or
"How shall I breathe?" There is no *one* best way of breathing that is the
right way or *the* best way to be aimed at for all times. We breathe in
many ways, and many ways of breathing may be appropriate. Breathing
is right not when it functions all the time in one particular 'ideal'
manner, but when it works in a way that lets it freely adjust, changing
its quality according to our needs of the moment, so that it will
adequately support us as we face the diverse challenge of our lives. ...
There is just no right way of breathing. (Speads, 1986, p. 42)

Dychtwald has pointed out that it is not only the diaphragm
that is important, but that "the ability to take a full, deep breath
is dependent on the flexible and healthy psychosomatic
inter-functioning of the belly, diaphragm, and lungs."[11]
We cannot, however, just get people to change their breathing.
Robert Fried warns,

Persons with seemingly functional breathing disorders may be referred to
non-medical psychotherapists for treatment. You are cautioned that these
conditions may not be functional. Hyperventilation, for instance, may
compensate serious metabolic disorders of the acid-base balance -
possibly caused by heart disease, diabetes, or kidney failure. Alternately,
there may be blood disorders, lung disease, lesions, or other disorders of
brain regulation centres. Consequently, you should not undertake to treat
anyone until a medical examination has determined that behavioural
alteration of breathing is not contraindicated. Organic breathing
disorders should be treated only with the approval of a competent
medical specialist. (Fried, 1993, p. xvii)

This means that in illnesses like diabetes, heart and kidney
disease, wrong breathing may be a survival mechanism and
hyperventilation may be a means to health!

Breath in different systems of Medicine
    In Western medicine, the accent is on breathing retraining
through biofeedback done by physiotherapists. They have,
however, appropriated non-western methods such as yoga and
meditation. These methods have had a great deal of success with
problems as diverse as menopausal hot flushes and agoraphobia.
They have leaked into respectability, as has the need for
psychotherapy. Fried favours breathing retraining done with
professional respiratory physiotherapists, in co-ordination with
clinical or counselling psychologists. From what Fried says,

[11] Dychtwald, 1977, p.140

however, it is clear that the breathing therapist should know how to use the breath psychotherapeutically and particularly how to deal with emotions. Dinah Bradley, too, recognises the need for 'talking' therapy in her six-part method for the treatment of hyperventilation. This method includes breathing retraining, exercise, total body relaxation, talk (both learning to measure one's breath when one speaks and talking therapy are included), esteem, rest and sleep.[12]

Please note that none of the various contemporary forms of Breathwork such as Rebirthing, Conscious Breathing Techniques, Vivation, Holotropic Breathwork™, and so forth, have yet taken up a place in what is recommended, despite their proven success. I know that some of the claims for success in the early days of Breathwork were grandiose, unconvincing and unsubstantiated, but Kylea Taylor, for example, who is highly trained in conventional therapy and, as her outstanding books show, who is not at all predisposed to grandiosity, attests that there is anecdotal evidence for healing with regard to symptoms such as back pain, hip pain, hyperthyroidism, irritable bowel syndrome, menstrual cramps, obesity, Raynaud's disease, urethral stricture, and asthma:[13]

> Many participants have experienced a decrease or complete remission of asthmatic symptoms after they participated in a series of Breathwork sessions. Breathwork is a useful adjunct to therapy if emotion is the main factor in the asthma. (Taylor, 1994, p. 11; see also p. 21)

I myself can offer case history information for a long remission (cure?) from cancer in which Breathwork played a significant role.[14]

It is unfortunate that contemporary forms of Breathwork do not receive more recognition. There is quite enough anecdotal evidence for the healing that takes place during Breathwork to convince qualified people to undertake appropriate research projects.[15] One reason for this may be the absence of sensible literature. We need more sensible and intelligent books like those by Kylea Taylor's about Holotropic Breathing and Gunnel Minett's about Rebirthing, as well as more books with case histories and techniques that will show what problems Breathwork can succeed with.

With regard to the new medical systems of healing, many of those now adopted into conventional medicine as it expands its field and goes back to its origin, when it was a healing art, are conscious of the importance of breathing. This is certainly true

12 Bradley, 1991, p. 47.   13 Taylor, 1994, p. 20.   14 Manné, 1997, p. 154f.   15 This seems now to be happening. See International Breathwork Foundation Newsletter, 3/97/1.

for Osteopathy,[16] Cranial Osteopathy, Polarity Therapy, and all of the diverse methods that make up the rapidly growing field of Somatics.[17]

Further, there are many originally non-western medical or healing systems that use the breath. I have called these 'originally non-western' because it is since their adoption and adaptation by Western practitioners that we know about them, and, frequently, also that their own practitioners have become more conscious of their importance.[18] Among these techniques are Ayurveda (prana), Tibetan, Chi Gung,[19] Chi Yi[20]. One could say that these are systems of breathing for health.

BREATH IS A LANGUAGE OF PSYCHOTHERAPY

Breath is a language of therapy. Appropriate therapy is the route from illness to health. If breath is "the fulcrum for the balancing act which we call health," as Fried has proposed, this is not limited to physical health, but includes mental health and well-being as well. Breath is the fulcrum for the balancing act which we call psychological health! As Kylea Taylor says,

> The breath is our key to reconnecting with aspects of life from which we have become split off. We may have unresolved issues from the past that are affecting everyday life. These issues can keep our emotional or physical energy from flowing naturally and may even appear as physical illness or unwanted recurring behaviour patterns. If this energy continues to be stuck, our ability to respond fully to life decreases. When the breath energises the psyche for healing, it does so in much the same way as our bodies enlist forces when we are injured. We do not have to think about or direct the healing. The body just goes to work spontaneously, sending more white cells to the injured area, repairing tissue, and bringing wholeness and healing to the body again. The psyche also has this ability. When the body and mind enter a state of nonordinary consciousness through controlled breathing, our inner wisdom uses the opportunity to work toward physical, mental, emotional, and spiritual healing, and even developmental change. (Taylor, 1994, p. 3-4)

It is no wonder then that Breathwork is a very special form of therapy. Whereas in many schools of therapy the client is required to work within the model and advance according to the theories to which the practitioner is committed - in other words, to perform - this structure cannot be imposed in Breathwork. As Kylea Taylor has so wisely observed, "There is no way to program the content of a Breathwork session. Even if we could,

16 Grossinger, Modalities, p. 190, especially the practitioner's breath cue-ing the patient's breath. 17 For information about Somatics, see Grossinger, Johnson, and the journal Somatics. 18 This is also the reason why my references are to a Western book. The West has appropriated these techniques. I would say that all contemporary native practitioners are today influenced by Western ideas. 19 Information to be found in Grossinger, Origins. 20 Zi, 1994.

it would be counterproductive to do so."[21] This is what gives Breathwork its authenticity and profundity.

Breath is a language of emotion
Breathwork is effective in bringing up deeply affecting and traumatic experiences. In psychoanalytic terms, breath is the language of defence: it is the language in which we defend our-selves against our feelings and emotions. It is also the language in which we release them. We hold our breath or breathe shal-lowly to prevent emotions and feelings from overwhelming us, and we breathe more deeply and/or faster to release long-held emotional material, and to integrate it.[22]
In psychoanalytical terms, breath is the language of repression:
> ...breathing is one automatic way tears are kept down. Shallow
> breathing doesn't dip into the body where feelings are stored. It aids
> repression. (Janov, 1990, p. 335)

Breath is the language in which we repress and hold down our emotions, and the language in which we release them. It is the language of catharsis.
In psychoanalytic terms again, breath is the language of resistance. This is how Hendricks describes the connection between breathing and resistance, and the efficacy of using Breathwork to get past resistance:
> Breathing can be one of the fastest ways to get past resistance. The
> reason is that resistance exists on the borderline between the
> unconscious and the conscious. So does breathing. It is the one system in
> your body that you can control with your conscious mind or that you
> can forget about completely, leaving it to be run by your unconscious.
> (Hendricks, p. 29)

As Taylor says, undoubtedly making an understatement,
> If we participate in several Breathwork sessions...it is likely that some
> unresolved traumatic stress would surface. (Taylor, 1994, p. 93)

Body language is a dialect of breath language
I once heard a lecture in which a doctor was describing an experiment he had done with patients with severe lung disease. He reported that he had had to stop the experiment because his patients were getting worse. I looked at the speaker. He was a little man - little in every sense of the term: small in stature, small in mind, small and tight in his body-holding, cold, unfriendly, closed off against new ideas, tight-chested - and I

21 Taylor, 1994, p. 93.   22 Taylor, 1994, p. 29; Janov, 1990, p. 119; See also Campoli, p.36, Rosenberg, 1985, p. 106.

thought, "What else could possibly happen? How could anyone get better from any ailment with a therapist (from any discipline) like that?" and in particular, "How could someone who cannot breathe help lung-disease sufferers?" What was quite obvious was that the man's breath did not flow![23]

There's no cheating in Breathwork or bodywork. How we breathe is the indicator of our psychological health and well-being or the absence of it, and it communicates itself to our clients and patients. Transference and counter-transference happens also through the nature and rhythms of the breath! Neurolinguistic Programming would call this matching. Here's an example from one of Hendrick's case histories to illustrate this point,

> George was in a great deal of physical and emotional pain. Many times during the session I noticed that I was holding my breath, probably in a misguided attempt to help him hurt less. Each time I noticed I was holding my breath, he seemed to be holding his, too. When I remembered to breathe, so would he. (Hendricks, p. 37)

If we want our clients' breath to be free, we must model this through our own free breath.

Fried, who practices Rational-Emotive Therapy and biofeed back, mistrusts the body,

> The body has no wisdom. .. it often limits us to repeat what we did in the past. While this may in some cases be helpful, it hardly qualifies as wisdom. The future may be different from the past, but the body seldom modifies its instincts even when they doom it to extinction. Due to conditioning, it responds blindly to the future or to its anticipation. (Fried, 1993, p. 28)

However, he also says,

> One cardinal rule in behavioural medicine is that unless it is interfered with, your body knows exactly what it is doing and always does the best thing to do under the circumstances. Consequently, if you have a disorder, you may reasonably assume that the disorder itself is the body's best adjustment to the circumstances. (Fried, 1990, p. 59)

People who use the breath psychotherapeutically have understood that the body collaborates in the healing process. I will discuss their work below. Meanwhile, here is a case history that shows the strong relationship between Breathwork and body language. It is the report of a man doing Breathwork on his own:

23 See also Timmons, 1994 ii, p. 269.

> As I breathed, I felt like the energy was getting stuck in my hands and arms. I couldn't figure out how to let it go. This happened for several sessions in a row. This may sound strange, but I finally asked my arms what they needed in order to let go. A few seconds later, I had the urge to reach out with my arms, even though I was sitting alone in my bedroom. Suddenly I was flooded with tears, and I had the realisation of how much I hold back from reaching out to people. Immediately the tension melted and never returned in subsequent sessions. (Case history from Hendricks, p. 28)

Breath language is a language of communication with the body. We can intentionally breathe into various parts of our body, bringing them energy and healing, and we can exhale from various parts of our body, releasing tensions in them with our out-breath.

Relationships are a dialect of breath language
The way our bodies are, or have become constructed, influences and our breathing style. Our breathing style is also our relationship style. Try this exercise: Take a deep breath and then exhale as deeply and as fully as you can. At the end of your exhalation, stop, and then take time to experience your body posture and your psycho-emotional attitude. You have now become what Dychtwald calls a chest-contractive person. He describes chest-contractive people in this way:

> (They) have narrow, fragile chests. The pectoral muscles are often under developed, permitting a minimal flow of feeling and energy through this region....The chest-contractive person will look and feel as if he is always exhaling. Muscle tension is chronically held and is usually associated with the blockage of proper energy flow upward from the belly and the diaphragm.

Through the exercise, you have become a chest-contracted person. Let's do it again. Take a deep breath and then exhale as deeply and as fully as you can. At the end of your exhalation, stop, and then take time to experience your body posture and your psycho-emotional attitude. This is what Dychtwald says about your relationship potential in this position:

> In all likelihood, your body has assumed a kind of sunken, collapsed posture, and your feelings probably range from ones of general emotional weakness to more specific constellations of insecurity and depression.

This is how chest-contracted people relate to themselves and others, and to energy, health and well-being,

Psycho-emotionally, this person will have difficulty building and sustaining an energetic charge in this passionate, life-assertive body region. His actions will be more passive than aggressive, his feelings will be prone to depression, his actions will tend to be more motivated by a chronic sense of fear and inferiority than by a sense of confidence and self-motivation. This person will tend to suffer from great many chest-centred diseases such as asthma, bronchitis, and chest colds and pains. By approaching the world with a deflated chest and correspondingly insufficient air and energy, this individual will have difficulty 'taking it on the chest' and moving comfortably through the world of self-assertive action. Because he continually experiences only a small portion of his own self-generated feelings of love and connectedness to all things, he will need to be charged and inspired by the life energies of other people. As a result, this person might tend to assume the interpersonal role of 'taker' more frequently than 'giver.' The combination of chronically held fear and self-protection, with the habitual experience of too little air and life energy might force him into regular moods of anguish and despair. (Dychtwald, p. 153-4)

Now let's do another exercise: Take a deep breath and this time overfill your chest, and, before you exhale, hold this breath for a while. While holding this extended inhalation, experience your bodily feeling and the corresponding psycho-emotional attitude. You have now become a chest-expansive person. Dychtwald describes chest-expansive people in this way,

They ... tend to have a large, over-developed chest. This sort of psychosomatic structure encourages an overcharge of energy and excitation into this region to the detriment of some other body-mind area, usually the pelvis or legs.

He says of himself, when he takes up this posture,

When I (do this), I feel as thought I am pumping up my aggressiveness. This 'overblown' attitude is accompanied by my losing contact with the more tender aspects of myself. When I blow up my chest I feel tough, strong, and powerful. I also notice that when I hold my inhalation in this fashion, my belly tightens and my diaphragm rigidifies, thereby blocking off my contact with my gut and the feelings that live there. When I am chest expansive, the general attitude I am presenting to the world is one that says, I'm OK, "I can take care of myself, you don't bother me." In fact, it seems to be as hard for the chest-expansive person to receive energy from other people as it is for the chest-contractive person to give it. I think that this is because before you can receive energy from other people, you first have to let down enough of your 'front' to let it in, something the chest-expansive person often has difficulty with. (Dychtwald, p. 156f.)

Having had both experiences, it is interesting to hear how Dychtwald describes the relationship between body, breathing and loving:

Neither chest contraction nor chest expansion defines the healthiest of all chest attitudes. Rather, it is the balance between these two exaggerations that describes the most vital and loving of all possibilities. Just as a breath is made up of an inhalation as well as an exhalation, and loving relationships are built on the ability to give as well as receive, true human creativity lies in the ability to experience the world anew each instant, to have each breath begin fresh, and to express freely and openly each passion of the body-mind. In the unrestricted individual, the balance of soft and hard, in and out, giving and receiving, expansion and contraction, defines the power and beauty of the thoracic region of the body-mind. (Dychtwald, p. 160)

Nose-breathing and Mouth-breathing are different dialects of breath language

Nose and mouth breathing are different dialects of breath language. They lead to qualitatively different experiences. The nostril which is predominant at any one time also has an influence on one's state of consciousness.

Minett explains the difference between nose and mouth breathing:

In most cases, breathing through the nose results in a more intellectual or spiritually-oriented insight into the experiences which emerge, while breathing through the mouth is more likely to lead to purely physical experiences. Nose-breathing is often said to have a more healing effect than mouth-breathing. It seems to be easier for the psyche to integrate and accept experiences that are linked with an intellectual or intuitive insight, than experiences on a purely physical level. (Minett, p.. 31)

Each nostril speaks a different dialect of breath-language.

During the day and night we alternate with regard to which nostril is doing the breathing. There are reasons for this which have to do with natural 90-minute ultradian rhythms (rhythms which happen more than once a day) in cerebral hemisphere dominance which are contralaterally associated with similar alternations in the nasal breathing cycle. Breathing through the left nostril stimulates right brain functions, and vice versa. Research shows that regularity of the nasal cycle is correlated with mental health and well-being.[24]

In his practice of Breathwork, Hendricks encourages alternative nostril breathing whose efficacy he explains in this way,

> The phrase right-hemisphere has come to symbolise feeling, emotion, imagery, and intuition, while left-hemisphere has come to refer to logic, mathematics, words, and linear thinking. The left side of the nose is connected to the right side of the brain , and vice versa. Breathing alternately through each nostril causes a shift from one hemisphere of the brain to the other....My sense is that shifting hemispheres is what gives the practice its power. Switching from one brain hemisphere to another a number of times, while breathing slowly and deeply, seems to bring about a balance. My personal experience has shown me that it improves mood, refreshes the body, and sharpens the mind. (Hendricks, p. 69)

Psychotherapists understanding breath language

Breathwork in psychotherapy has a long history. What I want to show here are some methods and case histories which show how various practitioners have understood that breath is a language.

1. Breathwork influenced by Psychoanalysis

Winnicott, a Freudian analyst, set up an experiment which allows him to observes the behaviour of an infant reaching for a spatula (his special case). He speculates as follows about breathing:

> In my special case, given to illustrate the application of the technique, control includes that of the bronchial tubes. It would be interesting to discuss the relative importance of the control of the bronchus as an organ (the displacement of control, say, of the bladder) and control of expiration of the breath that would have been expelled if not controlled. The breathing out might have been felt by the baby to be dangerous if linked to a dangerous idea - for instance, an idea of reaching in to take. To the infant, so closely in touch with his mother's body and the contents of the breast, which he actually takes, the idea of reaching in to the breast is by no means remote, and fear of reaching in to the inside of the mother's body could easily be associated in the baby's mind with not breathing. (Winnicott, 1941 in 1992: 63)

24 Rossi, 1993, p. 178-185.

Breathing, then, in this understanding, is the language of 'in' and 'out' - I hasten to say, one of the many languages of 'in' and 'out' in Freudian psychoanalysis, among them the 'language' of eating and the 'language' of excreting. Winnicott relates 'in' and 'out' to the goodness and badness of things taken in and given out, love impulses and destructive impulses, inner and outer reality, and fear, among other things. He has the concept of a dangerous breath and a dangerous breathing organ.

Winnicott is also interesting with regard to his understanding of the first breath of the new-born baby:

> I have found that the memory trace of restriction of chest expansion during a traumatic birth process can be very strong, and an important thing about this is the contrast between reactive chest activity and the chest activity of true anger. During the birth process, in reaction to the construction of the maternal tissues, the infant has to make what would be (if there were any air available) an inspiratory movement. After birth, if all goes well, the cry establishes the expression of liveliness by expiration. This is an example in physical terms of the difference between reacting and simply going on 'being.' When there is a delay and exceptional difficulty the changeover to normal crying is not definite enough and the individual is always left with some confusion about anger and its expression. Reactive anger detracts from ego establishment. Yet in the form of the cry anger can be ego-syntonic from very early, an expulsive function with clear aim, to live one's own way and not reactively. (Winnicott, 1941, in 1992: 188)

So Winnicott is saying that breath is the language of healthy normal self-assertion.

Winnicott recognises that breathing disorders can be the language of birth trauma. All contemporary breath-based methods confirm this.[25]

It is worth noting that Winnicott wonders if the mystical practice of doing without breathing is related to birth trauma.[26]

2. Reichian Therapy

Reich, the dissident Freudian, had a great understanding of the vocabulary of Breath language:

> Reich watched the flow of energy in the body. He worked with the breathing pattern to release chronic contraction in the tissue, which arrests the pulsation found naturally in life. Breathing, like the heartbeat,

---

25 See e.g. Orr & Ray, Leonard & Laut, Minett, Grof, Manné. There is also evidence from cranio-sacral osteopathy. See Weil, 1995, p.31, "If the first breath of life is not perfectly full, the cranial rhythms are restricted from the start."
26 Winnicott, 1941, in 1992, p. 188.

establishes the body's rhythm and flow. (Conger, 1988, p.45)

As is usual with everything in this world, the domain of
therapy included, not all of the people who worked with Reich
were completely satisfied with the experience. This is Hendricks
critique of Reich's Breathwork:

> Reich's Breathwork emphasised deep, rapid breathing through the open
> mouth. After a while, if this is done with care and/or with skilful help, it
> will result in an emotional catharsis or deeply pleasurable streaming
> sensations in the body. However, it can be an unpredictable and
> dangerous process. Reich and his followers, many of whom were skilful
> practitioners, precipitated psychiatric crises in many clients because of
> the profound anxiety released by too much deep, rapid breathing. For
> this reason I gravitated away from Reichian-style breathing toward
> gentler practices that I found more effective and completely safe.
> (Hendricks, p. 182)

Boadella explains,

> In Reich's work the therapist seeks to deepen breathing beyond the level
> of the repression. In doing so he has to be sensitive to the natural
> rhythms of the breath cycle and to the thresholds of anxiety in the
> client. Inexperienced therapists trying to provoke a patient to deeper
> breathing can easily induce a hyperventilation crisis and not recognise it
> as such. Skill is required in this work since a patient with chronically
> reduced breathing may easily go into hyperventilation as a response to
> the therapeutic situation. The crisis is avoided either by careful pacing of
> the rate of respiratory changes or by the patient becoming more
> expressive, either muscularly, emotionally or both....Reich warned that
> changing the patterns of a person's breathing was tantamount to
> emotional surgery and should only be attempted by those experienced in
> his methods. (Boadella, 1994, p.241)

Here is an example of a client who was completely satisfied
with the way Reich worked:

> I was extremely impressed by the way Reich worked with my body. He
> would have me breathe and then keep pointing out the way I avoided
> letting the breath expire naturally. Sometimes, he would press certain
> parts of my body, particularly my chest. A few times this was followed
> by very deep sobbing, crying in a way I could not remember ever having
> cried before. He would encourage me in an emphatic way. "Don't be
> ashamed of it. I have heard it by the millions. That sorrow is the best
> thing in you," (Myron Sharif, in Conger, 1988, p.21)

Reichian psychotherapy was further developed by Alexander Lowen as Bioenergetics.

3. Breathwork influenced by Analytical Psychology

Jungian analysts also were interested in Breathwork. "Magda Proskauer...was trained as a physical therapist...in European schools of movement, including Laban and Mensendieck. She became interested in breathing, which, she claimed, is a movement more than it is anything else. She came to New York in the 1940s and in practice there, found that breathing therapy could help not only patients with respiratory disorders but also those in pain or with postural or emotional problems."[27] Proskauer had a Jungian analysis and this influenced her work.

> Instead of correcting faulty habits one takes as the point of departure the individual breathing pattern, disturbed as it may be. One concentrates on the act of breathing, observing its inner movement until the breath, left to itself, can find the way back to its own rhythm. (Proskauer, 1968, 255f) One learns to visualise an inner body space, while simultaneously concentrating on one's exhalation, as if the breath were sent into that particular space. This might change blood pressure and lead to a sense of lightness....One is asked to concentrate on scanning [fn. focusing one's energy on] a certain area of one's body and to combine this with one's inhalation. Gradually the two tasks will connect, as if one were breathing with that particular area, or being breathed by it. (Proskauer, 1968, p. 258.)

This is one of her case histories, which illustrates trust and mistrust being expressed through breath language.

> A young dancer,...an overly intellectual woman who relied exclusively on her reasoning capacity. When I asked her to exhale gently, then wait and observe how the next breath came in, she became extremely anxious. She realised through this experience that she could not trust anything to happen on its own accord, not even respiration. Only what she controlled could occur. After an initial sense of confusion, this insight brought her great relief. It led her to the roots of her fears, which she felt went back to her childhood, in which no father was present to counteract an overburdened, domineering mother who knew no natural tenderness. She saw how far she had parted from Mother Nature and was glad to find this new channel through which she hoped to regain the lost contact with herself. (Proskauer, 1968, p. 258)

27 Timmons, 1994 i, p. 12.

4. Rebirthing.

Rebirthing is a particular form of Breathwork. It is very comprehensive, dealing with the whole range of human experience, from conception and birth trauma through to ageing; from the emotional, through the sexual to the spiritual.
This is how Minett describes it:

> Of all the modern breathing techniques available today, Rebirthing is the only one that focuses entirely on breath as the tool for cleansing, revitalising and purifying the body. In many schools of modern psychotherapy, breath is used as a tool to get in touch with subconscious thoughts and feelings. They are then dealt with through some form of mental and emotional catharsis. In Rebirthing, however, the focus is entirely on the breath. Maintaining a relaxed, open pattern of breathing is the key to our inner selves. The underlying assumption is that every thought and emotion is also a form of energy and can be expressed as such - through the breath. This makes the technique specially relevant, because an absolutely essential aspect of healing the body and mind involves changing the way we breathe. (Minett, p. 20)

Minett takes the position that Rebirthing is not a psychotherapy:

> Rebirthing is not in itself psychotherapy, but like other breathing methods it is used as a psychotherapeutic tool. Rebirthing acts as a cleansing process for the body and psyche causing everything, which blocks the body's natural flow to emerge. This emergence makes it possible for the obstructions to be integrated and dissolved. Because of this, it is not only important for the individual's therapist to be competent enough to guide breathing, but he or she also needs to be able to create an environment of trust and confidence, and to be qualified to handle the level of psychological problems that can emerge during this process. (Minett, p. 91)

While Rebirthing is not 'in itself' a complete psychotherapy, or only a psychotherapy, the original Rebirthing books contain many case histories that are clearly psycho-therapeutical. Here is one, chosen at random:

> In a split second I saw with total clarity and perfect understanding why every single relationship I had had with a woman inevitably ended in incompletion. Dissatisfaction. Separation. I saw in that moment that not one love relationship I had ever had even had a prayer of being whole, complete or lasting. I was too busy working out my revenge. This made me very sad and I cried. Cried for all the broken hearts and unfulfilled

hopes and aspirations. Cried for all the subtle cruelties and perpetrations.
My sadness was a sadness of remorse. (Orr & Ray, p. 136)

In just this one paragraph which describes a short period of
a long and powerful session are all the elements of good
psychotherapy: the realisation of a pattern, analysis or
awareness leading to comprehension, and catharsis or the
expression of emotion.

I consider the psychotherapeutic contribution of Rebirthing
so important that I will quote another case history, this one from
Minett herself:

> In the course of a breathing session I was guided by my therapist into
> mentally reliving my childhood. I returned to the time before my birth
> and experienced myself as a foetus, linked with my mother through the
> umbilical cord. At the same time I felt waves of anger and frustration
> crashing like tidal waves through the umbilical cord into my stomach,
> each one very painful. My initial reaction was to recede into a state
> resembling sleep. When the therapist asked my about my experiences, I
> could only repeat: "I don't know, I don't want to know, I don't want to
> feel." Despite this avoidance, she continued to insist on an answer. Still
> my only reaction was that of clinging to unconsciousness of the
> occurrence. When we later discussed this experience, I realised suddenly
> how often I handle unpleasant situations by making my mind insensitive
> and distant. (Minett, 1994, p. 110)

This personal case history, so courageously shared, shows
classical elements in effective psychotherapy: regression to an
early experience and reconnecting with feelings that had been
repressed on that occasion, and a healing understanding of its
influence on present behaviour patterns. As I have said, the
breath is the royal expressway to the unconscious.

I have shown elsewhere the relationship between Rebirthing
and other psychotherapies.[28]

5. Conscious Breathing Techniques

Rebirthing has led to the development of a variety of
Conscious Breathing Techniques. These are not a unified method,
but have been developed individually by various practitioners
among them Gay Hendricks and myself. Some of these may have
originated uninfluenced by Rebirthing.

Here are some examples of Gay Hendrick's work (others have
appeared previously in the text). The first is a case history

28 Manné, 1994, 1995.

showing a client using Breathwork to deal with resistance:
> [The client reports:] "During breathing one day I found myself getting
> bored. I felt sleepy and thought, 'This stuff is really stupid.' Suddenly I
> realised that the feelings and thoughts were just resistance. I remembered
> what someone told me once, that resistance is a sign that breakthrough
> is about to happen. So I kept on breathing, and I became aware of a
> tense place deep in my stomach. I breathed into it for just a few breaths,
> and the tension burst free like an exploding sun. I was filled with light. I
> had the realisation that I had lived my whole life like a robot, never
> thinking of what I wanted or needed. Doing this had put a ball of
> tension in my stomach that had been there for years." [Hendricks
> comments:] Through working with her breath, she (the client) had
> learned to let go of this ball of tension. (Hendricks, p. 29)

Breath is a way to communicate with unpleasant emotions.
Here is a case history that shows how Gay Hendricks worked
with a client with stage fright that sometimes became asthma:
> His habit was to hold his breath when his feelings arose, in a misguided
> attempt to make them go away. By doing this he actually prolonged the
> unpleasant sensation of the feelings....My client discovered something
> remarkable: When he let himself breathe through the feelings, he was
> often free of them within seconds. But when he held his breath, the
> feelings would sometimes linger for hours. The unpleasant quality of
> emotions come from not letting them through, from holding on to them
> by not participating with them. By directly participating with feelings,
> largely through breathing with them, you can rid yourself of much
> unnecessary negativity. (Hendricks, p. 14) This is how Hendricks works
> with feelings: I would ask my clients to listen to their bodies, to notice
> where and what they were feeling. Then I would ask them to breathe into
> the place where they felt those feelings. This never failed to produce
> results. They would come to deeper resolutions during the sessions than
> I had seen before. But more important, they left the sessions with a
> natural tool that they could carry with them into everyday life.
> (Hendricks, p. 183)

Hendricks uses a great variety of techniques. Here he uses
his breath to understand his pain:
> ...my righteous anger was a way of masking the pain I felt. I took a few
> deep breaths into the pain. It subsided and turned into sadness. I took a
> few more breaths into the sadness and a question formed in my mind.
> Why was criticism always such a big issue for me? Why was sadness just
> a few breaths under the surface of it? Then I realised that all this was
> really about my father....The realisation was helpful to me, but what

really moved me was how quickly I got in touch with it by using my
breathing as a searchlight. It was totally effortless. I just breathed a few
times and wondered; the answer was right there, as if it had been
waiting to be breathed on. (Hendricks, p. 183)

It is important for Hendricks that:

One should always deal with feelings and correct the breathing before
attempting to solve any problem on the cognitive level. (Hendricks, p. 184)

In other words, a person who is hyperventilating, or gasping
or any other form of uncomfortable breathing, is not in an
appropriate state to solve a problem.

In my own use of Conscious Breathing Techniques I have
developed a six-fold structure.[29] My first step is to teach awareness work with the breath or analytical Breathwork. Without
awareness, no-one knows what they are feeling and thinking and
so any form of personal or spiritual development or
psychotherapy is impossible. When clients are aware of what is
happening in their mind and body, I introduce independent
Breathwork. Here clients have their attention on their breathing
with their body providing the rhythm. They tell me what is
happening and we work with that. Nothing is forced or exaggerated. There is no attempt to make the breath larger or smaller,
faster or slower or to change or control it in any way. The body
is trusted to regulate the breathing and guide the process.
Through these first two steps a basis of self-knowledge is built
up. Painful experiences are recalled and integrated. Clients learn
how to work with and to contain their own process. All of the
experiences traditionally connected with Rebirthing, including
the famous reliving of the birth trauma come up through this
way of working, if they are ready to be integrated.

My third step is to introduce conscious connected breathing.
Connected breathing is more likely to lead to trance states
although it will not necessarily do so. It will certainly lead to
strong experiences. I introduce it when the client is grounded,
has a solid foundation of integrated self-knowledge, good self-
awareness and good self-esteem. Only then is the client ready to
integrate stronger experiences and to do advanced work.

My fourth stage is working the Breath. What I mean here is
any form and any rhythm of consciously connected breathing
intentionally undertaken and worked strongly in the same way
as a physical exercise. I discuss with the client what our goals
are for the session, and related to that I propose a rhythm of

29 Manné, 1995; 1997 ii.

breathing and perhaps a part of the body in which to focus the breath. The client and I have an agreement that if what has been proposed does not take place, we will not try force it, but rather we will surrender to whatever the breath brings up. At this stage I am doing classical Rebirthing including offering the client the choice to do augmented or super breathing.[30] Working the Breath induces intense emotional experiences, regressions and higher states of consciousness. When it has been well-prepared for, it is a way of playing with the breath and having adventures with it.

My fifth stage is advanced energy work with the breath. This uses the breath purposefully to clear from the energy-field unproductive thoughts, habits and attitudes, unnecessary influences, old relationship problems and tendencies towards relationship problems, and energy left over from past life problems and experiences. The sixth stage is advanced awareness work with the breath. This is meditation. A client who has reached this stage no longer needs accompaniment.

In the first stages, I am teaching clients to become sensitive to their own breath language. There is more interaction between me and the client during these stages. For example, if a clients sigh, or hold their breath when I ask them a question, or start breathing rapidly all of a sudden, I will immediately ask them, "What's happening." All clients are passionately interested in the way learning breath language advances their personal development.

V. BREATH IS THE LANGUAGE OF SEX

Here is a formal physiological explanation of the relationship between breathing and sex:

> Orgasm might be the result of hyperventilation tetany.... some of the sensations women experienced with orgasm (faintness, numbness, dizziness, floating) [have been attributed] to excited over-breathing....the normal heavy breathing that is necessary to achieve orgasm may lead to panic attacks. Clinicians caring for asthmatic patients confirm that over-breathing during intercourse can bring on asthmatic and then panic attacks....Research in the respiratory aspects of sexual physiology could benefit many clients. (Timmons, 1994.ii, p. 273)

Don't let this take the fun out of your sex-life!
Breathwork - whether accompanied or not - can lead to orgasmic experiences. Here are some more evocative

30 Manné, 1997 i.

explanations:

> The prime way of building sexual excitation - a way that is often over
> looked - is by breathing. Many people hold their breath during sexual
> excitement, despite the fact that it is a time when increased breathing
> occurs naturally. This natural phenomenon must then be taught and
> re-patterned since it is inhibited by fears locked into the body and made
> unconscious. Breathing is the major way to develop excitation in the
> body sessions, and in doing this one learns the development of internal
> excitement, independent of outside stimulation. (Rosenberg, 1985, p.
> 232f) After practising Breathwork for a few months, one person reported
> a particularly deep session: "I felt like I was plugged into a universal
> light socket. My body felt illuminated from within. I felt orgasmic rushes
> every time I took a deep breath." (Hendricks, p. 28)

Breath is important in tantra, Kundalini yoga,[31] and various
Chinese techniques which bridge sexuality and spirituality.[32]
These spiritual practices require great discipline in order for the
required control over energy and orgasm to develop. The sexual
act is linked to the quest for Enlightenment in which detachment
is fundamental. It is not dedicated simply to increasing the
frequency and intensity of orgasm, as is too often the modern
interpretation - to the great frustration of modern practitioners
who have turned sex into a spiritually materialistic practice in
which, as with all materialism, bigger and better is continually
being sought, and satisfaction is unattainable.

VI. BREATH IS THE LANGUAGE OF SPIRIT

Breath is the language of spirit. The symbolism of breath as
the life principle is universal.

> The ancient Greeks used the word diaphragm to indicate the mind, as
> well as for breathing. ... In most religions, chants and spoken prayers
> (intense exhalations) for the 'un- ordained' and special breathing training
> for the priests, were and still are the rule. All over the world - in fairy
> tales, legends, in secret societies - breathing plays a significant role.
> (Speads, 1995, p. 39)

Inspiration and expiration symbolise the production and
re-absorption of the universe,[33] what India calls kalpa and
pralaya, yang and yin.
Breath is the language of spiritual disciplines such as
meditation and yoga. Two famous suttas in the Buddhist
tradition are devoted to breathing exercises. These are the

31 Silburn. 32 Chang, 1977. 33 See Cranmer, 1994, p. 120; Weil, 1995, p. 204.

Anapanasati Sutta (MN, Sutta 118) and the Satipatthana Suttas (DN, Sutta 22) in the Pali Canon).

The sutta shows that our breath is our way into altered states of consciousness. Contemporary teachers too have observed that the breath is our way into the spiritual. Elsa Middendorf says,

> If a person finds his way based on the experience of his breathing, he finds his own power and creativity. (Ilse Middendorf, 1995 i, p. 69)
> Breath is a connecting force. It creates a bodily equilibrium and balance and helps us to make inner and outer impressions interchangeable. It connects the human being with the outside world and the outside world with his inner world. Breathing is an original unceasing movement and therefore actual life. The ineffable has given nature various autonomous laws which have still to come to fruition. Experiencing the breath means to start to live in a new way. Breathing became my 'guide rope' that enables me to lead the body and with it the spiritual and mental into a new 'opening' to life where meaning is, to achieve a wider consciousness and greater expansion in the inner and outer spaces. (Ilse Middendorf, 1995 ii, p. 77)

It is because the breath is the way into the spiritual that many forms of Breathwork lead to similar spiritual experiences, for example, unity, forgiveness, and love:

> I have seen many people have spontaneous experiences of love, forgiveness, and joy while doing Breathwork. These feelings are all the more important because they have emerged from the body rather than from the mind. For example, many people have reported that, while they had previously understood the concept of forgiveness, it was only during Breathwork that they actually experienced it internally. I have also seen people breathe themselves to a sense of unity with themselves, others, and the universe itself. Deep spiritual experiences like these have great healing potential because they put the person in touch with a power greater than their normal ego consciousness. The highest potential of Breathwork is in unifying mind, body, and spirit. (Hendricks, p. 30)

Breath is the language of trance states. Often in shamanic practice it is combined with dance and drumming. Felicitas Goodman, who induces trances using a rattle and postures from ancient figures and cave art, uses breath to prepare the concentration necessary for trance.

> At the outset of the session, everyone was to take fifty relaxed, normal breaths, in and out, in and out. Only during inhalation could one feel the air passing over the septum; it was not perceivable when exhaling. This

alternation was what the participants were supposed to observe. It was a natural, soothing rhythm... (Felicitas Goodman, 1990, p. 44)[34]

Breath is the language of our commitment to life in this world:

> Breathing and the circulation of air that it implies is the prefect metaphor of the obligation to live in the world, the obligation for exchange, sharing, giving, and also the common and shared dependence on the Law. As we must all be born and die, we must all breathe, and in doing so, we must all share a common substance with others; whatever may be our desire for independence, autonomy, individuality (personalisation), sometimes to break with (separate ourselves from) the world, we are all subject to the law and to the communion of breathing. (Lesourne, 1996, p. 100)[35]

Breath is the language of Energy

Breath is the language of energy, as Fried has so poetically said. This must be so, as it is through breathing that we receive the basic energy of life.

I have already given many examples how Conscious Breathing makes energy available for therapy. This is how conscious breathing works in a Rebirthing session to bring about an energy cycle:

> In order to achieve a successful Rebirthing session it's necessary to trigger a phenomenon known as 'the energy cycle'. The energy cycle will begin to operate when a pattern of intense, relaxed and connected breathing has been attained. This pattern should be effortless, despite being far more powerful and intense than normal breathing. All parts of the breathing apparatus are, at best, utilised and the entire body is energised. When the relaxation of the body, in combination with the increased breathing, has led to a sufficient opening of the body, the whole system will be directly affected by the breath. The breathing and relaxation will reach and penetrate every part of the body. The body starts 'to breathe energy as well as air.' This means that the body is starting to release inner, stored energy, while at the same time it is activated by the new energy brought in by the intensified breathing. This is a state referred to as 'inner breathing' in the yoga tradition....When this state is reached, the energy sweeps through the body and 'flushes out' all the previously stored energy. This energy has been stored in the form of organic chemicals or hormones which, when released, provokes memories. The energy cycle is the actual healing part of the Rebirthing process. (Minett, p. 30)

---

34 See also Minett, p. 153.   35 La respiration et la circulation de l'air qu'elle implique est la parfaite métaphore de l'obligation de vivre au monde, l'obligation de l'échange, du partage, du don et aussi de la dépendence commune et partagée à la Loi.
Comme nous devons tous naître et mourir, nous devons tous respirer, et ce faisant nous devons tous partager une substance
commune avec autrui; quelque soit notre désir d'indépendance d'autonomie, de personnalisation, parfois de coupure d'avec le
monde, nous sommes tous soumis à la loi et à la communion du "respir."

Conscious Breathing also enhances our ability to gain access to and to use energy simply for pleasure.

> Conscious breathing activities also increase our ability to handle more energy. Many of us have our positive-energy thermostat set very low, so that we do not allow ourselves as much pleasure as we could. Conscious breathing actually retrains your nervous system to tolerate a higher charge of energy... (Hendricks, p. 27-28)

Breath is the language of love

If breath is the language of spirit, it must also be the language of love.

Here is one of Hendrick's case history that demonstrates the release of love energy through Breathwork:

> As I was doing the breathing activity, I began to feel a new energy flowing through my body. This energy brought with it a sense of love. Once I felt this natural love flowing through me, a thought popped into my mind - I'm willing to do whatever I need to do to feel this love in my life all the time. (Hendricks, p. 27)

Case histories like this are frequent in the Breathwork literature.

Breath is the language of prayer

> Each breath contains two blessings: life in the inspiration and the expulsion of the air in the expiration. Thank God, therefore, twice for each breath. (Gulistan de Saadi de Chiraz, dans Dictionnaire des Symbols)[36]

Breath and Spirit: the task of the therapist/accompanist

Because breath is the language of spirit, Breathwork requires particular qualities and skills in its practitioners.

Breathwork induces altered states of consciousness, and clients in altered states require a particular form of accompaniment. Kylea Taylor has considered this profoundly in her important book The Ethics of Caring: Honoring the Web of Life in Our Professional Healing Relationships. Among the problems she has identified are those related to the intensity of the work, the depth of transference and unacknowledged counter-transference, the greater suggestibility of the client particularly as regards retrieval of memories, among other factors. Taylor is aware of the interface between altered states of consciousness and states labelled psychotic:

> The difference between psychosis and a nonordinary state of

36 Chaque respiration contient deux bénédictions: la vie dans l'inspiration, et le rejet de l'air dans l'expiration. Remerciez Dieu, donc, deux fois pour chaque respiration.

consciousness is sometimes difficult to discern from the outside. The dramatic symptoms may be similar or different in each state. The client's awareness of the process and his co-operation with it may be a key indicator that the client is in a transformative rather than a pathological process. Generally psychosis is a defensive pattern functioning to keep awareness and pain at bay. Nonordinary states...are openings for change and growth. Those experiencing nonordinary states are usually aware of the process they are undergoing and in some sense welcome the awareness and change that is happening. (Taylor, 1995, p. 32)

Unless the therapist has understood the problems of working with altered states of consciousness, there will be problems for the client. The client may be misled into misunderstanding the experiences that come up, including their relationship with ordinary consensus reality. Further, unless the therapist has made considerable progress with her/his own process of personal and spiritual development, s/he will be unable to support the client in these states.

VII. DIALECTS OF BREATH LANGUAGE

Breath language has many dialects, among them, relation-ships, sex and prayer, as I have said above. There are others that may surprise you.

Laughter is a Dialect of Breath Language

The International Journal of Humour Research published a study which demonstrated that laughter boosted the cardiovascular, respiratory, muscular, hormonal, central nervous or immune system - not the least by drawing more oxygen into the lungs.[37]

Laughter is good for health and well-being. There is a famous case of a person, who was also a doctor, and who was diagnosed as terminally ill with cancer. He took videos of Marx brothers and other humorous films home and spent hours watching them. The result was that he laughed himself to health again. This case is medically attested. As this is the section on laughter, I do not feel obliged to search out in the library for the references where I read about this. In any case, it is regularly cited and some people teach laughter therapy.

37 The Therapist, Vol. 4, No 2 - 1997.

Singing is a dialect of Breath Language

The deep and complete breathing necessary for singing contributes to the good feeling people have afterwards. Through the
tendency to match one's own breathing rhythm with that of the
singer the audience gets 'breathed' by the rhythm and the phras-
es of the singer's breath.

Music can be used in meditation as a means of guiding and
deepening the breath:

> Music for meditation .. creates an atmosphere conducive to stillness and
> inner contemplation. It is quieter and slower [than music for trance];
> melodic phrase may last as long as the inspiration phase of breathing. Its
> purpose is to slow and deepen breathing, altering perception of time by
> focusing us on the present moment. (Fried, 1990 : 286)

Speaking is a Dialect of Breath Language[38]

Our ease with our breath affects our ease with ourselves, and
so with our ability to speak. As Daphne J. Pearce has said so
succinctly, "Speech is the culmination of two essential human
functions: breathing and communication."[39] As our breath is
connected with our emotions, our breathing is a reflection of our
emotional well-being. The larynx, which is the physical
apparatus of speech, can be affected by dust and fumes, and
emotions. Pearce explains, "From the infant's screams, to the
quavering of senescence, the voice reflects feeling and well
being; it betrays fears and doubts, and proclaims intentions."
Problems with breathing may result in stuttering or other
speech disorders.

We can use, misuse or abuse our voices - and our breath. We
use our voice to project an image and to elicit a response, so our
voice is a tool to control ourselves and the environment. The
voice and the breath, can be abused through smoking and
alcohol.[40]

In this dialect of breath-language, pauses are important.

> If one wishes to carry breathing all the way to completion, it is necessary
> to be able to carry through the four phases of breathing: inhalation,
> pause, exhalation, pause. These pauses and the conscious feeling of them
> are of the greatest importance. The pause, or rest, after exhalation must
> not be lifeless. It should never be a matter of holding the breath. On the
> contrary, it should most closely resemble the pause we experience in
> music which is the vital preparation for what is to follow. It is wonderful
> to see how inhalation emerges from this living pause. There is an
> opening of the cells: the air enters easily and silently and we feel fresh

38 I thank my friend Brigitte Zellner who reminded me about this "dialect." 39 Pearce, 1994, p. 12. 40 Pearce, p.185.

and toned up. What happens, though, if we do not wait until the lungs have opened up? And when do we wait for it? Immediately after exhalation, we often take in air arbitrarily and try to pump the lungs full of air before they ask us for it. This is utterly inappropriate. We soon feel how the course of air in the lungs falters, and there occurs a thick feeling around the breast bone, the air is dammed up in the large bronchi and there is pressure and closure in the small ones. The air does not and cannot enter the lungs freely because the small lung vesicles have not yet opened. And it is these that must be supplied with oxygen while breathing. Access to them, the smallest bronchia, is provided by vessels more delicate than hair, so naturally the attempt to press the dammed-up air into them must fail. In addition, it often occurs that the air vesicles, at the time when the air is prematurely pumped in, have not yet emptied themselves of the old supply of air. They now do that, and the air stream trying to work upward and outward from inside collides with the air being pumped in from the outside so that there occurs a kind of piling up, and the result is a pressed, constricted feeling. But if we wait for the opening of the smallest vesicles we thereby permit a pause to occur completely. Then, as soon as the vesicles become empty, they suck in air automatically. The air then easily penetrates the smallest, hair-fine vessels. Nowhere does congestion occur, and nowhere is there a sensation of thickness or of lack of air. We do not need to bring into action any special activity for inhalation. (Elsa Gindler, 1986-7, p.11f)[41]

In the dialect of breath language called speaking, not only the utterance of language-words is important, but the fluency of the utterance, including the nature of its pauses. Pauses depend both on physiological aspects of speech motor activity and cognitive processes. Surprisingly, pauses also occur during the in-breath: "Physiologically inevitable pauses regularly occur during the inspiration phase of respiration, since phonatory activity is intricately connected with respiratory activity."[42] These pauses relate to the speaker's health. As Zellner says, "weak respiration, low muscle tone, and slow articulatory rate is associated with a greater number of pauses than a rapid articulatory rate and good respiratory capacity."

If we interfere with the length of the breathing pause, shortening it even slightly, we find ourselves feeling 'rushed' and 'pressured,' that well-known state that interferes so often with our sense of well-being and is such a generally acknowledged burden in our daily lives. We have all experienced how strained this kind of breathing leaves us. We pay dearly for it in inefficiency, weariness, and irritability. (Speads, 1995, p. 47)

41 Interesting to do in therapy - if someone stops breathing, get them to take their pauses consciously.   42 Zellner, 1994.

One variety of the breathing pause is the suspension of the breath that can happen in meditation. Fields defines this phenomenon as "Periods of breathing apparently suspended between 15 and 30 seconds. Further,

> Investigators who have reported such respiratory suspension periods equate it with the meditative state of 'pure consciousness.' Badawi et al. (1984) characterised it as having unique features differentiating it from other states of consciousness. It is important to note that these features occur during typical EEG configurations different from any found in biofeedback, relaxation, and hypnosis. (Field, 1993 : 275)[43]

Kylea Taylor has compared the breathing pauses that happen in Holotropic and other Breathwork when the breathing stops or seems to disappear with breathing pauses from yoga.[44]

Smoking Is a Dialect of Breath Language

Smoking is a dialect of breath language. The dialect of smoking speaks about dependence, traumatism and auto-destruction, anxiety, sharing, sex, and shamanism.

Smoking is a dependence issue. At birth, the foetus' dependence on mother is exchanged for the new-born's dependence on air. Dependence on breathing is painless, but the smoker makes it painful. Nicotine dependency is light and disappears within 24-48 hours. So nicotine dependency is the voluntary submission to an object with the purpose of escaping the involuntary submission to life. Smoking speaks about painful dependence.

The dialect of smoking speaks about traumatism, auto-destruction and the feeling of anxiety. The smoker repeats the first traumatic breath with every inhalation. Each time he feels aggressed by life, or 'penetrated,' he attacks and penetrates himself with air which he has polluted, to show he has no fear of being traumatised: that he remains in control. Anxiety affects breathing. A good slow deep breath eases anxiety and permits a person to make contact again with his life-force. The smoker eases or prevents his attacks of anxiety through smoking. When he feels unease or tension, he creates 'artificial respiration.' He knows he will not die because, through his cigarette, he knows that he breathes - as long as his cigarette burns.

Smoking is about sharing, and aggression. Air is communal, and to breathe is to share this communal element. The smoker, however, subverts this communion. He demonstrates his power of the air by marking it, as if marking a territory, so that all

43 Badawi, K., Wallace, R. K., Orme-Johnson, D., & Ronzere, A. M. (1984), "Electrophysiological characteristics of respiratory suspension periods occurring during the practice of the transcendental meditation program." Psychosomatic Medicine 46: 267-276. Farrow, J. T., & Herbert, J. R., (1982), "Breath suspension during transcendental meditation." Psychosomatic Medicine 44: 133-135; Kesterson & Clinch (1985)   44 Taylor, 1991, pp.5,7; 1994, p. 81.

others breathing it know that it was his first. Smokers poison and pollute the air for their neighbours. They are like babies who have not been successfully potty trained, leaving their 'bad smells' and 'bad objects' for others to see. They project the role of parent onto society, waiting for their 'badness' to be received and transformed into goodness by the good mother who admires their kaka and makes it good and clean for them. They express their hatred by polluting the air. Air that smells of old cigarette smoke makes an atmosphere charged with tension and aggression. The smoker keeps what is good in breathing: the warmth, the fire, the burning, the smell, life; and puts out for the others the smoke and the grey ashes, the colour of the earth that evokes death and corpses.

Through smoking, the smoker separates himself from the world, protecting himself, marking his limits and his territory, fighting suffering with auto-erotic activity. But by preventing himself from feeling his suffering he does not learn to bear it.

Smoking speaks about sex. Smokers are giving themselves a symbolic penis, to compensate for a hidden, inadequate or missing penis. Smoking is a sexual act: inhaling causes the smoke to penetrate the mouth of the smoker; exhaling causes it to penetrate the communal air shared by all others. Smokers want to add to the neutral breathing, smell and taste: to make it good. They make a food of the air, something they can swallow, bringing air into an erogenous zone, the mouth through which enters the goodness given by the mother. Smokers try to get pleasure out of the neutral act of breathing, as if inhaling the 'mother-universe,' devouring it, absorbing it like a food and not surrendering it, allowing it simply to be there, supporting, containing, protecting.

Can only negative things, then, be said about smoking? No. Smoking is about fire. Smoking, like suffering, speaks about shamanism. Smokers want more of what air brings: more activity, more life. They want combustion in the form of fire, exchange, transformation; faster heart beat, more rapid neurone activity, quicker processes. More dependence, more pain, more pleasure, more everything. Hence many creative people smoke (Freud, Picasso) as if seeking inspiration, ... and to activate their inner fire.

And Farting?

Everyone farts, but as far as I am aware, although the biological reasons for farting are known, there are no serious studies regarding the when's and because of farting. Surprisingly, the psychology of farting remains unexplored. I have heard people call farting 'Le deuxième souffle' - 'the second breath.' Is farting, I wonder, a dialect of breath language too?

BIBLIOGRAPY

1. Abbondio, Irène (1994), *Traumatisme de la naissance et souffle dans la psychologie occidentale : manual de référence à l'usage des Thérapeutes du Souffle.* Irène Abbondio, Cité Derrière 4, CH - 1005 Lausanne.

2. Boadella, David (1994), Styles of Breathing in Reichian Therapy, in Timmons & Ley, 1994, pp. 233-241.

3. Bradley, Dinah, (1991), *Hyperventilation Syndrome: a Handbook for Bad Breathers.* London: Kyle Cathie, 1994.

4. Chang, Jolan (1977), *The Tao of Love and Sex: The Ancient Chinese Way to Ecstasy.* London: Wildwood House.

5. Chevalier, Jean & Gheerbrant, Alain (1982), *Dictionnaire des Symbols.* Paris: Robert Lafont / Jupiter.

6. Campoli, Collette (1996), 'Les mots du souffle.' In Sapir (ed), 1996.

7. Conger, John P. (1988), *Jung & Reich: The Body as Shadow.* Berkeley, California: North Atlantic Books.

8. Corsini, Raymond, ed. (1973), *Current Psychotherapies.* Itasca, Illinois: F.E. Peacock Publishing Co.

9. Cranmer, David (1994), 'Core energetics,' in Jones, 1994.

11. Dychtwald, Ken (1977), *Bodymind: a Synthesis of Eastern and Western Ways to Self-awareness, Health and Personal Growth.* London: Wildwood House.

12. Eliade, Mircea (1969), *Yoga, Immortality and Freedom.* New York: Bollingen Series LVI.

13. Fried, Robert (1990), *Breath Connection: how to reduce psychological and stress-related problems with easy to do breathing exercises.* New York: Plenum.

14. (1993, with Joseph Grimaldi), *The Psychology and Physiology of Breathing: in Behavioural Medicine, Clinical Psychology, and Psychiatry.* New York: Plenum Press.

15. Gindler, Else (1986-7), 'Coming to our Senses.' In Johnson, 1995.

16. Goodman, Felicitas D. (1990), *Where the Spirits Ride the Wind.* Bloomington & Indianapolis: Indiana University Press.

17. Grof, Stanislav (1997), 'Holotropic Breathwork™ and the Hyperventilation Syndrome,' in *The Inner Door,* Volume 9, Issue 2.

18. Groddeck, Georg (1951), *The Unknown Self.* Plymouth: Vision Press.

19. Grossinger, Richard (1995), *Planet Medicine: Vol. 1, Origins.* Berkeley, California: North Atlantic.

20. (1995), *Planet Medicine: Vol 2, Modalities.* Berkeley, California: North Atlantic.

21. Hendricks, Gay (1995), *Conscious Breathing: Breathwork for Health, Stress Release, and Personal Mastery.* New York: Bantam Books.

22. Janov, Arthur (1990), *The New Primal Scream: Primal Therapy Twenty Years On.* London: Abacus.

23. *The Inner Door, a Publication of the Association for Holotropic Breathwork International,* ed. Kylea Taylor. P.O. Box 7169, Santa Cruz, CA 95061-7169.

24. Johnson, Bob Hanlon, ed. (1995), *Bone, Breath & Gesture: Practices of Embodiment.* Berkeley, California: North Atlantic Books.

25. Jones, David, ed. (1994), *Innovative Therapy: A Handbook. Buckingham:* Open University Press.

26. Kellner, E., ed. (1994), *Fundamentals of speech synthesis and recognition.* Chichester: John Wiley.

27. Leonard, Jim and Phil Laut (1983), *Rebirthing : the science of enjoying all of your life,* California : Trinity Publications, 1983.

28. Lesourne, Odile (1996), 'Variations sur l'air, le souffle, et le fumeur.' In Sapir (ed), 1996.

29. Ley, Ronald (1994), 'Breathing and the Psychology of Emotion, Cognition, and Behavior,' in Timmons and Ley, 1994, pp. 81-95.

30. Manné, Joy (1994), 'Rebirthing, an orphan or a member of the family of psychotherapies' *International Journal of Prenatal and Perinatal Psychology and Medicine,* Vol.6 (1994), No. 4, 503-517.

31. (1995), 'Rebirthing, is it marvelous or terrible?' *The Therapist: Journal of the European Therapy Studies Institute,* Spring 1995.

32. (1997 i), 'The Language of Breath: The Use Of Conscious Breathing Techniques In Psychotherapy,' paper presented at the International Society for the advancement of Respiratory Psychophysiology (ISARP) conference, 1995, in Rapp, Hilde, ed., (1997) *Experiences of Difference.* British Institute of Integrative Psychotherapy (BIIP): New Controversial Discussions Series. London: BIIP (21 Priory Terrace, GB- London NW6 4LG).

33. (1997 ii) *Soul Therapy.* North Atlantic Books, Berkeley, California.

34. McNeely, Deldon Anne (1987), Touching: *Body Therapy and Depth Psychology.* Toronto: Inner City Books.

35. Middendorf, Ilse (1995 i), *Interview with Ilse Middendorf by Elizabeth Beringer,* in Johnson, 1995.

36. (1995 ii), Preface to *The Perceptible Breath,* in Johnson, 1995.

37. Minett, Gunnel (1994), *Breath & Spirit: Rebirthing as a Healing Technique.* London: Aquarian/Thorsons.

38. Mithoefer, Michael (1997), 'The Physiology of Hyperventilation,' in *The Inner Door,* Volume 9, Issue 2.

39. Nierenberg, Gerard I. & Calero, Henry H. (1980), *How to Read a Person like a Book.* Wellinborough, Northamptonshire: A. Thomas.

40. Orr, Leonard et Sondra Ray, *Rebirthing : in the New Age.* Berkeley California : Celestial Arts. Revised Ed. 1983.

41. Pearce, Daphne J. (1994), 'Breathing and vocal Dysfunction,' in Timmons & Ley, 1994.

42. Proskauer, Magda (1968), 'Breathing Therapy,' in Timmons and Ley, 1994, pp.253-259.

43. Rapp, Hilde, ed., (1997) *Experiences of Difference.* British Institute of Integrative Psychotherapy (BIIP): New Controversial Discussions Series. London: BIIP (21 Priory Terrace, GB- London NW6 4LG).

44. Rossi, Ernest L. (1993) *The Psychobiology of Mind-Body Healing: New Concepts of Therapeutic Hypnosis.* Revised Edition. New York: W. W. Norton & Co.

45. Rosenberg, Jack (1985), *Body, Self, & Soul: Sustaining Integration.* Atlanta, Georgia: Humanics New Age.

46. Sapir, M. ed. (1996), *L'air et le souffle.* Champ Psychosomatique No.6. Ed. La Pensee Sauvage.

47. Schutz, William (1971), *Here Comes Everybody.* New York: Harper & Row.

48. Sharaf, Myron (1983), *Fury on Earth: A Biography of Wilhelm Reich.* New York: St. Martin's Press.

49. Silburn, Lilian (1983), *La Kundalini: ou l'Energie des Profondeurs.* Paris: Les Deux Océans.

50. Somatics, 1516 Grant Avenue, Suite 212, Novato, California 94945, USA.

51. Speads, Carola (1986), *Ways to Better Breathing.* Great Neck, NY: Morrow. In Johnson, 1995.

52. Taylor, Kylea (1991), 'Yogic Sleep and Meditation States During Holotropic Breathwork,' in *The Inner Door,* Volume 3, Issue 1, July 1991, pp. 5 & 7.

53. (1994), *The Breathwork Experience: Exploration and Healing in Nonordinary States of consciousness.* Santa Cruz, California: Hanford Mead.

54. (1995), *The Ethics of Caring: Honoring the Web of Life in Our Professional Healing Relationships.* Santa Cruz, California: Hanford Mead, 1995.

55. Thich Nhat Hahn (1996), *Breathe! You are Alive: Sutra on the Full Awareness of Breathing.* Berkeley, California: Parallax Press.

56. Timmons, Beverly H. (1994.i), 'Introduction,' in Timmons & Ley, 1994, pp. 1-13.

57. Timmons, Beverly H. (1994.ii), Breathing-related Issues in Therapy, in Timmons & Ley, 1994, pp. 261-292.

58. Timmons, Beverly H. & Ley, Ronald, eds. (1994), *Behavioral and Psychological Approaches to Breathing Disorders.* New York: Plenum Press.

59. Tristani, J.-L (1973), *Le stade du Respire.* Paris: Ed. Minuit.

60. Weil, Andrew, M.D. (1995), *Spontaneous Healing: How to Discover and Enhance Your Body's Natural Ability to Maintain and Heal Itself.* New York: Alfred A Knopf.

61. Whitmont, Edward C. and Kaufman, Yoram (1973), Analytical Psychology, in Corsini, 1973.

62. Winnicott, D.W. (1941), 'The Observation of Infants in a Set Situation,' in Winnnicott, 1992.

63. (1992), D. W. Winnicott: *through Paediatrics to Psychoanalysis.* Collected Papers. London: Karnak.

64. Zellner, Brigitte (1994), 'Pauses and the temporal structure of speech,' in Kellner, 1994, pp. 41-62.

65. Zi, Nancy (1994), *The Art of Breathing: A Course of Six Simple Lessons To Improve Performance and Well-being. Glendale,* California: Vivi Co.

GLOSSARY

dyspnea - "can't catch my breath. I feel like I am choking." (Fried, 1990 : 83)
hyperpnea   - increased respiration rate
hypocapnia - end-tidal carbon dioxide decreases
hypoxia - decrease in tissue oxygen
Tachypnea - increased respiration rate

Pranayama – A key to Atman
The four types of breathing

REINHARD SCHOLZE

Reinhard Scholze is a psychotherapist working in Austria and Germany who uses Pranayama Yoga in psychotherapy.

Prana, the subtle life force, is maintained at the biological level by twin processes of internal and external breathing. External breathing is activated by complementary actions of the nervous system which picks up the subtle movement of Prana and triggers the breathing mechanism, the pumping action of the heart and its distribution of oxygenated blood through the circulatory system to all the organs of the body. Internal breathing takes place at the cellular level and consists of various metabolic processes of which oxygen reduction is the most important.

The act of breathing is one of the most obvious and tangible manifestations of Prana and it constitutes the tool and the object of experimentation in the science of Pranayama.

The ancient Yogis concentrated their attention on their own breathing mechanisms, experimented with and discovered the cosmic laws that united them to the cosmic power. A methodical regulation of breath allowed them to enter the plane of subtle energy and to draw from it the vitality and power needed to give health and longevity to their physical frame.

This ancient science of breathing and control of the subtle energies is know as *Pranayama*, a Sanskrit word composed of the terms *Prana*, the energy and *Yama*, its extension, expansion and control.

One of the main purposes of Pranayama is to control and equalise the energy that is pulsating through the body and the mind. When this mastery is gained with the appropriate asanas and breathing techniques and when all parts of the organism are working in harmony, a power greater than the physical energy can manifest itself in humans. Moreover, the science of Pranayama allows practitioners to discover their fundamental divine vibration, attune it to the cosmic vibration and find a resonance with all the vibratory rhythms of the universe.

To achieve this goal, Pranayama techniques have been devised to intensify the rate of absorption of energy by the physical body. These techniques use the nervous systems as communication mechanism capable of increasing, reducing or modifying the energy potential in an individual.

Moreover, these Pranayama techniques have a profound effect on the mind helping it to concentrate through the regulation of the breath. And finally, Pranayama is used as a spiritual discipline for the higher forms of Yoga, by tuning the breath to subtle vibrations known as mantras.

Pranayama allows practitioners to draw Prana from the main sources; the atmosphere, the sun, the cosmic and tellurian radiation, to store this Prana in subtle energy centres situated along the spine, to move the Prana in harmonious and rhythmic manner along the pranic pathways, and finally to remain in constant harmony and union with the universal energy.

Thus, Pranayama covers a vast range of practices from the physiology of breathing, breath management, to the purification of the respiratory organs and the mastery over the subtle energy pathways and centres.

The physiology of breathing
The basic physiological needs of the human body are predominantly met by the supply of oxygen and glucose. Whereas oxygen has an elimination function through the oxidation of waste matter, glucose mainly carries out the function of supplying energy in the cells. The respiratory organs perform this process during breathing. The main function of these organs is to take the oxygen from the air, to transform it and to make it available to the cells as well as to expel the carbon dioxide accumulated in them. Ordinary breathing is thus a self-regulated mechanism of gas exchange. This self-regulation determines the rate and intensity of breathing through a control mechanism of the respiratory centres in the central nervous system which integrates the information from mechanical and chemical receptors. When the carbon dioxide level in the arterial blood increases, the proportion of hydrogen ions in the cerebrospinal fluid is changed. This, in turn, influences the respiratory centres in the medulla oblongata that send impulses to the phrenic and vagus nerves and trigger the movement of the diaphragm and the rib cage. When the muscular, nervous and skeletal structures surrounding the lungs start operating, the breathing mechanism starts working. This happens when a new-born child emits its first cry and produces its first breath: the

breathing process begins to function and it will continue throughout life in the twin movement of inspiration and expiration.

In ordinary breathing, the lungs will inflate and deflate about sixteen times a minute and the heart will pump the blood through the body at an average rate of seventy times per minute. This kind of breathing depends on the automatic co-ordination of the nervous system, heart, lungs and circulatory system coupled to the smooth movements of the rib cage and the respiratory muscles.

Inspiration consists of an active expansion of the chest, which allows the soft, and spongy lungs to be filled with fresh air richly charged with oxygen. This takes place when the rib cage expands and the diaphragm is lowered, causing a reduction of pressure inside the lungs with a concomitant drawing in of air from the atmosphere. The oxygen from the atmosphere penetrates into the alveolar sacs of the lungs and diffuses into the blood stream through the capillaries surrounding the outer walls of the alveoli.

Expiration consists of a passive recoil of the elastic rib cage which pumps the vitiated air out of the lungs. This recoil takes place when the respiratory muscles are relaxed and when the surface tension inside the lungs keep them contracted. At the moment, the pressure inside the lungs is greater than the atmospheric pressure and the air is driven out of the lungs through the respiratory tract. The expiration phase is completed when the abdominal muscles push the abdominal organs against the relaxed diaphragm and the residual air in the lungs is thereby expelled.

A retention phase separates the inspiration from the expiration: a pause at the end of each breathing phase in which the heart muscle is allowed to relax and the heartbeat is reduced.

The respiratory organs and their purification
Oxygen is vital to life. The intracellular metabolic processes, which use oxygen for their sustenance also, produce carbon dioxide, a waste product. In simple single-celled creatures, this gaseous diffusion occurs according to pressure gradients whereas in a complex system, like the human one, an elaborate blood circulation system activated by an even more refined system, the nervous system carries out the function to and from the bodily tissues.

The gaseous exchange constituting the act of breathing takes place in paired specialised structures, the lungs, which are connected to the outside air by a breathing tube, the respiratory tract, constituted by the nose, the pharynx, the larynx, the trachea and the bronchi. This respiratory tract is supplied with a great number of nerves and blood vessels that play an important role in the breathing process. Finally a number of respiratory muscles come into play in the breathing process.

The management of breath
Breathing is absolutely natural for a living being but it is usually performed under capacity and can be greatly improved. By a gradual awareness of the respiratory process, practitioners can bring the involuntary breathing act under their conscious control. This is done by a progressive discovery and regulation of the periodicity and rhythm involved in the breathing process during the practice of asanas, pranayama and mantras.

The regulation of the four phases of breathing: inspiration, full lung retention, expiration and empty lung retention, is needed to maintain the energy balance in the organism at a positive level. From the pranic standpoint, breathing represents the mechanical action and Prana the electromagnetic force. So, energy spent in daily routine activities is automatically compensated for through conscious breathing and the organism is continuously recharged with pranic energy. In ordinary breathing, the quantity of oxygen substituted for carbon dioxide is greater than the quantity of the latter by 0,60% because the former is also used for physiological functions other than breathing. In conscious breathing, the emphasis is different: the carbon dioxide has to be expelled efficiently (rather than inhaling more oxygen) so as to allow the remaining portion of oxygen in the lung to carry the prana to the different organs of the body and induce an adequate cellular or internal breathing. This is achieved by the regulation of the four phases of breathing, the practice of the four types of breathing and by other pranayama techniques which train the respiratory organs intensely, rhythmically and consciously.

The four phases of breathing
Inhaling or *Puraka* is the act of receiving the cosmic energy through the air that is breathed into the lungs.

Exhalation or *Rechaka* is the act of giving the individual energy to the cosmic energy through the impure air and the carbon dioxide that are expelled from the lungs. During inhalation, the pranic energy is stored in the brain and the central nervous system and during exhalation, the pranic energy unites with the mind and the soul and dissolves itself in the cosmic prana.

Retention of Kumbhaka is the act of retaining the breath in the lungs between inspiration and the following expiration or retaining the breathless condition between an expiration and the successive inspiration. It is called *Antara Kumbhaka* and *Bahya Kumbhaka*, respectively.

During Antara Kumbhaka, or full lung retention, the cosmic energy is merged with the individual energy and the senses and mind are stilled.

During Bahya Kumbhaka, or empty lung retention, the individual energy is surrendered to the cosmic energy and the sense of ego tends to disappear at the moment. Since the breath is the common link between the body, the energy and the divinity planes, it is of the utmost importance to start any Pranayama practice by experiencing, directing and mastering the four phases of breathing.

This disciplined breathing known as *Sukha Pranayama* produces subtle chemical changes in the organism, brings the functions of the autonomic nervous system under control and calms the mind. This introduces harmonious and positive changes in the psycho-physiological complex while improving the rate, rhythm, intensity and quality of breathing. It is recommended that the practice should concentrate first on the inhalation and exhalation phases and, later, on the full lung retention followed by the empty lung retention phase. To achieve mastery over the four phases of breathing, practitioners should perform this breathing for fifteen minutes twice a day for a period of four to six weeks.

Apart from a temporal experience of breathing, practitioners should also become aware of the spatial dimension of breathing by practising regularly the four types of breathing.

Diaphragmatic, abdominal breathing or Adham Pranayama
The lower lobes of the lungs are activated while the upper sections of the lungs remain less active. This is accomplished by specifically directing the awareness to that portion of the abdominal wall just above the pelvis. On inspiration, the anterior and lateral abdominal muscles contract and, since these muscles are attached to the rib cage and to the pelvis, their

action lowers the diaphragm and increases the thoracic capacity. On expiration, the diaphragm moves up again and, by elastic recoil, the lower lobes are emptied of their residual air.

Intercostal, thoracic breathing or Madhyam Pranayama
The right middle lobe and the left angular region of the lungs are mainly activated in this type of breathing. On inspiration, the lower rib cage expands in an ascending movement through the full activity of the intercostal muscles while the diaphragm and the abdominal anterior walls remain contracted. On expiration, the intercostal muscles relax the rib cage narrows and the lungs are emptied of the vitiated air.

Upper chest, clavicular breathing of Adhayam Pranayama
The upper lobes are chiefly activated. On inspiration, the higher intercostal muscles and the muscles connecting the upper ribs, sternum and clavicles to the neck an skull are contracted and the rib cage expands to its fullest capacity. On expiration, the entire rib cage deflates as the diaphragm returns to its natural position.

Full yogic breathing or Maha Yoga Pranayama
The three sections of lungs are operating at full capacity by successive movements of the muscles of the abdomen, chest and neck in which each series of movements prepares the way for the next series of movements. This enables the lungs to be filled at maximum capacity and the gaseous exchange to be performed efficiently. When the first three types of breathing are practised in stages, they constitute *Vibhaga Pranayama* or Sectional Breathing. When they are practised in direct succession, they become the Mahat Yoga Pranayama or full yogic Breath. When this latter type of breathing is accompanied by the vibration of *OM*, it becomes Pranava Pranayama or the Cosmic Breath.

Basic Elements of Psychotherapy

GERHARD STUMM

Stumm Gerhard, PhD, is a psychotherapist (Person-Centred psychotherapy) in Vienna. He is a clinical and health psychologist, trainer and leader in trainings of the 'Arbeitsgemeinschaft Personenzentrierte Gesprächsführung, Psychotherapie und Supervision (APG)'(The Association for Person-Centred Approach, Psychotherapy and Supervision in Austria). He is the author of several publications about psychotherapy, among them editor of 'Psychotherapy - schools and methods' (Falter 1994) and 'Encyclopedia of psychotherapy' (Springer 2000).

One of my great concerns has been to establish psychotherapy as a profession in Austria. In many countries, this work is not even legalised and acts in an undefined space. Austria has a law on psychotherapy. I have always been interested in a comparative approach so that a lot of streams could find a shelter. In my view we have been successful to establish psychotherapy as a recognised discipline in Austria. Here I'd like to give an account of the discussion in the international literature of the necessary elements when defining the field of psychotherapy.

What are the necessities for psychotherapy?

1. It should be based on a professional training that should have a certain quantity and a certain quality as far as self-experience, supervision and theory is concerned.
2. A certain scientific method should be applied.
3. It should take place within a professional relationship and should have a process conception which is not prejudiced. It should have an open space where whatever can develop out of the relationship. Of course this should be based on certain theoretical perspectives and regulations.
4. Psychotherapy should have an indication; for example a behavioural or a personality disorder should be diagnosed. This is the external site of the indication. The subjective indication is the individual suffering. This is included in the

definition of psychotherapy in Austrian law. This shows that we have successfully moved away from the medical conception.

5. A goal or intention of where the psychotherapy should, lead should be defined. This could be the reduction of symptoms, the healing of the self or the reorganisation of the personality structure. It can also be personal growth, emancipation and/or improved health. Developing all our potential - is also a step away from the medical conception.

These five elements should be formulated as a consistent theory and application. We also need to establish what we mean by 'scientific'. We are all interested in how a certain method works in practice: How therapy works and how the quality of relationship is conceptualised theoretically. But that is only one principle to consider, since what we do is primarily based on our theoretical assumptions. These should consist of the following elements:

1. A philosophy of the nature of man. This could be humanistic, existential, transpersonal or positivistic views, which should form a base and be consistent with all the other elements.
2. A theory of reality: How do we establish what is real? There are different methods: Hermeneutic, critical realism, constructivistic or positivistic methods.
3. A personality theory that will act as a clear base to establish which functions and dynamics are important, for examples Freud's theory of the Id, Ego and Superego, or the person centred approach of the self and the organism.
4. A motivational theory to establish the sources and motors of our development.
5. A developmental theory to establish the 'normal' stages in a person's life - what is healthy and what is ill and the conditions we need in order to develop in our childhood.
6. A concept of health and illness and its aetiology: What causes the deviation? How do I define someone as sick or mentally disordered and what is the concept of health? We should have a perspective similar to Carl Rogers' 'fully functioning person'.
7. A practical theory: A concept of how you should act as therapist so that the misconceived development can be re-conceptualised. This should contain theories about the therapeutic relationship and the therapeutic process.

All of these elements should consist of a logical and consistent combination. An example is when Dollard & Miller some thirty years ago tried to combine psychoanalytical and behaviouristic theories. It did not work since the positivistic position and the concept of a deep subconscious does not fit together. It is also difficult to combine person centred work with theories based on the assumption that we have learned our behavioural patterns and that we have to relearn the new patterns planned step by step. Rogers held a very different view, arguing that the person, facilitated under certain circumstances and psychological conditions, i.e. attitudes experienced by the therapist, such as congruence, empathy and unconditional positive regard, will develop on the basis of his inner potential, as a result of the tendency that is actualising the organism.

If I try to combine Breathwork with the person-centred approach I must be very attentive to the fact that I should avoid being directive. Rogers was almost afraid of being ahead of the client, leading the client in a direction where he does not want to go. A person-centred therapist would therefore be very reluctant to tell the client to lay down and breath deeply. That would not be appropriate.

Here I'd like to add the political comment that I think that a new and fresh school should be very careful and make sure that nothing damaging happens as a result of their therapy. There are people who are waiting for something negative to happen that they can criticise. So it is probably good advice to be extremely cautious in this stage of development.

Rogers pointed out that the therapeutic relationship is just a special form of an overall relationship. Although in one of his articles he made a very interesting differentiation: In everyday relationship such as a partnership, congruence is the most important part of the relationship. In a relationship between mother and child it is the unconditional positive regard, the love and caring. In the therapeutic relationship it is the empathy. Of course all three are very important, but there are gradual distinctions.

The professional relationship gives us the opportunity to grant the space for the client to explore. Of course we should be transparent and authentic, but it is ultimately the client that does the job. G.Gendlin has characterised psychotherapy as leading a person away from structure-bound behaviour. A real and enduring reorganisation of the gestalt, of the configuration of the self, will then take place. That is why the process takes so long.

Breath is Your Companion

WILFRIED EHRMANN

Dr Wilfried Ehrmann is a psychotherapist from Vienna who integrates Breathwork, counselling and systemic approaches in his practise. He is head of Atman, the Austrian Breathwork Association and editor of its newsletter.

"Soul is a wide land", according to Arthur Schnitzler, the brilliant Viennese writer. He was contemporary with Sigmund Freud, who was among the first to draw a systematic map of this wide land a hundred years ago. Since then many more maps have been drawn of this landscape. Of these, the breath-map still shows several white spots. We do not know much about how working with the breath influences the functioning of body, soul and mind. We have accumulated many interesting experiences from therapeutically working with the breath but we still lack a systematic background and theoretical framework.

Breath is our companion - on our travel to the deep levels and wide horizons of consciousness - in search of the true self. Breathwork means to recognise and accept this companion in his specific quality.

If we want to lead Breathwork away from being a stubborn orphan child and introduce it to the well-respected therapeutic society we have to work on the presentation. One part of this presentation will have to be to demonstrate the specific impact that Breathwork has for the psychic and psychotherapeutic development of mankind.

1. Basic forms of Breathwork

We have two basic ways of using the breathing in psychotherapy: 1) to cover up (activating the sympathetic nervous system) and 2) to calm down (activating the parasympathetic nervous system)

1) activating-cathartic breathing is useful for moving deeper feelings and can be achieved by stronger and faster breathing. This pattern works well when there are blocked feelings, but also in cases of hysteria where it helps to open access to true feelings. In some forms of depression, which involve lack of energy, enhanced breathing can raise the energy level.

2) relaxed and calming breathing is appropriate when we deal with traumatic opened inner wounds. A depression connected with restlessness, fear and torturing compulsive thoughts, but also neurotic anxiety, compulsive neurosis and some forms of paranoia react positively to a relaxing breathing pattern.

Both these basic forms of Breathwork can of course be combined in one session or in a series of sessions. Eventually the breathing pattern will balance itself.

2. What is the specific therapeutic effectiveness of Breathwork?

2.1. Breathing enhances our physical wellbeing

We are familiar with some of the reasons why we feel good after a breathing session - endorphins are released in the brain, there is an increase of carbon dioxide pressure in the tissues and enhanced cellular metabolism etc. The fact that we cannot isolate physical wellbeing from emotional wellbeing is of therapeutic use to us. A depressive person who is talking only about his/her depression can reinforce his/her negative self-reference even deeper. During a breathing session, on the other hand, the body will experience, at least momentarily, a very positive physical change caused by the breathing, which will help to dis-empower negative thoughts and to build up counter forces against the inhibiting negative patterns.

Furthermore, if someone suffers from actual physical problems such as painful tensions or chronic stress breathing can bring relief and open to the flow of new energies. During my years of practical work with the breath there have been very few incidents where the client did not feel well after a breathing session. Even if the experience was just a minor relief, it has been a new message to the consciousness, which helps to lighten up the horizon of the suffering person, step by step.

2.2. Breathing changes the cognitive landscape

If we manage to let go of our thoughts while breathing - which is what should happen in a good breathing session - and which sometimes happens by means of periodically drifting away - this tends to make us change our thought pattern. So in this sense 'Rebirthing' can take on the meaning of the mind being reborn.

What happens is that our normal thought patterns get interrupted in their usual way of functioning at the same time as other parts of the brain get activated which allows new connections to be made. This is why the client often comes out of the session with an 'aha' experience.

2.3. Breathing strengthens the emotional intelligence

We assume that the neuronal ways between the cognitive and the emotional centres of our brain are opened up by the changed breathing pattern. Deep memories can rise on a sensational level without diversion of cognitive associations. By activating the interconnected systems of the body, which we experience as feelings, the body's associative power is triggered.

The ability to discriminate and identify emotions is of specific therapeutic importance: What is anger, what is hunger, what is frustration, and what is tiredness? How do I feel loneliness, how do I feel ecstasy? Anorexics and people with other forms of addictive behaviour lack this ability to discriminate. In many cases Breathwork has proven to be a positive exercise in becoming sensitive towards physical sensations.

Another field of learning is the ability to find the appropriate distance to emotions. Clients who tend to get overwhelmed by feelings can learn with the help of the breath that they are not the feelings they feel.

So in a variety of cases breath-therapy functions as an emotional education: By making up for the lessons we may have missed in our childhood and by having new lessons where we can learn more about our feelings, in a field where we all are illiterates, according to Ingmar Bergman.

2.4. Connecting with natural rhythms

The breathing is a natural organic rhythm controlled by the most ancient parts of our brain. In Breathwork we rely on the power of organic self-actualisation which we give space by restoring the original flow of inhalation and exhalation. There is an inner logic in the timing of a breath-session and its completion. The breath has its own melody and is in deep contact with the inner movements of the soul and of the whole universe. In Breathwork we balance our nervous system and connect with the root feelings of trust and harmony. This closeness to the powers of nature forms links to shamanic techniques.

By following the path of our breath we can be guided over the borders of time and space. Pictures from the past and visions of the future can rise. By entering the realms of non-linear and subjective experiences of time, the linear dimension of time becomes less dominant. On the psychological level, experiences like these imply the weakening of problems connected with clinging and needing control.

2.5. Opening for a spiritual horizon

From a certain level onwards Breathwork transcends the emotional and mental restrictions of the ego. The flow of high vibrational energies which emerge as a result of overcoming emotional blocks opens up for transindividual contexts by transcending the narrow frameworks of our daily life patterns. So Breathwork often leads to cosmic experiences - as described by Stan Grof in many books. The direct and immediate evidence of these experiences have helped many people to discover their own spirituality.

In terms of therapy these experiences can efficiently clear up problem areas where the client has a feeling of being 'stuck' and thus minimise the impact of the problem in his/her life. According to C.G. Jung, the real problems in life are never 'solved' but overcome and transcended until they at some point in time lose their inhibiting power. Breathwork has proved to be a good help in this process, especially when it enables us to open up enough to allow us to get a glimpse of our own spiritual path.

2.6. Breathing is surprising and creative. Breathwork is fun!

A good Breathwork session is like a good joke. The surprise comes at the end. The results of Breathwork sessions are rationally unpredictable. They are like miracles and magic, sometimes expressing the inscrutable humour of the universe.

3. Different ways to apply Breathwork in Psychotherapy:

There are three ways of combining Breathwork with other approaches in psychotherapy: Breathwork per se, complementary Breathwork and supplementary Breathwork.

A) Breathwork per se

This application requires some conditions:

A stable character structure and no inner need for therapy:
Some clients come to improve their physiological mechanisms of breathing or they look for a way to reach deep relaxation and explore the inner world of body sensations.

Therapeutic pre-experience and high degree of self responsibility:
Some clients have experienced their opening on verbal and imaginative levels and want to deepen their self-explorations on the body level. When they find their way to Breathwork they are usually very self responsible in dealing with their personal issues and are easily guided through the breathing cycle as they have learned that they have to rely on themselves and not on the therapist to get good results.

The practise of meditation:
As meditation in most cases is linked with breathing, clients who also practise meditation find it easy to open up to the breathing in a session and to reach deep inner levels. But it is good to be aware of whether they use Breathwork to access their emotional barriers or to avoid them and to always offer them the opportunity to look at their issues.

From the therapist: Gentle and careful approach
In cases where the therapist does not apply additional therapeutic support it is crucial to choose a very gentle and careful way of breathing, especially in the beginning of the session. Breathwork can stir up strong emotional processes, which should never be triggered without first carefully considering the client's individual case history and level of inner growth. If or when such a process is triggered, therapeutic support should be offered to help the client integrate the experience properly.

B) Breathwork as complementary therapy

By this I mean Breathwork as a process connected with different therapeutic methods of other origin.

One reason why Breathwork is so efficient is that it connects the pre-personal, the personal and the transpersonal realms of the psyche.

To deal with these kinds of powers requires specific awareness and responsibility. To overpower the inner wisdom of evolution by applying energetic tools to people who have not yet reached the appropriate level of inner development can cause severe damage, sometimes even crossing the borders to psychosis.

Most people need to discover and to utilise their own individual therapeutic tools to master their challenges in life. Breathworkers who want to work with people on different levels of development need complementary therapeutic approaches. In these cases, Breathwork can be used under the pretext of psychotherapy.

There is a ground rule for combining different approaches with Breathwork: Breathwork refines and widens subconscious material brought up by other types of therapeutic work and connects these issues with the body-mind-systems so that they are finally reduced to sensational patterns that change all the time. This way problems can be transformed into physical experiences which take away a lot of their inhibiting power. Breathwork may not always be the preferred therapy for solving clearly defined problems but is invaluable as a transforming factor for the subversive and dissipative[1] transformation of deeply rooted behavioural patterns.

The following remarks are aimed at providing some hints for possible combinations without claiming any form of completion. In every case, detailed research is needed as the possibility of combining different methods should not only depend on pragmatic points of view according to the principle that everything that works is good, but also on the mutual suitability of basic anthropological and scientific theories.

Breathwork and Psychoanalysis
This combination seems to be one of the most difficult. Clients come, in my experience, to Breathwork, when they have finished their analysis. Psychoanalysts often think that alternative

---

1 This term means 'Self-similarity' and is used in systems theory. It indicates that changes achieved by changing the breath can transform the mental and emotional structures on different levels in an unpredictable way.

therapeutic processes will disturb the analytical work. The strong influence of the rules of abstinence[2] in psychoanalysis, the predominance of verbal interaction, and a strong tendency to interpret verbalised material, as well as a many other theoretical and cultural differences, such as the sophisticated academic background of psychoanalysis, add to the big gap between psychoanalysis and Breathwork.

Breathwork and cognitive therapies
Many turn to cognitive therapies, as this realm is well known due to our way of cultural imprinting which favours the cognitive approach to reality to the emotional or spiritual approach. The weak points of these therapies are to be found in the nature of the mind with its big repertoire of self-deceptive tricks. The mind is always prone to find excuses and ways to avoid issues connected with embarrassment, shame and fear. Breathwork helps to focus on physical sensations and emotions, pleasant or unpleasant. As the thinking process almost automatically withdraws, the door for suppressed feelings opens up. As a result, new ways of thinking emerge during or after the session.

On the other hand, therapists who work mainly on the cognitive level are often sceptical towards Breathwork, due to its lack of elaborate theoretical frameworks. The same way many Breathworkers have a critical or simplistic attitude towards cognitive approaches and judge any form of cognitive insight to be a distracting 'mind trip'.

Breathwork and verbal counselling
There are a number of common theoretical concepts, which connect Breathwork, and the person-centred approach of Carl Rogers (underlining the tendency of self-actualisation and self-responsibility, a basically non-directive way of interaction, and the importance of empathy and acceptance). Maybe this is the reason why many clients see Breathwork as a logical continuation of their verbal therapy. Usually Breathwork sessions are combined with some kind of verbal counselling. The more experienced the Breathworker is in the area of empathic and congruent interaction, the better he will be at detecting and focusing on important issues. This will enhance the therapeutic process mutually as the issues can be condensed through verbalisation, and integrated and deepened through the breathing. When verbal counselling is criticised as being

2 the term abstinence in psychoanalysis means the limitations in the interaction between therapist and client, e.g. not talking to the client when meeting her on the street.

superficial, Breathwork can provide an efficient remedy to this lack.

Breathwork and NLP - Neuro Linguistic Programming

Many methods developed by the Neuro Linguistic Programming can be applied complementary to Breathwork. Process oriented Breathwork is the ideal combination with the strongly structured approach of NLP which is frequently considered to be 'technical'. To experience that we are not just the sum of our different information processing systems but that we are also one with ourselves can be easier to achieve in one Breathwork session than through a series of NLP exercises.

Breathwork and Gestalt

The breath serves as an excellent example for the functioning life intended by the gestalt theory. Simplified, life works when the breath is flowing in the right way. Connected breathing as such is the symbol of a completed gestalt. Since the breathing rhythm mirrors the whole landscape of feelings it soon becomes obvious when observing our own breath which 'gestalts' are energetically open and which are complete. As long as the breath cannot flow easily and relaxed when considering certain issues, there is still work to do to close the 'gestalt'.

To use methods from the wide and creative range of gestalt therapy, helps to open up new perspectives on deeper rooted feelings. To do a breathing session after gestalt work can help to deepen the expression of the emotions and also the understanding of their origin to integrate them and to access new levels of awareness in the here and now.

Since gestalt therapy has been associated with a non-dogmatic and pragmatic approach by strongly emphasising the experience in the here and now, there are a lot of natural links between these two schools in the practical field.

Breathwork and imaginative therapies

There are many ways of combining these approaches when working with relaxation. There is also a common assumption that the relaxed state of consciousness enhances the rise of suppressed material. Many experiences assert the strong healing power of the world of inner images. On the other hand we have to be careful about the seductiveness of this world. Many clients are highly talented in the art of going to 'their inner cinema' to experience amazing stories without ever changing anything in their life. When images get connected with emotions and body sensations through Breathwork, when they get seated in the body, they gain an elementary form of reality and evidence. By this, they leave a deep imprint on the consciousness and sub-consciousness, which provides a good ground for efficiently changing behavioural patterns.

Breathwork and body therapies
The breath is one of the most important instruments in body therapy. Starting with Wilhelm Reich, all body therapists have stressed the role of the breath and have used it in their practical work. Reich's concept of the organic or orgiastic flow of energy and his concepts of blocked energies have influenced the theories of Breathwork in a large area. Although body therapists, who are proud of their repertoire of techniques, have sometimes a low opinion of pure Breathwork, there are advantages in the highly unstructured process in a breathing session. To let issues rise spontaneously by themselves opens a direct door to the client's inner self, so that feelings are not provoked by some exercises from the outside but arise from within and can be experienced and observed in their own way of unfolding and declining.

Exercises from bodywork before a breathing session can also open up the space for feelings and add greatly to the intensity and depth of the session. During the breathing session, interventions like massage, or applying pressure at some points etc. can [also] increase and accelerate the process of opening up. So a combination of guided bio-energetic exercises and Breathwork guided from inside can be very effective in many cases.

C) Breathwork as a supplementary method

Focussing on the breath at certain points of the therapeutic process, can be used as an additional tool in a number of different therapeutic approaches. To encourage the client to deepen the breath can enhance any process aimed at opening up to feelings. It can also deepen any imaginative method.

There are a lot of examples in this area. Below are a few to give an idea:

- NLP: using breath in pacing or anchoring

- Family reconstruction: feelings come up during reconstruction of the family which can be intensified by deepening the breathing
- Using the breath as a tool for getting in touch with sensations and feelings.
- In counselling, watching the breath of the client can give valuable information about the therapeutic process.

COMPLETION

Breathwork is an important and valuable therapeutic tool, which has been developed and refined during the last decades. In most cases though we also need other approaches to succeed in profound healing. On the other hand, Breathwork can offer its resources with pride to many other forms of psychotherapy as an efficient complementary method.

Breathwork has to claim its place in the repertoire of methods of modern psychotherapy. This requires to be able to offer a solid theoretical framework. We have already established a solid ground to build on. Let's continue to build, so that Breathwork can contribute more to society and help inspire and improve life for all of us.

Breathwork-Therapy of Choice for Whom?

JIM MORNINGSTAR

Jim Morningstar, PhD, ABPP, is a clinical psychologist who was one of the first 12 certified Rebirthers in the 1970s. For the past 14 years, he has been the director of Transformations Incorporated, which includes the School of Spiritual Psychology and Creative Consulting and Counselling Service in Milwaukee, USA. He is the author of the books, Spiritual Psychology, Family Awakening and Breathing in Light and Love.

Is Breathwork a therapy? Breathwork is a broad rubric designating the use of a directed breathing process for healing or self-improvement. As a form of Yoga it has been used for centuries for physical, mental, emotional and spiritual change and renewal.

Modern psychotherapy refers to a healing process contracted between a client and a trained health professional working from an established theoretical framework. Psychotherapy uses specified techniques to effect change in behaviour, thinking and/or feeling states leading to more productive life and sense of well-being. Early forms of psychotherapy using the psychoanalytic model employed the projections of the patient onto the therapist (transference) as a major tool in understanding and giving feedback (interpretation) to the patient. Medical models of doctor/patient relationship and illness/health were assumed. Later developments in psychotherapy do not rely on the transference and interpretation tools. Many are more cognitive or behaviourally based, but they do retain the model of a professional contract for a specified change in feelings, thoughts and behaviour.

Breathwork can, I believe, be effectively employed within the framework of some psychotherapies, but in itself goes beyond psychotherapy and is used in educational models, e.g. yoga classes using a student/teacher relationship, physical healing arts e.g. massage or physical therapy for pain or stress reduction using a client/technician relationship, or a spiritual seeker model using a disciple/master relationship.

Breathwork is not under the domain of any one discipline or confined by a single model. My intent is to share my thoughts and experience of how it has been used, within appropriate psychotherapy models, and what are precautions and advantages to its usage with different conditions, as seen from a traditional diagnostic model, and an alternative diagnostic framework, and the differences between the two points of view.

First let us look at the traditional diagnostic nomenclature. These diagnoses are divided into the organic disorders, related to specific lesions or physical causes, and functional disorders for which there are no observable organic lesions. Most of my work has been with functional diagnosis. The functional diagnosis are divided into psychoses displaying major mood or thought disorders, neuroses characterised by anxiety, personality disorders dealing with behavioural problems and situational adjustments.

A major impairment of thought or mood refers to one which inhibits the individual from functional self-care. These are known as psychoses. I have had very little experience or success in using Breathwork with those diagnosed with schizophrenia, a major thought disorder. Their terror of any breakthrough of real feelings and their defences against this makes them unlikely volunteer candidates for this process. To try to require this treatment for them is antithetical to the philosophy of self-responsibility and flirting with the disaster of their further entrenching into their split.

One ambulatory schizoid individual who was genuinely seeking change from his isolated monochromatic life continued to come for Rebirthing with me even though he would invariably go into tetany with a few breaths. He explained to me that even though it was painful, he actually felt alive in his body for the first time. The voluntary seeking of the Breathwork is critical here and the Breathworker's sincerity, sensitivity and warmth are important. It is also critical to adjust your expectations for how much can be handled safely by someone so tenuously defended and to proceed with infinitesimal patience.

When thought disorder is combined with paranoid delusions there is the risk of striking out toward others when the perceived threat is increased as may happen by increasing their energy level or reducing their defences. I would exercise great caution with Breathwork under these circumstances.

People with major mood disorders, manic depression or major depression, are more likely to voluntarily try Breathwork. Here again we are dealing with very shaken defences and Breathwork, a very powerful technique that if used to rip away their walls of fear, can produce quite dramatic reactions. Again my experience is that adjusting ones expectations for speed of progress is critical. I would have great caution in raising the energy level of someone already in a manic state and myself would not use Breathwork with them until they were not so pressed. The propensity for their acting out and not grounding the increased energy is great, not just during but especially after the session. One needs to help them get safety and grounding firmly integrated. Breathwork has greatest potential with depression. It is well to note that the largest suicide risk is when the depression is lifting It is most important to stay in contact with your client at this time. Underneath the feelings of worthlessness is great rage and this can be redirected to themselves when their energy is mobilised.

I have much more experience with the anxiety states and Breathwork. Here is where Breathwork is an invaluable tool. Anxiety is marked by a sense of dread and uneasiness that does not have a logical focus. Thus there is a paralysis in taking any effective action to alleviate it. In Breathwork clients learn to consciously change their energy level, identify what physical and psychological indicators go with their fears, feel and express emotions underlying their fear, remember life situations leading to their trapped energy and address the people and circumstances involved in their original blockage. I have used Breathwork with everything from panic disorder, hyperventilation syndrome to more mild and generic anxiety states. Challenging the fears on their own grounds (the Breathwork session) rather than unexpectedly in their life, starts building the all-important confidence that they are in charge of their life more and more.

States of combined depression and anxiety are likewise amenable to Breathwork. The tendency of the depressive to defend, however, through drowsiness in the Breathwork session, makes the use of Bioenergetic techniques very helpful in maintaining their energy level and keeping them consciously working with you. Getting the client to hit, kick, twist or bite a towel, verbalise or make a sound can get them past the repressive drowsy state and aware enough of their underlying emotions to continue their breathing rhythm. Short of this you may get into the trap of feeling and expressing the depressed person's anger for them as they 'sleep' through your Breathwork session.

When anxiety is associated with posttraumatic stress such as from childhood sexual abuse, it is very important to help the client release and not just recreate the trauma. Breathwork has also been invaluable in this area for me when combined with directed visualisation. Clients must be helped to access their adult strength and not just collapse into the victimised child position during Breathwork. I repeatedly encourage them to be with or even speak for their 'injured child' rather than simply feel their feelings when they get overwhelming. We can recover and psychologically re-enter situations that were abusive letting their child know that we arc not going to abandon them there or let them fend for themselves. They can then speak as a protecting adult or give the voice to the child that they were incapable of at the time of the original trauma. Further they can take the child psychologically out of the abusive setting in their mind and bring them home to a current safe environment. This is all when the 'child' part of them is ready to (a) leave the old setting and (b) trust the adult part of them. Breathwork helps ground this in the heart and guts and not just keep it as a nice fantasy. Breathwork surfaces the emotional body more powerfully than verbal or visualisation techniques alone and helps integrate the heart and the head. I give assignments to daily consciously breathe and communicate with and listen to their inner child to help build a track record of trust. Also helpful is to have a daily reminder of their intention to heal, such as putting a picture of their inner child or a favourite childhood toy where they will see it regularly. This helps integrate the Breathwork into life.

Personality disorders present a broad range of challenges. In this arena the advantage of Breathwork is that it takes the client to levels of the unconscious beneath their behaviour patterns. The disadvantage is that if this is not handled appropriately, this unconscious material may spill over into more inappropriate behaviour. The borderline personality is a prime example of presenting this possibility. Clear behavioural contracts can be useful when working with this high potential for acting out. It is important, however, not to get into a 'critical parent' role, but to help them deal with the thoughts and feelings, e.g. shame, when they do not stay within the boundaries of their stated intentions. Some may touch in with your services only sporadically. This can provide a valuable resource for them even though it may challenge your criteria for effective behaviour change. I have one such client who comes in for short periods every six months to a year and at present can tolerate little more. We serve in many ways.

When dealing with situational disorders or adjustment reactions, Breathwork has the potential to crack the illusion that the grief, sadness or anxiety is all about one event. This may be disconcerting for those wanting a quick fix. Breathwork, of course, can be adapted to handling situational anxiety. Sooner or later, I believe, following the guidance of the breath will take the serious applicant to deeper roots when they are underlying. As the Breathworker or therapist, our job is to point out the potential or possibilities for further work or deeper processing, and be available should the client choose to pursue it, not to sell it to them or force it upon them.

Though I am not a great proponent of psychotropic medications, they may be useful if used judiciously as a bridge to help bring some clients back to a drug-free condition of self-care. I do not refuse to do Breathwork with someone on medications, but want to know what symptoms are being suppressed through their usage. In general the medications tend to mute the effectiveness of the Breathwork. The Breathwork, though, can diminish the length of time the client relies on the medications.

I use a form of Bioenergetic diagnosis in my therapy and Breathwork. I prefer it because it gives me a framework for interpreting not only psychological, emotional and behavioural cues but also character structure as reflected in body types. Bioenergetics also gives a developmental model of both health and illness, the strengths and weaknesses of each body type. Clear goals are presented for each body type along with exercises on the physical level to augment the mental and emotional work. Adding Breathwork to this form of therapy is a natural fit as free and easy breathing and a spiritual core are already main components of the theory. I have modified Alexander Lowen's typology to increase focus on the wellness components of each type and have added the indications for Breathwork with each type.

The Psychic Sensitive patterns developed pre- and post-nataly are most concerned with basic safety in their bodies and their worlds. In the held fear state their basic belief is 'The world is not a safe place.' Their compensating belief is 'I am a free spirit, unattached to the material.' Their bodies are disjointed, frozen and unfocused; their breathing is minimal. Under any stress they split off. Breathwork helps them unlock their chest and free their breathing mechanism, gain more comfort with their bodies and move towards releasing their rage and fear. It is important for the Breathworker not to give double messages or control covertly. Breathwork can help bring out their high vibrational qualities with safety, bring agility and responsiveness to their bodies and show more productively their sensitive artistic natures.

The Empathetic Nurturing patterns formed during the first year of life are concerned with the issue of deprivation/ abandonment. In the held fear state they believe 'I'll never get enough.' Their compensating belief becomes 'If I love enough, I'll be loved' or eventually 'I'm self sufficient.' Their bodies take on a posture of deprivation with a collapsed chest affording a shallow inhale and a breath by breath experience of lack. Their pelvis is forward with knees locked, having learned to hold themselves up prematurely. They can also be tall and thin, looking undernourished. Though being oral and highly verbal, under stress they will tend to collapse. Breathwork helps them find their true source within so they can support themselves and their feeling of vitality. It is important for the Breathworker to be there as a support but not 'do it for' the Empathetic Nurturer. The depletion and abandonment themes then fade and their empathetic qualities are shared with the world out of choice and pleasure rather than fear of loss.

The Inspirational Leader patterns, solidified during the first to third year of life, are focused on control issues in relationships. Having been either overpowered or seductively manipulated, their held fear position is 'To give in to feeling is weak.' Their compensating belief is 'I'm in control.' Their body reflects the identification with the controller in taking on either an inflated upper body, muscle-bound, overpowering appearance or a more evenly proportioned, approachable looking, but inwardly controlled style. Under stress they will try to control by rising above or manipulating seductively. Breathwork will help them release their exhale, start to trust and feel pleasure in their vulnerable feelings, and to eventually let go and surrender appropriately with others. The Breathworker serves as a model for caring strength rather than struggle for control. Their head and heart working together bring out their loving leadership qualities and releases the old tyrannical control of the Inspirational Leader.

The Steadfast Supportive types, developed during the second

to fourth year of life, struggle with freedom of expression issues. Squashed in their expression of the 'bad me' and smothered with controlling guilt, their fear-based attitude is 'No one appreciates me.' Their compensating belief becomes a martyr like position: 'My struggle is noble.' Their bodies take on a squashed appearance, with a thick neck, pelvis tucked in, waist short and thick.

Their muscles are under continual pressure. Since direct expression of anger is repressed, under stress they often provoke others in passive-aggressive ways. Breathwork helps them complete and release their exhale and shed their experience of being under continuous pressure to please. They are able to deal more directly with their anger. It is crucial that the Breathworker avoid going into collusion with their struggle and end up struggling to help them feel better. The strengths of the Steadfast Supportive Type are their abilities to stay with challenges and be helpful to others. When their creative spirit is released, their helping no longer has hidden expectation attached. Their bodies show solid and enduring qualities, along with being truly tender and huggable.

The Gender Balanced patterns set in during the third to fifth year of life. Their theme is gender confusion. How do I safely express myself as a male or female? The held fear posture dictates 'If I assert myself spontaneously, I will be rejected.' Trying to gain comfort with their dilemma of not being reinforced for their natural initiative, they adopt a compensatory belief that 'My assertion is safer than others of my gender.' The males adopt a very passive, soft style, their bodies have a rounded exterior and a compliant expression. Their true strength is often cloaked with sarcasm and covert manipulation. The females take a very assertive stance, often very competitive with males. Their bodies show a split between upper being quite rigid and lower being more full and weak. Their jaw is characteristically tight. Under stress the males will tend to undermine and the females resort to attack. Breathwork addresses this male/female imbalance by helping to balance the inhale and the exhale, to gain safety in both their vulnerability and their strength, and to accept safety in their sexual identity. The Breathworker provides a new model of acceptance in this regard as they expose their deepest fears of rejection and punishment beneath the surface. As this happens their true potential for blending their male and female sides comes to blossom and they are able both to enjoy themselves as full, balanced humans and share this model with their world.

The Energetic Grounded types, formed during the fourth to sixth year, have as their theme disappointment in intimate relationships. Feeling a deep sense of rejection and betrayal from their initial attempts to relate as a sexual being to their parents, their slogan becomes 'No one is going to hurt me again.' Their compensatory belief becomes 'I am a loving person who no one understands.' Their bodies portray stiffening for the anticipated love rejection and are armoured in the torso region and have a stiff back. Their eyes tend to be bright and they handle affairs of the world well. It is in maintaining intimate relationships that they falter. Under stress they express anger readily. Breathwork helps them integrate their exhale and inhale as well as their heart and their genitals. The Breathworker, avoiding getting competitive with them, is able to handle their underlying anger without rejecting them. They begin to learn safety in vulnerability with others and let their natural attractive, alert, capable qualities be shared in healthy, whole relationships.

The Bioenergetic framework accounts for the extreme cases described in the traditional diagnostic nomenclature. Schizophrenia is an extreme case of frozen Psychic Sensitivity. Depression is found in the collapsing of the Empathetic Nurturing and the inner morass of the Steadfast Supportive. Behaviour disorders are typical of the Inspirational Leader who has not integrated and is under high pressure. Anxiety is the hallmark of many of the types when beginning to deal with their basic themes before they identify and release the emerging fears deepest in their patterns. The difference in the Bioenergetic schema, however, is that their model includes a psychosocial etiology to suggest an approach to dealing with underlying causes and not just a biological predisposition. Bioenergetic analysis also includes a continuum of dysfunction to integration, and illness to health, for each type. The Bioenergetic approach gives a holistic plan for integration using body, mind, and spirit that is documented.

We all deal with the basic themes of safety, abundance, control, freedom of expression, sexual identity, and intimacy and can identify with the postures humans take toward them. Few want to be labelled psychotic or neurotic. When answering the question of with whom to use Breathwork, the diagnostic framework that is used will have a large bearing on your prognosis, treatment approach, and subsequent success. The label 'psychotic' or even 'neurotic' does not point to the way in or the way out of the stuckness for that individual. It tends to reinforce that position in the helping agent also.

Notice how hopeful, or fearful, you felt as a prospective practitioner when the diagnostic categories were being discussed from the traditional versus the alternative approach. I still would have caution in using Breathwork with the extreme frozen or held fear position in any of the Bioenergetic Types. I would calibrate my prognosis according to the standards of individuals using this style of life defence who range from dysfunctional to very productive versus the standards of the 'severely mentally ill' to the general population. This helps me, the practitioner, to put their defensive patterns in the perspective of a continuum of wellness, and moving toward integration at their own individual rate, not one dictated by statistics or standards foreign to them.

In summary, Breathwork is not psychotherapy, but can be very effectively used as an adjunct approach in some systems of psychotherapy that utilise a mind/body approach. Cautions and recommendations for the application of Breathwork are offered from my experience using both a traditional psychodiagnostic framework and from Bioenergetic analysis. The wholeness of the theoretical diagnostic approach is seen as influential not only to the categorisation of candidates for Breathwork, but also to the expectations of the practitioner on how well they will do with it (prognosis) and the success of the treatment (outcome).

Breathwork-Instant Charm and Hidden Dangers

SERGEI GORSKY

Sergei Gorsky is one of the key organisers in the Russian human potential movement. During the last years, Sergei and his colleagues have carried out extensive research on the medical, physiological and psychological aspects of various forms of Breathwork.

It makes sense to me to describe Rebirthing as a tool, not as a method and not as a technique. This tool can be used in different techniques, methods and even paradigms. Many use Breathwork in different techniques; some of them can be called therapy, others cannot. There are even different paradigms that utilise Breathwork.

The arguments about Breathwork being a therapy or not, can be compared (with some exaggeration) with the question if a knife is therapy. A knife is a tool which is totally neutral by itself but which can be used therapeutically under a certain paradigm: Under the paradigm of the surgeon, the butcher or the killer. In the same way, Rebirthing is a tool that has been used in many different forms and methods.

If we look at the destructive side of Breathwork, it's shadow, then we can see that the side effects of it make it quite dangerous in some cases. When the jump from a pre-personal to a transpersonal state is too quick, the personality can be left in a very disturbed situation.

What does Breathwork do when we use it?

There are several answers to this question but two main consequences. The first one is; it creates altered states of consciousness. The second consequence: it brings the subconscious material to consciousness or to awareness. These two effects are connected, but it is good to look at them separately.

How does Breathwork achieve these effects?

Physiologically, Breathwork uses a very simple mechanism like a lot of other methods. We can describe it as a pendulum between the sympathetic and the parasympathetic branch of the autonomous nervous system. At the beginning of a breathing session, we change the chemistry of our body and activate the sympathetic branch with all the symptoms of the body, tetany, pain and emotions. It shows that subconscious material is coming to awareness through the body: memories, images, and thoughts. The main mechanism for getting this material from below the threshold of awareness, is the change in chemistry that Breathwork creates. So Breathwork can also be viewed as a shovel that we use for going through the stuff of our unconsciousness. It is a very effective shovel, and the problem is not how we shovel, but what we do with the things we discover.

After some time of the shovelling, the chemistry of the body changes. We cannot permanently provoke shifts in the body. If we push the organism in one direction it will eventually go in another direction. It compensates itself to keep its homeostasis. After all these pains and tensions, at one point we start to feel the wonderful flow or the electric current or the energy - the activation of the parasympathetic branch of the nervous system. If the sympathetic branch represents our suppressed ego structures, our unconscious material, the parasympathetic branch gives us access to the deeper, transpersonal layers of our consciousness. It is like a swing children use when they run in the opposite direction and then swing out and jump into the river.

If we worked hard at the first stage and surrendered well at the second stage, then we have a little shot of the transpersonal flow at the end. That brings us a lot of pleasure - endorphins running through the body.

Like anything that works with altered states of consciousness, it is addictive. By definition, altered states of consciousness are addictive, no matter how we reach them. So any strong techniques are addictive.

What happens after the session?

That has a lot to do with the relationship of the conscious and the unconscious part in that specific person. To illustrate that, we can parallel that to the relationship humankind developed to nature especially in the last hundred years. Nature was conquered and controlled by mankind who considered itself at the peak of evolution with the right to decide for the rest of nature. From nature we got back ecological catastrophes, decreased immunity, AIDS, and many other problems. We see the same parallel in the antagonistic relationship of consciousness and subconscious: a majority of persons in the western civilisation see the subconscious as dangerous, dark, void, death, something that needs to be healed, conquered, enlightened, changed, transformed, at least as something we need to handle somehow. We look for more and more tools for conquering the subconscious.

The divine balance of order and chaos is disturbed. The order took and structured a lot of chaos in our external and internal life. Notice that chaos is much more tolerant and patient and loving towards us than we are in the other direction. There is a limit of all tolerance. Nature gives us messages: You better stop. And the subconscious gives us the same messages. When we quickly and dramatically go into the subconscious and start messing up with the protective mechanisms of the ego, we take the ego off guard. First we can go very quickly for some time, and the subconscious will withdraw, allowing us to play with insights and revelations for a while. But deep inside there it will mobilise itself and strengthen its defences, and at some point we will face the walls, we cannot go deeper. And then we look for a bigger bulldozer, for stronger techniques. Every technique we start practising only works for some time and then stops working. The ego defences learn the techniques quicker than we do.

This all is true for the antagonistic relationship between consciousness and subconscious. I do not speak about the situation when there is some kind of trust and friendliness. Rebirthing was built up with a very negative attitude towards the subconscious. Leonard Orr and Sondra Ray treated their subconscious in a not very friendly way. Five biggies, birth trauma, parental disapproval, specific negatives and so on. In the Breathwork movement we have a not very co-operative and trusting relationship between consciousness and subconscious. If we use any strong technique, especially Breathwork in this context, it creates more antagonism and polarity. We become more conscious, more aware, but get more separated on the other hand and create more division between what we are aware of and what we are not aware of.

That creates another consequence. What is this subconscious we go for, get aware of and integrate? These are the blocks of identity of the personality - unconscious identity like the foundation of the house. We can argue that the ego defences are not effective, they are full of pain. But the personality is built on that foundation. We are identified with these ego structures. When we take a big shovel, we very quickly shift to the transcendental. We take away their identification. Then we find out that we are not ready to live a transcendent life.

If we use a lot of transcendental techniques, if we overuse meditation and Breathwork, we start dissolving the unconscious identity of the personality and then the social life starts dissolving as well - especially in the antagonistic relationship. People get divorced and lose their jobs; they get socially maladapted, although they are happier and freer, more playful. But somehow they cannot earn money and have difficulties with permanent relationships. On the one side it is an indication of more transcendence, but on the other side it is not very comfortable to be transcendent in the modern social structures.

Breathwork can shake the foundations of the identity of the personality, and an immature personality that is not ready to transcend itself becomes very mushy. These people are easily influenced and look out for any kind of guru, because they want something to identify with. The indication of social adaptation is a very good criterion for whether working with a client is successful or not.

The healthy ego has a natural tendency to transcend itself and open up to transpersonal messages and values. Within everyday life, the mature ego does not need an altar to pray to, or a guru.

Now I look at the possibility when consciousness and subconscious communicate well and trust each other. Subconscious naturally is very trusting and open. If we torture it long enough, the shadow can become very large. If we objectify and personify the shadow and name it like birth trauma, even if we see it as wounded and talk about healing, we still think that something needs to be changed in the subconscious. The only thing that needs to be changed is the conscious model of perception. There is nothing wrong with the subconscious. It was whole and divine and will always be so.

C.G.Jung showed that all the attributes that Chinese philosophers put into the Tao were exactly the same attributes as for modern psychology for the subconscious. So Tao and subconscious are absolutely the same.

So in the situation of a conflict between consciousness and subconscious, Breathwork is dangerous, and in the situation of trust between consciousness and subconscious, Breathwork is useless.

If we start using any strong technique in the situation of mistrust and antagonism between consciousness and subconscious we bring more conflict, more separation into the personal structure.

Where then is the place for Breathwork?

We can use Breathwork to shift from the untrusting relationship to a trusting one.

There are two brain centres for breathing. One is much younger than the other. The very ancient one is positioned in the limbic part of the brain. This centre allows breathing to go by itself, whether we are asleep or awake. The other one is in the front part of the brain. It was created to control the breathing and is used for conscious breathing. This control is needed for controlling the breath while talking which is connected with thinking. We control the breath in a way which is exactly opposite to the natural breathing pattern. We control the breath on the exhale when we talk, and our inhale is almost compulsive. In the natural breathing pattern, the exhale is totally relaxed and the inhale is active. Every time we think we control our breath whether we want to or not.

The unfriendly relationship between consciousness and subconscious is reflected in our breath to a large extent. If you watch your breath, you will notice that it has a lot of tiny tensions and blocks.

We have a conscious control over our breathing. And that is very tempting. We can develop Breathwork techniques. We can use our crazy imagination to imply different breathing patterns in order to get into altered states of consciousness. When we use an artificial breathing pattern like Pranayama or Holotropic Breathing, we disturb the ancient breathing centre. The surrounding of this ancient breathing centre is the locus of our personality, a very deep-rooted block of identification. If we disturb this, we disturb the foundations of personality.

So how do we shift from an unfriendly to a friendly relationship between our consciousness and our subconscious?

We can use the personal and the transpersonal side of the breath. We can look and find the harmony between the way we breathe and control our breath and the way breathing happens. When we establish trust, friendship and dance between the two breathing centres, we establish trust, friendship and dance between the conscious and subconscious parts of our psyche. It is important to limit our experimentation with the breath and to become aware of the natural breathing pattern that happens by itself, when we do not control our breath. Then we can align and harmonise both sides. It does not mean we have to give up our personal breathing. This would create another imbalance. Between these two polarities we can find the middle path, the ritual path.

Whenever we make any transpersonal step, we need to go back to the social and ground the inside revelation into the social. Whenever we see signs of dissolution of social structures it is good to stop with strong techniques for a while and start to clean the house.

Thank you for your attention.

From therapy to spirituality
– stages of the path

EIRIK BALAVOINE

Being half French and half Norwegian, Eirik Balavoine brings qualities from these two distinctly different cultures into his personality and teaching - passion, presence and precision. He has trained and worked with meditation since 1973, Breathwork since 1978 and psychotherapy since 1982. Leader of groups and silent retreats since 1984. His professional work has mainly been centred in Norway but he has recently moved to France to live and teach.

Good morning.

The following is a presentation of my work to join the two major paths of development we have in the West, psychotherapy and spirituality, to see how they work together on the way to enlightenment.

There is today an evident need for guidelines in the development process after basic psychotherapeutic groundwork has been done. Without such guidelines, people with the impetus to continue their development after psychotherapy tend to repeat psychological clearing processes they already have been through, in an effort to keep moving.

Regarding these higher realms of development, we in the West have up until now been very dependent on knowledge coming from the East. As our cultures are so fundamentally different this has created a lot of confusion: For example, when I started my training in meditation in 1974, I was trying out different types of meditation from different teachers. I worked diligently with them all, but not much progress was really made. This was simply because the different techniques neutralised each other. Instructions given in one school with its related methods were not necessarily appropriate when working with other seemingly similar ways of working, and moreover some of them were not at all appropriate to my unripe state of maturity. It was when I finally concentrated on one and let go of the others that I began to see results of my efforts.

It dawned on me how fundamentally important it is to deeply understand what all these techniques we are using, psychotherapeutic and spiritual, are doing to us. We need to understand what they produce in us related, to the state of our progression in the work we are undertaking. Only then will it become possible to know when it is appropriate to use a certain technique, and when it is not; when a technique is no longer potent for us and when we are ready to proceed further to more advanced methods.

There is an old myth from when Buddhism was spreading to Tibet: An Indian scholar/mystic called Padmasambhava was sent to Tibet to teach Buddhism. He did not really want to go, because Tibet was not at all important regarding Buddhism at that time. It was looked upon spiritually as a 'third world country'. What he found when he finally went there was a shamanic tradition called Bön, with deep roots in the hearts of the Tibetans. Bön had developed very advanced techniques enabling the practitioners to mobilise the powers of the psyche, but they had not evolved above that. Padmasambhava realised that there was going to be a power struggle between himself representing Buddhism and the Bönpriests. The myth tells that he found himself a cave outside the Tibetan village and submerged himself in deep meditation. When settled there, he psychicly went into the subconscious mind of the Bön priests, deeper than they could access themselves, and planted the seed of Buddhism. Returning to the village he challenged the Bön priests, defeated them and thus convinced them of the higher validity of the Buddhist practises.

Because of the seed he had planted and the ground he had already prepared in their psyche, the truth of Padmasabhavas arguments were welling up in the minds of the Tibetan people and the Bön priests themselves. That is what the myth tells us of this important moment. For me this story contains the very reason why the Tibetan Buddhism, which I deeply respect, has survived and is vital today: Padmasambhava did not suppress, but incorporated the deep roots of Bön into the Buddhist teachings, and thus created a branch of Buddhism that has been thriving and strong for more than a thousand years, and still remains so today.

Modern gardeners today do the same thing to produce rose plants. They take the root of a wild rose, and graft a beautiful cultivated rose onto it. In this way they manage to produce very healthy, sturdy long living rose plants using the natural ability of the wild roses to access local nourishment from its native soil, but giving that strength to a rose much more developed than its own.

A similar process is now happening in our culture. We have deep empirically sound roots in our knowledge of psychology and therapeutic techniques, among them Breathwork. We know how to access the deep levels of our psyche, but we may not know how to evolve from there. If we want to proceed further and not be repetitious in what we are doing, we need to go beyond working with our emotions into Self, then Union, and in the end realise the deepest truth. We need practical and theoretical knowledge of how to do this, what laws to respect.

The techniques we have developed to deal with suppressed states of emotionality were not available in the old days. This is unique to our times. At the same time we have all the wisdom of the old traditions and masters available, and we cannot dismiss 5000 years of refined knowledge! A handle of a knife looks like it does simply because it has shown itself to be the most functional, through thousands of years of refining. There is no need to reinvent it. Similarly the traditional spiritual knowledge is what it is because all the unnecessary bits has been taken away. There is gold for us in there, but we have to make it our own!

Very early in my life I got suspicious of the objectivity of my perception, because I had spontaneous psychic experiences that convinced me it was not trustworthy. I was thirteen years old and travelling for the first time alone on a train climbing up a narrow valley in Norway. Coming around a bend the view suddenly opened for a few seconds, and I got a tiny glimpse of a vast area of snowy mountains. Something snapped in me at that moment and everything became exquisitely beautiful. Everything in me and around me suddenly got a new lustre, a brilliance, and a deep silence filled me. Something so real, that life up until that moment suddenly seemed trivial and in a way beside the point. This experience established itself in me from then on as a reference of how it was possible for me to be, to feel and to perceive. A completely different mode of being.

A little later another experience happened where I walked by a concrete wall. A grey, boring, completely ordinary concrete wall. I looked at it in passing, not really seeing anything noteworthy, but when I returned some moments later it was so beautiful! Again the beauty, but I did not understand it. Just that something had changed in me during those few moments. Something that made me understand that I could not trust the stable objectivity of my own perception. And if I could not trust my own perception, what then could I trust? The only thing that was sure was that there was something inside me that had the power to shape the way I perceive the world.

In that same period I also almost broke my back and I also had serious sinus problems. Two different doctors told me that I was going to have those problems for the rest of my life! That started my search. I wanted to know why I had these problems, and I wanted to understand the underlying laws governing my perception, my mind and my body. I was led to meditation and to yoga and in time I found the underlying emotional structures behind my health problems, and the symptoms gradually disappeared.

I am giving you a little of my background, because in these relatively simple experiences lies the seed to the work that I am presenting today.

The development process as I see it is divided into four stages which I name: the Ego, the Authentic self, the Higher self and the No self. You will see from the posters behind me that I have tried to find the points that characterise a person when his or her consciousness is dominated by the reality defining each stage. How a person dominated by his ego is experiencing himself, how it is to be a person governed by the self, how it is to be a person resting in the higher self and also some indication of what no-self is. I have structured it so that the same theme shows up at the same physical place in every map, so it is possible to see the progression from state to state, bearing in mind that no two persons develop in the same way, and no growth is linear.

First of all I need to make some definitions: When I speak about mind I speak about the content of mind. I make this distinction of the 'content of mind as distinct from 'the Universal Ground' or 'God' or 'Nirvana' or' Rigpa' or 'The Absolute'. The content of our mind is what covers and blocks us from the Absolute, like clouds covering the blue sky behind it. It is the content of our mind that stops us resting in the Universal Ground.

In short, to truly evolve is first to develop a sound relationship to the mind and its content, then to make it transparent and finally to realise both as illusion.

Another aspect to understand is energy. Energy exists in us on the one hand as potency and on the other hand as mind-pictures, meaning and movement. Our mind is energy crystallised into concepts. These concepts are the building blocks of our personality, which is the illusory entity we are dealing with in personal development. First it is something to understand and develop, then it is the main hindrance to basic sanity and freedom.

THE EGO

The ego, which is the most usual level to find ourselves in, is a state of mind completely without control. Here we are utterly governed by the subconscious forces and by previous experiences in life. The Asians call it the monkey mind. One of the reasons for this is because it jumps away every time you try to get hold of it. Another reason comes from the way monkeys are trapped: You take a coconut, drill a hole in it, fill it with food and hang it in a tree. Then a monkey puts his hand in the hole and gets hold of the food. But when he tries to pull his hand out, he cannot. The fist full of food is bigger than the hole and he is captured! The delicious food is so close that he does not want to let go of it. He thinks that he can get both; the food in his fist and his freedom. But he cannot, and so he is captured: In our story this means that if we want to evolve into freedom, we have to learn to let go.

As I said, energy related to mind has two aspects: One is potential. The other is that energy formulates itself in our mind's eye as feelings, emotions, pictures - anything the mind can conjure up. If for example, we get angry and habitually, unconsciously in the moment understand 'I am angry', then we put our fist in the coconut. We are identified with the anger and become submerged in it and turn spiritually blind. If we instead learn to understand: 'My mind is coloured by anger', or love or self-pity or whatever, then it becomes possible to separate the two; the mind and its colours. It will then also be possible to recognise that anything that happens within the content of the mind is cyclic; anything that comes also goes! When you have realised that, then it becomes self-evident that not striving after pleasure and not pushing pain away is the smartest thing to do to maintain detachment. And to be detached from what is going on in our mind opens up the road to what is beyond mind. That realisation is one of the main pillars of inner personal freedom.

What is the motivating force in a person at a certain stage? What is the typical focus of attention that repeats itself at that stage? What attitude towards emotions and imperfections, one's own and others, do people have at this stage? What is the main challenge to focus on if we want to grow, and what is the main training corresponding to that challenge? What is appropriate to do to meet that challenge? What is needed to progress? What is the structure of mind at that stage? These are the points I have chosen here as important to look at now, bearing in mind that, of course, they only represent a tiny fraction of what is needed to be worked on in real growth.

The motivating force in the ego-person to spur growth, is a general dissatisfaction with life. There is a longing for satisfaction, for something more real and for personal fulfilment. The ego-person is centred around himself. Emotions govern him and he is obsessed with imperfections, in himself and in others. For example: If an ego-person has a slight humpback and someone comes up to him and says, "What is this funny thing on your back?", he will immediately deny the existence of the hump and say, "What do you mean? There is nothing wrong with my back!" He is caught by his need to be perfect. That tendency needs to be released if you want to transcend the ego-personality. You have to find an ease with imperfections, your own and others.

To be able to move along the path of growth, we have to learn to express what is in our hearts and minds. What we don't get out rules us. But once we manage to express and own our imperfections then things start to move and get easier.

Another challenge on the ego-level is to confront our own shadows. Whatever is lurking in the basement of your personality, confront it. If you do not confront it, it will rule you.

Expression is the main change-inducing ingredient in working on the ego-level, because expression is followed by clarity and understanding: Without expression, there is shallow or no understanding.

Another work that has to be done on this level is to unravel and understand your biography, your personal history. You should do this in as much detail as possible. It is when going into the details of past experiences in your life that you find that the re-living and release of old suppressed memories and emotions can happen. It is a well-proven fact that if you do not understand your history, it will repeat itself.

One way of working with this is to take a book with blank pages, reserve one page for every month of your life, and then fill it in. Start with the period before your conception and, if it is possible, find out the atmosphere between your parents that was predominant at the time you were conceived. If you do this work in that much detail, then you will find that your personal history has a much greater chance to find rest and peace.

Another important aspect to spur growth at this stage is to learn about conscious centering, and to experience the spontaneous centering that at this stage happens at the moment of expressing emotions.

Progress normally depends on our own effort, but we cannot as an ego-person do it all alone. We need somebody to mirror us, somebody to see through our clever schemes of avoiding what we find difficult, and finally somebody to be with when melting happens and separation is replaced by connection.

THE AUTHENTIC SELF

When the consciousness of the Authentic Self shape the mind, the outside world starts to become less important. The consciousness of a 'Self-person' revolves around finding ones true qualities and to follow ones own intuition. A person that is starting to discover his own Authentic Self, has already learned to express emotions. He has also discovered the difference between feelings and emotions, where feelings are natural responses to a present situation while emotions are repetitious feeling-patterns with unresolved roots in the past. Taking responsibility for our feelings and emotions prepares us and opens us up to the next stage in our possible evolution: Containing and transforming emotions rather than expressing them. This step is dependent on training in uncensored and uninhibited expression. Otherwise, containing emotional energy will just end up as another act of suppression.

The main challenge for a person getting to know his Authentic Self is to follow a subjective, intuitive path in life - daring to test what is seen in glimpses of clarity and intuition by taking the consequence of them into physical reality. The beauty of doing this is that in the long run you will find that by following a subjective, intuitive path you end up discovering more and more of the reality that is universal and shared by everyone. This is why for example. a master can speak to many people at the same time, and each person present will feel that the words spoken are aimed at him or her specifically. He speaks directly from that shared reality.

For an Authentic Self-person, feedback from other people is not so important anymore. More crucial are the impulses coming from his own depth. He finds out that leading a life guided by intuition produces a moment to moment experience of life that increasingly becomes more real and intense.

If again we take the metaphor of the glasses, then at this stage the glasses are getting much cleaner, but they are still tinted as sunshades are. What you are seeing is much more true, but your awareness is still coloured by the shade of your personality.

Evolving through these stages is not a linear process where you steadily work from one stage to the next. Normally everybody starts at the ego-level, but even at this level of consciousness you can have sudden glimpses of higher self or no-self, often without understanding what is going on. The beauty is that these glimpses of higher consciousness create a longing, which gives us a sense of a direction to our development.

THE HIGHER SELF

Going from the Authentic Self to Higher Self is moving from having much of your attention captured by the outside reality, to more and more focusing on the inside of yourself. You are putting your sense-faculties to rest. Your personality is what it is, you use it as a necessary tool much like you use your hands and feet, but you are constantly drawn to what is beyond. Your outer world is in order. Your emotions are more or less worked through, and if they appear you are free to choose to express or contain them, but basically you do not bother about them.

There is this story of a master who repeatedly told his students that everything is illusion, especially feelings and emotions. Then one morning he received a message that his brother had died, and he started to cry. This greatly confused his students who came to him and said: "For years you have been telling us that all feelings and emotions are illusions - and now you cry"? "Yes", he said, "that is true and this is the saddest illusion of all!"

You discover that the movements of the mind come and go like the waves on the ocean. You let the mind do its own thing without interfering, accepting rather than rearranging the reality of things. Only then you will get the chance to discover the deeper reality, beyond mind.

There is a Zen Koan pointing at this: You take a baby goose, put it into a bottle and let it grow up with its body on the inside and the head on the outside. Then comes the Koan: "How can you get the goose out without breaking the bottle and without killing the goose?" There are two answers to this paradox. One belongs to the ego-level and says: "You should not worry about other peoples problems", clearly telling you not to be distracted away from being centered. The other answer goes much deeper and belongs to the level of No-Self: "Neither the goose nor the bottle ever existed", indicating the goose as the soul and the bottle as the body are mere illusions.

There is another story that so nicely pictures the nature of attachment - the stickiness of the content of our mind. Two monks are walking along a muddy road on a rainy day. One monk is old and experienced, and the other is a novice. Suddenly they come across a young noble woman in her beautiful clothes, standing on one side of the road, not able to get to the other side without getting her shoes dirty. The old monk picks her up and carries her across. They then walk on, but the young monk is furious. He has caught the old master breaking one of his ordination wows. A while later he cannot contain his anger any longer and bursts out, "Don't you know that we are not supposed to have anything to do with women, and especially not carry them"? The old monk turns to him smiling and says; "I am not carrying that woman. You are!"

At this stage there is one aspect of training that is unavoidable; the training in concentration. If you want to evolve beyond mind you must train yourself to be able to hold your focus for a longer period of time without being distracted by the movement of your mind. If your 'concentration-muscles' are weak, you will always be at the mercy of the whims of your mind. Your consciousness will be stuck in repetitions without any possibility of going beyond.

In Higher Self mode you learn to view all content of mind as distractions. Even if while meditating you get a vision of Buddha coming towards you blessing you as very special, you ignore this image as you ignore any other content of your mind in this training.

The stages of concentration are well known and very useful to have as a background in this work, even though knowing them puts you in danger of becoming ambitious and even more stuck. It is very sobering to have this theoretical knowledge. It bursts the bubble of the self-delusion of 'mastery'.

These are the stages of concentration you will have to go through:

1) At the onset at stage one, an untrained person has a mind that is basically immersed in the external reality. Then for the purpose of training, some kind of object of concentration is brought in. It can be the breath, some part of the body, an image or an external object.
2) Stage two is that the trainee internalises the object, and with closed eyes recreates the object. He manages to create mind-pictures of the chosen object, but loses it to distractions immediately again.
3) The third stage, which is the highest state most people normally reach, is characterised by managing to recreate the image of the object, but having to re-visualise the object over and over again. You see it and you lose it repeatedly in a meditation-session.

One example of this kind of training is the Shinè practise in the Tibetan Buddhist Karma Kagyu lineage. The procedure is simple, you just count on each In-breath up to 21. When you have done 21 in-breaths you restart at 1 again.

Sounds simple? It's not. When you lose yourself to distractions then you also restart at 1. This makes you very aware of where about you normally lose it. The sobering effect of this method is that you can always measure the degree of your progress. If you tend to get side-tracked at, let's say, ten, then you know precisely the level of strength of your concentration.

4) The next stage appears when you do not have to restart your contact with the object so often. To get this far you have gradually passed through a process of having to restart fewer and fewer times in a session.
5) Now at the fifth stage the image has become stable, so you don't need to recreate it. You simply rest with all your attention intimately linked to your object. Something happens here, that is full of beauty. Like the dawn of the day, something indescribable like a mental balm is creeping in from somewhere and filling you up. It is so welcoming, this nectar, that you may think; this is it, this is the goal,

and fail to notice that however nourishing and full of rest and spirit this experience is.... it's really just another distraction. The mental attitude that is produced in you at this stage is what I call Focus. It is not produced by you in your meditation, because the clue is that you really have to be completely non-doing, but it is given you as a by-product of your ability not to be distracted. I call this stage 'Focus with effort', because you still need to be somewhat active in your attitude not to be caught up in distractions.

6) Your ability to remain in Focus increases with time and becomes more and more effortless, natural and stable. This stage I call; 'Focus without effort'.

7) The next stage is characterised by Focus happening spontaneously to you in active life.

8) The final stage is Continual Being. This stage is close to the enlightenment experience, a stage of bliss. Everything is open, and you see everything in complete clarity. If you do not have a master to kick your butt now, then you probably will end up here, because alone, it is hard to find any reason to evolve further. It is so complete. But there still is an experiencer experiencing something, a viewer that views something, so we are still in relativity. We are still within the sphere of the mind.

When you go from the Authentic Self to Higher Self, you naturally exchange self for others. Your main focus is not your-self anymore. Your expression now really needs to come from your heart to be able to evolve further. You are realising that whatever you do to anybody, you really do to yourself. If for example you get the impulse to help somebody, and you resist that impulse, then that interruption of the flow from the heart immediately turns to psychic weight and a lowering of your present consciousness back into personality. In other words, you create karma.

Another thing that comes with the Higher Self-consciousness is a sense of humility and a natural acceptance of things as they are. You may even find yourself in a situation where you know you are a victim of injustice, you are right and the others are wrong. But you accept even that with a light mind, because you trust and know that what is happening is coming from a reality deeper than your own limited vision. And listening to this reality in the long run produces results that are fundamentally best for everyone. And not reacting keeps your mind clean.

An old story illustrates this well.

A very well respected old monk had a beautiful noblewoman as
a student. One day she came home to her parents and told them
she was pregnant, and that the father was the old monk. This was
a big catastrophe for her, her family, the monastery and the
whole community. They charged the monk, and he answered. "Is
that so?"

The monk of course was expelled from both the community
and his monastery, and when the woman gave birth to the baby
they came to him with it. "You are the father, you take care of it".
The monk accepted and raised the child for several years. Then
one day the pressure of guilt became too strong for the mother
and she could not contain her secret anymore. She admitted that
the real father was the stable boy, not the monk. This was
another big catastrophe, because they had done the monk such
wrong. They immediately went to the monk and apologised
profusely. He answered: "Is that so?", and gave the child
back again.

The attitude of acceptance is very, very important. At this
stage you regularly get influx from the divine, or the Absolute if
you want, but we often don't see it and take it in. Understanding,
which is not dependent on the intellect, comes with acceptance.
If we don't maintain the attitude of acceptance we often push
away, in ignorance, the 'golden messages' coming from the
divine. Our intellectual intelligence is based on what is known.
Everything coming from the divine is unknown, it has to be,
because it emerges straight from the uncreated. So how can we
understand it? These impulses often come like condensed
packages of knowledge, too compact to be immediately understood and assimilated by our limited minds. It takes a long time
for an untrained student to unwind these riddles, but slowly with
patience it will dawn on us that we are never going to get any
answers, but our questioning mind will be dissolved, and the
riddles evaporates with it.

Another beautiful Zen story points us in that direction: Two
monks were looking at a flag waving in the gentle morning
breeze. One monk said to the other; "Look how beautiful the flag
is moving". But the other said: "It is not the flag that is moving,
it's the wind!" They did not manage to agree and soon they were
quarrelling without being able to settle the argument. In the end
they decided to ask their master who had the right answer. Being
posed the question he quietly looked at them and said: "Neither
of you is right. It's your mind that moves!!!!"

Our mind is moving all the time, and there is really nothing we can do to stop it, except to leave it alone. This attitude gives us a chance to dis-identify with the content of our mind. This is a very important step in our spiritual evolution. It turns our attention completely around and directly points us in the direction of inner freedom: Our mind exists only on the energy that we feed it through the attention we give it.

THE NO-SELF

When we come to no-self confusion really sets in. To move from the higher self to no-self is not something you evolve into. No-self is not the next step higher than the higher self, it is beyond self, higher self, the mind and even beyond the notion of no-self itself! It is emptiness! Empty of any content of mind, empty of all concepts, labels and labelling, empty of personality and of course empty of emptiness. Do you get it? From the perspective of no-self you will see that anything that is within mind or the personality is a prison. You will see that the personality is merely a habitual way of organising impressions coming through the senses.

There is a fine story from Japan of a nun struggling to understand all this. She had a hard time for a long period and was on the verge of giving up, feeling that she was the most hopeless of all nuns. What she did not know was that her confusion was doing a very good job of helping releasing her from the grip of her personality. One full moon evening she was carrying a water basket full of water out from her cell. She stopped for a moment admiring the reflection of the moon on the surface of the water in the basket. Suddenly the bottom of the basket fell out and the water with it. Right then and there she got enlightened and exclaimed: "No water, No moon". Do you get it? Once the mirror of the mind goes, there is nothing there to reflect what is coming through the senses. Both the reflection and the reflected is realised as the illusion it always was. That's the simplicity and beauty of it.

When the fifth patriarch of the Ch'an School of China felt that death was coming his way, he wanted to appoint his successor. He asked his students to write a poem that reflected their state of progress. The one who showed the highest degree of attainment was going to succeed him as the sixth patriarch. All his monks tried, but the one who everyone expected to be his successor wrote this outstanding stanza:

Your body is like a bodhi-tree
and your mind is like a mirror.
Moment after moment continuously
dust it impeccably.

The patriarch read it and said it was very clear, but he was still
not quite happy and asked everybody to try again.

At the monastery there was also this young boy, who once hearing the diamond sutra recited at the marketplace had had a spontaneous enlightenment experience. He then wanted to become a
monk but he was so poor that the only place in the monastery
available to him was in the kitchen. Hearing the stanza of the
star student read to him, he exclaimed: "But this is wrong!.....
This is how it is," and got a monk to write:

Your body is not a tree at all,
and your mind is not a mirror.
When everything is empty
where could the dust collect?

Isn't it beautiful?

He finally became the sixth patriarch.

When the clarity produced by the training in concentration
merges with the compassion of the heart, then no-self happens.
You prepare for this by viewing everything as illusion, even no-
self itself.

The main characteristic of no-self is absolute compassion.
Compassion is what saturates the non-experience of no-self and
the main training for that is practising relative compassion,
meaning being compassionate in your daily life.

Thank you for listening!

EGO

Some points characterising the personality.

Motivating Force

- General dis-satisfaction with life.
- Longing for Calm.
- Longing for personal fulfilment.

Typical Focus

- Craving for recognition through
  feedback and gratification
  from others and the outside.

Attitude to emotions

- Governed by them both consciously
  and unconsciously.

Attitude to personal imperfections

- Hiding them.
- Obsessed by them.

Main Challenge

- Expressing personal thoughts and
  emotions.
- Getting to know and confront your
  shadows.

Main Training

- Understanding your biography.
- Expressing thoughts and emotions.
- Learning to center, for your self to
  shine through.

Progress
- Your own effort, plus help.

Structure
- Cyclic, Relative.
- Within mind.

Glasses

- Dirty sunglasses.
  (The dirt of karma).

THE AUTHENTIC SELF

Some points characterising the personality.

Motivating Force

- Tired of mundane living.
- Curiosity; "Who am I"?
- Wanting to find and use your true qualities and talents.
- Fame.
- Longing for spirituality.

Typical Focus

- Wish for recognition and feedback both from inside and outside, but the last means much less than before
- Discovering intuition.

Attitude to emotions

- Accepting and expressing them.
- Realizing the difference between feelings and emotions.
- Beginning to contain them.

Attitude to personal imperfections

- Taking responsibility for them, and being willing to work through them.

Main Challenge

- Following your own subjective, intuitive path, no matter what.

Main Training

- Being productive with your talents and your qualities.
- Realizing the energy that is released when in tune.
- Starting meditation and other inner silent work.

Progress

- Your own effort, and help more out of want than need.

Structure

- Cyclic, Relative.
- Within mind.

Glasses

- Clean sunglasses.

  Your view is clearer but still very much tinted.

HIGHER SELF

Some points characterising the personality.

Motivating Force

- Longing for stillness and bliss.
- Kicks from your master.
- Sheer delight in the spiritual
  life you are experiencing.
- Knowledge of the path.

Typical Focus

- Borders between inner and outer life
  are disappearing.
- Accepting things as they are.
- Listening.
- Subjective awareness & universal
  ground realized as same.

Attitude to emotions

- Witnessing feelings and emotions,
  not buying the package.
- Viewing all content of mind as
  distractions.

Attitude to personal imperfections

- Total melting & acceptance.
- Detailed knowledge about their nature.
- Discovered as source of sacred
  humility.

Main Challenge

- Simplification of external life.
- Not following distractions.
- Letting go of personhood.
- Not being seduced by super natural
  powers.

Main Training

- Concentration / Meditation.
- Empathy.
- Exchanging self for others.
- Compassion also as atunement to the
  atmosphere of the Absolute.

Progress
- Your own effort, plus something that
  takes over.
Structure
- Cyclic, Relative.
- Within mind.

Glasses

- Sparkling clean glasses.
  As if they were not there.

NO SELF

Some points characterising the personality.

Motivating Force

- Nowhere to go.
- Nobody to motivate.

Typical Focus

-Compassion.

Attitude to emotions

- None.

Attitude to personal imperfections

- No imperfections.
- No perfection.

Main Challenge

- Not being drawn back into relativity.
- Fear of extinction.

Main Training

- Total surrender of self.
- Viewing everything as illusion.
- Realizing that the self never existed!

Progress
- Nowhere to go.

Structure
- Non-cyclic, non-dual.
- Beyond mind.

Glasses

- No glasses, no not glasses.
- Realizing that
     - the glasses never existed,
     - the tinting never existed,
     - the dirt never existed.

What does Breathwork have to do with Psychotherapy?

ALFRED PRITZ

Dr. Alfred Pritz is psychoanalyst and president of the World Association for Psychotherapy, the European Association for Psychotherapy and the Austrian Association for Psychotherapy.

I observe Breathwork from the very outside. Breathwork is a very ancient method practised for a few thousand years. In the eastern tradition (Yoga) the observation and awareness of breathing is a main issue. And it is not surprising that many of us include breathing, which is a basic human function, in our modern techniques for handling relationships - individual and in groups. Today we are losing the non-observational basis. Just as in breathing we develop techniques to get a deeper breathing that will function better for the body and use hypnosis to re-leave emotional pain.

Breathwork and psychotherapy: What do they have in common?

When I say psychotherapy I refer to the broad scope - not only psychoanalysis. All these methods have the following aspects in common with the Breathwork:
- Concentration and focus on the self.
- A theory of radical subjectivity: Psychotherapy is investigating how an individual, a group, or even a nation perceives reality and the world around. It is always how the client sees it, holding back the own view of the world.
- The awareness of one's own being - How do I feel?
- The tendency of precise observations of one's own abilities
- Awareness of time - especially in letting time flow and looking for timelessness when we get into regression
- The cautious tendency for change of the own structure and the structure of the client
- When someone says "We just want to observe and we do not want to change", it is probably a game because when we observe, observation is already a move, in the same

way as when the baby feels observed by the mother it feel connected.

- The awareness of the inner behaviour - the awareness of ideas, thoughts and reactions - which are not observable from the outside only internally. The inner dialogue is constantly working. This is one of the reasons that every psychotherapeutic method claims positive results. So many non-spoken ideas about the world are constantly exchanged by body language. Common ideas are not shared. They just happen.
- The intimate and sacred situation where the outer reality does not seem very important.

Now to the critical points:

The conceptualisation of what most schools do. Following Austrian law, the Ministery of Health established a commission to evaluate psychotherapeutic schools and methods from a scientific point of view. That lead to the question to which science psychotherapy should belong? Basically it is a hermeneutic science between theology, medicine, psychology and pedagogics with sources in all these areas, but a science of its own since it perceives reality form a subjective point of view.

Some criteria:

A psychotherapeutic method needs a theory. As Einstein said, we can only observe what we have a theory of. According to constructivism we are constructing reality. Many psychotherapeutic methods believe in this philosophy. Without theory, a method can be useful and helpful but it is not a school of its own. The psychotherapeutic theory is not like a theory in physics or chemistry but has specific elements of its own: A Menschenbild - a concept of human nature like the concept of self-actualisation or the concept of genetic determination.

For a model of normal and pathological behaviour with the differentiation of normal and pathology we need a classification of illnesses that crosses the borders of the various schools and is understandable for other people. This is one of the big short-comings in many psychotherapeutic schools. They formulate theories that are incomprehensible for others. Psychoanalysts in particular are very good at this. It is clear that every school needs their own way of formulating observations. The student has to learn their way of formulating. But sometimes schools formulate theories for pathological behaviour and classifications that are not explainable even after studies and leave the students at a point of believing or not believing. This is not scientific.

Although we know that believing is very important and psychotherapy is a science about beliefs, a psychotherapist should not be a believer but a researcher of beliefs.

There are also some other, maybe more local criteria. A psychotherapeutic method should be teachable. It means that it should not be based on a system of Guru teaching where one person has the truth and the others have to learn.

The psychotherapeutic school should be ready to be tested externally. The client and therapist (in Austria every therapist has to do 250 hours of therapy for himself) both have the right to test the method internally. Mao Zedong once said that, "The objective world will never be fair to the subjective world". It is also necessary to research the outcome of psychotherapeutic methods.

There is a weakness in a school that is not willing to be tested by external researchers, to establish for whom the method is useful and when it is not useful. This also means quality control and responsibility towards the national health systems and authorities.

In my view all psychotherapeutic schools belong to a family - a big family with many children, older ones and younger ones, bright ones and less bright ones. With this view it is easier to handle fights between the schools.

Thank you for your attention.

Chapter 5

Body, Breath, Bliss

Social Integration

BO WAHLSTRÖM

Bo Wahlström is a pioneer in Swedish Breathwork and co-founder of the Swedish Breathwork Training Institute and has some 20 years experience of Breathwork. Since 1988 he has become a much sough-after Breathwork teacher and workshop leader in several European countries. He also travels extensively to India as a group leader conducting spiritual quests.

I had my basic Breathwork training in 1979-80. I stayed in USA for six months and went to California to see Leonard Orr. I do not know how many Rebirthing sessions I made these six months but they were many. When I began to get more aquatinted with the power of breath, I thought, "This is gold". I really felt like my fellow Swedes who went gold digging in America 150 years ago. I struck lucky.

Already at that time I was interested in the idea of social integration - the strive for inner development to have an impression on the social structure. When I came home I wanted to save Sweden - all of it in one go - but the whole of Sweden did not want to be saved. Not by me anyway. So I had to save myself first. Then six years later, slowly and with help of fellow Breathworkers, we could start to "save" Sweden together, with our " Breathwork Training Programme". Another way of putting it is that it took me six years to get mentally grounded and socially integrated enough to be able to express myself in public. But since 1986 we have been running the Breathwork Training and so far we have trained around 800 people.

When we played with the idea of saving the country we made a sort of mathematical calculation to see how many people we reached and touched with Breathwork, including the spin off effect that occurs when one Breathworker starts to work with other people. The reality is that we have not yet reached 1% of Sweden's population. Maybe this will be our first goal. On the other hand I think our training programme has been quite successful with the social integration aspect. This success I think is due to our common vision not to become a sect or a private VIP club. We wanted things to happen in the common reality, also known as society, which, as you known by now, has been my interest for a long time.

Why should we strive for this social integration? What is the purpose of social integration? My answer is that society will give you feedback on your behaviour, which is healthy for your growth. A reality-check if you wish. Another way of putting it is that reality is real. I know that we have seen discussion groups at this conference around the subject "*Thought is creative, is it?*" We are not the only people in history that have been discussing this issue. This discussion is actually recorded in Indian scriptures around 2,000 years ago. Open metaphysical debates between the three classical schools of thought, the Vedanta school, the Samkya school and the Yoga school. They were often discussing different issues. One really interesting debate concerned the meaning of the word "Maya" which in Sanskrit means "illusion". On this issue, Samkya and Yoga were on one side and Vedanta was on the other. Vedanta claimed that the physical reality, the physical universe, is pure illusion where as the Samkya and Yoga schools said that our way to perceive the physical universe is an illusion but it has a reality in itself.

This is also my standpoint. I believe that there is something out there, outside my head. When people use the words "*Thought is creative*", these days, you don't know whether they are coming from the Vedanta perspective or from the Samkya-Yoga perspective. You may not agree with me, but I perceive that "*The Course in Miracles*" is more like the Vedanta philosophy. "This chair does not exist", "This table is not really there", it is all pure illusion. I recommend that you find out for yourself to see from what perspective you come. Personally I come from the Samkya-Yoga perspective. I really care about the physical reality and it is obvious to me that if you want a good relationship with reality you better perceive it as real. This is my reason for being interested in society and also for being interested in real transformation. I have seen so called New Age development techniques as well as more traditional therapies helping people to create personal illusions to make them happy. I do not believe in teaching people how to create personal illusion.

I would therefore like to explore the essence of transformation. It is interesting to look at different techniques and methods to see what they say about transformation. It will inevitably lead to generalisations but I would still claim it to be generally true.

It would probably help our perspective if we divide the different kinds of development techniques and therapies into four categories:
TALKING, FEELING, TOUCHING and BREATHING
- the first category concentrates on talking and conceptualising. Here I include psychotherapy, psychoanalysis, counselling, consulting, etc
- the second category focus on experiencing and expressing emotions. The classical method here is primal therapy, but there are many other methods that can be brought into this category.
- the third is oriented towards physical touch. Here we have body-work and of course all various kinds of massage techniques, bio-energetic etc.
- the fourth category is Breathwork

What do these different schools say about transformation?
Well, people in the first category who use talk to change usually claim that insight is the key to transformation. If you get a clear insight about your problem you will change. Just to conduct a bit of scientific studying here - how many of you here have seen people with great insight and no change? Quite a few, I can tell by all the raised hands. So insight may not really be the key to transformation. Just because you get clear insight does not mean that you transform.

When it comes to feeling and expressing emotions the transformational key would be to relive. So if you relive this terrible traumatic moment that happened in your childhood, would you then be free of it and be transformed? Being scientific again - how many of you have the experience of reliving a trauma over and over again? Not so many hands this time. Maybe it is true then. Still, the way I see it is that this is not really the key issue. I have seen people relive their traumas over and over again with no noticeable change. If I include myself I can speak with absolute authority when I say that this is true!

As regards touching, the key issue would be to release tensions. If you release your tensions, transformation would take place. It is my experience that when I receive a bodywork sessions, I can have a beautiful blissful experience, getting a fantastic experience of heaven on earth almost. But sometimes it lasts one week, sometimes it lasts only one day, so for me it does not seem to be the key issue either.

But we mustn't only disclose mythology in other schools, we

must also look at ourselves. In Breathwork the key concept is opening the energy. In my experience, both personal and with my clients, it is fairly easy to bliss out with the help of Breathwork, focusing on energy. All problems are gone, until you go home and have the next encounter with your wife, husband, children or parents. What happened to the transformation in the Breathwork session?

I hope you are curious to find what the key issue is, if you have not heard me before. For me the key issue is to change both thought and behaviour. I think this is the real key issue. A therapy called cognitive-behaviourism has very good results. They don't care about insights, nor do they care about reliving, they don't touch the body, and they don't know anything about breath. Still their technique creates a lot of change. I had a medical doctor in one of my trainings. He was an expert in pain therapy. With the help of cognitive behaviourist therapy they could lower the use of painkillers by half. They could cut the medication by 50% just by getting people to change their thoughts and change their behaviours. But the weakness with the method is that it takes away the symptoms that might appear somewhere else in a different form. Although the physical pain has an emotional level underneath, they could still lower the pain by just changing thoughts and changing behaviour. But until the underlying emotional problem is addressed properly it could have a tendency to surface somewhere else in another similar situation whether it is relationships or communications problem or something completely different. Cognitive behavioural therapy replaces an undesirable conditioning by a desirable conditioning in so far as they make proposals, they analyse your thinking patterns and they propose other ways to think. They analyse your behaviour in certain situations and make suggestions to behave in a different way in that specific situation.

What I am aiming at is that all the methods I have mentioned are valuable. But if you don't look at changing your thoughts and behaviour at the same time it does not work. If you get all these beautiful insights and still go home and think negative thoughts about yourself or address your wife in the same manner as you always do, there is no change. The same applies to all methods. Breathwork can just be like a drug kick without side effects if you don't let it affect you thoughts and your behaviour. I suppose this is why the Rebirthing movement has talked about creative thought from the very beginning. But it does not have to be done in a superficial way. It can be done in a very realistic and practical way.

It is sometimes said that when the energy moves it can change our thoughts but I'd say that when we move the energy we get aware of limiting thoughts. Your way of thinking and behaving creates psychological and physiological tension. If you release this tension in one breathing session but then go back to think and behave in the same limiting way you will eventually re-create the tension.

I strongly advocate this totality, to adopt a holistic perspective. All these methods reinforce each other. The work does not end in the workshop. There is homework to do as well. And if you don't do your homework you may well fail your exam, which is to participate in the flow of life and to integrate its essence into your being, flow and change.

In the holistic perspective, nothing in the whole universe has one single cause. Everything affects everything. You cannot even fart without affecting every galaxy in the whole universe. Now I know why my mother did not want me to do so. She was a very modest person and she did not want her son to affect the galaxies. Of course my minuscule influence on the universe as a child had a very minimal effect on the galaxies. So if you look for causes of anything, you have to look for main causes.

What are the main causes that create self-respect and social integration in the holistic perspective? To answer this I will use the symbol. (Fig.1). A star of self-respect and social integration.

It is my belief that self-respect is the basis for transformation. A friend of mine, who trained in Breathwork at the same time as me, later abandoned the Breathwork and went only with affirmations. She became a very successful therapist. Her trick is to start with affirmations about self-respect. Without a certain level of self-respect, no affirmations will work. But there are several factors to self-respect and social integration. To illustrate them I'd like to use the form of a star.

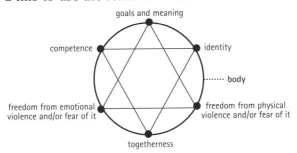

Fig 1.

The first factor is very basic. I call it freedom from physical violence and/or from fear of it. We know that the best way to give a child poor self-respect is to beat them up. It is very important when you work with clients to check if this is the reality for them. If they are living in a relationship where there is physical violence, or threat of physical violence, don't be surprised if the therapy does not work. Freedom from physical violence is to learn to put very clear limits to relationships but it is also about caring about the physical environment. Because the violence is real! If you live in a very violent neighbourhood you do not say to yourself, "How did I create this?" and "Maybe if I do some affirmations it will all go away." No, it doesn't work that way! But if you take physical action and maybe try to do something to change the physical violence in your neighbourhood, you care about your physical environment at the same time as you do self-therapy. This difference is important to notice.

The next factor is called freedom from emotional violence and/or fear of it. Freedom from emotional violence is also to check your relationships. Emotional violence is when people make each other feel guilty or constantly blame each other for wrongdoing and similar. Your client comes to you once a week and you give him or her a lot of attention, love and positive thoughts. The rest of the week s/he goes home and is fed with an abundance of negative thoughts and negative feedback. What you tell your clients does not work very well if you do not encourage them to also change their situation. So this is also about setting very clear limits to our relationships and communicating very clearly with our friends, or sometimes even changing friends.

The third factor located at the base of the star, I call togetherness. As human beings we have a basic need for togetherness with other people. Togetherness is about having a positive we-feeling, to belong somewhere where you are seen and welcomed and getting some kind of recognition. This could be a good family, a Rebirthing group, a religious setting, a sports club, or whatever brings you that positive we-feeling. Of course there are many levels of this positive we-feeling but it is extremely strong. This is often the reason why even very destructive groups such as skin-head-neo-nazi-associations or motorcycle gangs hold such an attraction to people who do not have any we-feelings with society. In these groups they become somebody. They receive individual recognition in the group. So the feeling of togetherness is very seductive. Here I'd like to identify five different levels of group participation.

They are like different stages in our biological development as well as inner stages of psychosocial participation. We often jump between the different levels in the course of our development but also in different social settings.

The first stage I call dependent. The dependent stage corresponds to the very small baby that needs the mother constantly for its survival. There are many people who are stuck on this level in our society - people who can't do anything unless somebody tells them to.

The second level I call semi-dependent. It corresponds to a small child who needs its mother but also is prepared to make small private excursions.

The third level that corresponds well to most teen-agers I call counter-dependent. They are totally against their parents. They think they are free but they are still in someway dependent. This may well be a necessary phase in their development process, but they are stuck in being against. This level of participation is of course easy to find in our society.

The fourth level I call independent. Many people think this is the highest state but for me it is not. It corresponds to a young adult.

The highest state I call interdependent. It is totally different from co-dependent. This state corresponds to a mature adult - an independent adult that chooses to co-operate with others to achieve an even better result. That is a co-operative individualist. The co-operative individualist is not really dependent on others, for other things than to achieve practical results, for social, financial, economical, ecological or spiritual reasons. In fact, I think that Global Inspiration and IBF are fantastic examples of co-operative individualists coming together. This is one of the exciting aspects that bring me here. But co-operation demands more of everybody. It is easier to do things yourself, sitting in morning meetings, discussing various organisational topics, trying to find ways to agree at the end of each discussion. But when you finally succeed you often accomplish so much more. So my advice to you is - don't stay in the independent state. Go on and take up new challenges as they come your way. This is what I consider to be a high level of togetherness.

But let's return to our star so that we can complete it. The next factor I call competence. Competence means to be aware that you are good at something and to be willing to come out with it and to get feedback from others, from real people. This can be extremely therapeutic. There are at least three ways to raise your competence. The first is to get clear about what you already know and what you can. The other two are more education and more experience. I have seen clients taking giant steps in transformation, just by starting a training course. They grow in self-respect. You could have continued to take them through 10 or 20 more breathing sessions but if you instead guide them and support them towards educating themselves in order to achieve what they really want, you will probably do much more for them.

The next factor I call identity. Identity is what most therapy is all about. To know who you are, know your wounds, know your longings and your behavioural patterns. Traditional therapy is of course very important although I consider Breathwork to be traditional too, these days. Or maybe this is still just an affirmation. Still I am sure that it will become a reality, as real as reality itself.

The top factor I call goals and meaning. Meaning in your life. Meaning answers the question "Why". Why am I living? Why did I get born? Why should I participate? Whereas goals have to do with "How", How do I want to participate? But of course these two border to each other, which is why they are together.

What I have described so far are six nice parameters but there is also a seventh, which is symbolised by this encompassing circle. This is the body. And it embodies all the others - to have a friendly relationship with your body. You are okay with the way you look and with your sexuality. You care about what you eat or drink. You care about giving your body massages, exercise, or whatever.

So here we have seven factors and again it has to do with balance. People often have a tendency to over-emphasise one aspect to compensate for the other. One example of this is high-level business people who are very competent. They are functioning well in society and have a good self-esteem. But if they lose their job, they may well fall apart. They often have a very low level of identity and maybe they lost contact with their family while they were involved in their career. People in therapy sometimes over-emphasise the identity factor. If you have a problem at home you go to get more therapy. I once said to a client, "You cannot breathe away your husband. Go home and talk to him and get clear on what you will do with your relationship." It worked, better than my breathing sessions.

I should perhaps add that all these methods work only if they lead you to change your habitual thinking and your habitual behaviour. All these methods are good but it is important to know what makes them work and what does not make them work. Any therapy can become just a repetitive escape from reality. "My life is horrible but I love my therapist. It's so nice to go there, he gives me such nice feedback and good attention that I never get at home." If you want to keep your blissful state even between the sessions with your therapist, you need to work on reality too.

The way to measure where people or clients stand as far as these various key issues are concerned is simply to interview them, to talk to them and try to find their specific imbalances.

Since we are talking about social integration, I also like to present a socio-economic model of our society, which also incorporates transformation, more today than ever. I know that this is very pretentious of me, but I must confess that I like this model very much, even if I am not totally addicted to it. I like to draw a map (Fig. 2) of how our society has developed. Since our time together is limited, we have to restrict ourselves slightly. We'll start 10,000 years ago.

	the farming society	the industrial society	the Information society	the Inspiration society
dominating tool	plough	machine	computer	body
common purpose	survival	prosperity/ abundance	personal development	spiritual development "holism"
main production	food	goods/ products	information	more life
strategic resource	land	cash/capital	knowledge	"human humans"
main form of organisation	family	company	network	"organic cooperation"
main sources of energy	animals and plants	coal/petrol and oil	brain	breath
main profession	farming	worker	entrepreneur	healer
means of production	local	mass production	individual	united efforts

Fig 2.   present time

10,000 years ago there was a great revolution in the human socio-economic setting. People started to farm the land. This was the start of the farming society. There are certain key factors that characterise the farming society. In the farming society, the most important tool is the plough. It brought about a great change for people. The common purpose in the farming society is survival. The main production is food. Of course they produce other things too but food is the main production. The strategic resource is land. The main form of organisation in the early farming society was the family. Not the small family we have today but an extended family. The main sources of energy were animals and plants. The main profession was of course farming. This was the reality in Sweden up until a hundred years ago. The majority of people were farmers. The means of production were mainly local.

Just a couple of hundreds of years ago, some countries started to move into the industrial society. The dominating tool here is the machine and the common purpose is prosperity or abundance. The main production is no longer food, it is goods or products. The strategic resource is cash or capital. The main form of organisation here is the company and the source of energy is coal, and later petrol and oil. The main occupation is manual work. The means of production is mass production. All this is significant for the industrial society. If we move from left to right on our map and move on to current time, we end up somewhere close to the end of the industrial society. We have not left it yet, but as you all know, we are moving fast into the Information society.

In the Information society the dominating tool is the computer. The common purposes here becomes personal development. The main production, when this society is in full blossom, is the production of information. The strategic resource is knowledge. The form of the organisation is the network. As you can see the IBF is already a bit ahead of the society in general. The source of energy is of course the brain and when this society is fully developed, the main profession will be the entrepreneur. Just think about the scenario where the majority of people are entrepreneurs. It means that instead of a majority of people being workers or working for a company they will start their own business. The means of production is mainly individual.

But what comes after this? Yes, even if we are not there yet, there is something ahead of us which to some extent is already apparent. If we know about it we can all more consciously move on and support the process. So what do we do with all the information if we don't have inspiration? In my view the next era approaching will be what I would call the Inspiration society. It is a very optimistic scenario, it gives a good feeling to think about it, doesn't it? But what is significant of this society? The dominant tool will be the body. The common purpose will be what you either can call spiritual development or "holism", to expand consciousness according to a more holistic perspective, which of course includes spirituality. What will be produced in the Inspiration society? More life! The main production will be more life. A kind of immortality if you like.

As I told you already I have been interested in society for a long time and I have been very concerned about the ecological situation on the planet. My perspective on where we are going right now, is that we are really going downhill. I truly believe this is objectively true. We are producing more death and less life on the planet at this point in time. The ecological consciousness that has been raised in the last decades has made us go downhill a little slower. I am looking forward to the day where we reach the bottom and start to go up again. Producing more life is not only producing more life in your own body but also taking on ecological responsibility. What is the strategic resource in the Inspiration society? I call it "human humans", - human beings who are whole. Since we no longer can produce just a lot of information, we must embody it and live it out. This would be a great strategic resource. The form of organisation I call "organic co-operation". In the Inspiration society, this will be the main form of organisation. You will need a network and perhaps also a company, but there will be several organic corporations emerging everywhere. They will not necessarily come from a family or need a legal form like companies do and they will not necessarily be structured as a network. A good metaphor is musicians that come together. When a special set of musicians get together they will make unique music and produce a C.D. Then they will move on and do something else. In the organic co-operation we do not need as much structure. Things will happen spontaneously. The source of energy in the Inspiration society is of course our breath! And the main profession is the healer. The healer is somebody who produces more life, more life in the body, or somebody who is an ecologist and produces more life in nature, or protects or preserves natural life. The means of production are united efforts since if you unite your efforts you can make many more things happen, especially if you unite as co-operative group of individualists. As you all know there is something magical with group energy. With good group energy everybody gets more than what they put in. Where does this extra come from?

I think this is what we need to do. Just because society is changing does not mean that we totally leave the old societies. We need to keep a foot in the farming society as well as the industrial society that is also producing valuable goods. In the Information society we use the computer to communicate with each other. This enables the Inspiration society to happen. To do personal development means that you need a lot of information. You also need contact, real physical contact, with people. In the Information society you are in contact with these people through your computers, E-mail and whatever you are using to build a very high-quality network. So at the moment we are preparing the way for the new society. In the Information society we will not necessarily have enlightened leaders, or enlightened people in power. Anybody in the Information society who has a vision or a good project can communicate their thoughts on the internet without using the usual media. Anything can be used creatively or destructively. Still, the plough you built for tilling the land to grow food for your family can if you want also be used to bang somebody on the head.

As you can see, I am still trying to save the world. I never really gave up, I just became more realistic. I realised I could not do it alone. I had to co-operate with people. And I am pleased to say that it is fun too. Someone said "It would be so easy to save the world if it was not for all of the people in it". I hope my beloved latest model will give you something of value. It works like a map where your personal values, ethics and highest ideals are the compass. Just take a look at how you can move through this map. Where are you now and what is your next step?

Thank you for your attention.

Beyond Bliss

EIRIK BALAVOINE

Being half French and half Norwegian, Eirik Balavoine brings qualities from these two distinctly different cultures into his personality and teaching - passion, presence and precision. He has trained and worked with meditation since 1973, Breathwork since 1978 and psychotherapy since 1982 and is leader of groups and silent retreats since 1984. His professional work has mainly been centred in Norway but he has recently moved to France to live and teach.

To stand before an audience and speak about what my heart is full of is a wonderful opportunity to establish a sharing condition where magic can happen. So, my own wish for the time I'm going to spend talking to you is that as I speak I will be able to convey truth so that our minds will sometimes blend in understanding, and I hope that in some moments, our heart's will merge in communion.

For those of you who don't know me I think perhaps I will start by giving you some essentials about my background - to make it easier to understand where I'm coming from when I'm speaking.

Most important is the fact that I have been meditating for most of my adult life, meaning that I have had a strong and steady practice of silent meditation for about 20 years. Meditation and the inner landscape that is revealed when the sense impressions gradually become quiet is really the basis of what I do. In that silence and I'm not speaking of the silence that is the absence of sound, universal truth can be discovered. This experience which is also an extreme clarity, reveals the laws governing human life with astonishing precision. These laws are described in abundance in traditional mystic literature, but I believe every time period has to rediscover and formulate them in the language and style of the present culture to be of fruitful use.

I work as a psychotherapist and rebirther as my everyday activity – I use many of the basic modern psychological techniques in my work, but I don't stick to anyone in particular anymore. I rather choose method according to each individual person and the present situation. Moreover I use my personality and consciousness as a therapeutic and diagnostic instrument, to assist in aligning the person to his or her own truth. My attitude and intention is definitely transpersonal.

In this talk I intend to look a little deeper into bliss and the consequences that searching for bliss has on someone involved in personal development or someone on a spiritual quest.

Fundamentally as human beings we are always on a search for happiness. This normally starts with fulfilling basic physical human needs and naturally evolves through various intermediate steps to, in the end, a genuine spiritual quest. The aim is always for something more fulfilling, more true and often for something more intense. This is fundamental for all of us, and functions well as a true motivation for development. However, when we look deeply into the nitty gritty of what really works in inner development, then we see that the story is a little different.

My use of bliss in this talk refers to a variety of experiences, but common to them all is that for the experiencer they are experienced in the moment as a profound freeing of the body-mind from the non-physical constraint of the present situation. Often as an existential revelation into something higher. In the later stages of development, bliss is often labelled as deep religious experiences. This labelling is independent of the life conditioning of the person involved, and is not really important for us in this talk. What I intend to consider is our attitude to bliss itself, rather than the content of the experience, as I find that this attitude has consequences that are fundamentally important for our development process to be fruitful.

Some years ago, investigating my own practice I found that often in meditation I was always half consciously hunting for some kind of bliss. Some kind of heightened more real and intense experience. As a youth I had some experiences of bliss that had profound effects on me. These later became a blueprint reminding me what my life could be like. Through the years though, bliss experiences came and went as a result of my practise, but when they disappeared, it often left me feeling that there was something wrong with me since I always sooner or later returned to 'normal' again. I reached some kind of bliss experience, remained submerged in it for a while, but then it faded and disappeared again. This produced in me an attitude that there was something wrong with me that needed to be 'repaired'.

In the Rebirthing sessions for example, ecstasy came and went, again and again. It was always the same cycle - the rise, the peak and the fall. And I kept pounding on myself. "What is wrong? Why is it that when I come from a retreat or a workshop full of energy and power, wholeness and clarity, it always disappears again?" Because that is what it always did.

It was when I took a step back and looked at my own expectations for bliss to last, that I remembered some comment from my old teacher, Bob Moore in Denmark. He said that every-thing that exists does so in the pulse of contraction and expansion - in nature, in day and night, in man and woman. And so it is with our consciousness when it's locked in the personality. When our attention is locked in there, it always exists and functions in opposites, in relativity. That's the way it is. The continuous creation of our personal consciousness happens in this dialogue between opposites. What I didn't see was that in my striving to reach bliss and in my striving to get the bliss to last, I was going against the pulse of life.

So this was one of the fundamental 'letting go' I had to do. I stopped striving for bliss and started to watch the movements of my mind instead. In time I could see that in all the stages of per-sonality, in all the stages of consciousness, this cycle of increase and decrease happened, including bliss, including unity, but it stopped at the level of the Void, at the level of the Absolute.

I started instead to look at my attitude towards the content of my mind, especially my emotions. After having investigated for a long time it seemed to me that it was possible to extract from my mass of experiential knowledge a progressive way to deal with emotions that could be used as a bridge between psychological work and spiritual development.

Emotions have a profound way of shaping our perception, and to work with them means in essence to progressively under-stand them and then to dis-identify from them. It is possible to identify stages in this development that are valid for everyone that cares to look closely. And to understand them is to possess a key to work fruitfully with them.

I will go through these stages to clarify what I mean.

Suppression
The first level of dealing with emotions is suppression. We all know about this. When we are dealing with emotions on the

suppressed level, the emotional energy appears as projections. We're all banging our heads on this all the time, so this is of course nothing new for you, it's just to put it in place. We've all been through this attitude: "Something is wrong with the world, something is wrong with our parents, something is wrong with our teachers, brothers, sisters, friends, etc". We are not aware at this stage of the consciousness-shaping force of emotional energy, so we project it out. And of course it doesn't lead anywhere. This is often one of the reasons why we go into therapy. The feeling of not getting anywhere frustrates us.

Relief
The next level of attitude towards dealing with our emotions is what I call relief. This comes about when we have learned not to suppress anymore, but to express instead. We still project, but we express instead of keeping everything inside. In the relief that is felt in the moment of expressing what is going on inside, we experience a kind of bliss. (Relative to the stage we are on now, not bliss in the more powerful complete sense that comes later). There's no real growth in this - but since we're no longer holding it back there is nevertheless some evolvement from the suppression stage. Compared with the everyday body-mind feeling of someone, who is still suppressing, this relief is bliss. In dealing with emotions it is worth noticing that bliss is always experienced in the moment when the energy is so activated that it somehow bursts, and also in the calm deflation period that remain for some time afterwards.

Release
The next stage, when we move a little further, is what I call release. This occurs when we are aware of the emotion, we are taking responsibility for it, and we have learned to express our own subjective truth as an action, not as a reaction. With the ability to express emotion as truth, something new happens – instead of becoming stuck in self-righteousness, we fall back into ourselves. This is the first real return of the energy. The consciousness starts to generate on the inside, and the sense of a sound separate self start to emerge. We can say that we develop in this a wholesome ego. In Norway for example, we have the expression 'holy anger'. This is the anger that is not frustration, not projection - but you are so angry, so rightful, that the moment you express it, the fullness of the expression creates a feeling of clarity. You are so angry that the heat of truth in it

transforms the energy. This is not merely the explosion of held back frustration. Finally, you are expressing truth. The movement of energy in that moment is the first stage of bliss in a more spiritual way. Although it is just a tiny fraction of clarity, at the moment it is expressed it feels like a revelation.

In this we are at the very beginning of starting to learn about transformation of consciousness. It is vitally important to understand the basic principles of this as early as possible, since they are valid and necessary in all the later stages as well. Acceptance and dis-identification allows us to progress on the path as no other attitude can do.

The transformation stage.
After the release stage, the transformation stage is introduced to our consciousness. In the clarity that evolves with responsible expression, we start to understand the cyclical nature of emotions. We understand that emotionality consists of structure and energy. Energy is built up around the repetitive personality-structure, and is emptied through emotionality when the pressure is high enough. The body-mind feeling after an emotional outburst is usually lightness and clarity, but this disappears again as soon as the energy starts to accumulate again around the personality-structure. In the transformation stage it dawns on us that we can go on emptying ourselves for a lifetime, without progressing any further. If we understand that emotionality is cyclical – we can realise the wisdom in taking a step back to observe what is happening instead of merely acting it out. This means we are beginning to develop the witness position. This stage may in the form look a little like the suppression stage, but is completely different. We are refraining from mindlessly expressing our emotions, but we are containing them rather than suppressing them. This allows us in time to develop the witness position, which leads to maturation of our personality structure rather than the more immature reaction of simply releasing energy.

When we are working in the Transformation State, more bliss states happen in our everyday lives. For example; in our work we are now usually at a stage where we are deeply familiar with the technicalities of our trade, so the expression of what we are doing has a much greater chance of coming from our core being. It may arise from a subjective state that is so deep that it ceases to be only subjective – we are starting in our work to express from what I call the universal state, often experienced as a luminous creative flow.

Another example; Intimate relationships where the partners are both doing development work on themselves, and have progressed to the transformation stage, will find that in establishing the witness position they may experience that communication often turns into communion. This is an experience I am sure most of you are familiar with. It brings a kind of silence and togetherness into the relationship where words often becomes superfluous. Thought transference takes place more and more. There is stillness and frequent occurrences of synchronicity. We get the feeling that instead of being two people moving in different directions, we slowly become two people heading in the same direction.

Personally I have often had experiences of the transformative state out in nature. Often I went to the mountains alone. It would take me about three days to let my consciousness move from being preoccupied with the external reality to the internal reality. What I mean is that in my normal everyday state my attention is often focused on what is happening on the outside, but during the first three days alone in nature I go from being preoccupied with outside events to reaching the core in me, and states of clarity, of transparency, and of unity start to emerge. There are of course many other ways to experience such states but nature has always been one of my main sources for getting in touch with expanded states of awareness.

To proceed from there, anyone who wants to move further into bliss needs to develop the ability to focus the mind. If we do not acquire the ability to focus one-pointedly through training, the mind will always stay too linked with outside events. If we do not develop the ability to focus, the mind will not develop its innate ability to penetrate the apparent reality of things either. People who haven't developed their ability to focus tend to get locked into repetitive states of emotionality. But to know these stages makes us more independent in our personal development process in that we may recognise where we are in our progress. It is so easy to get an inflated ego as to how developed we are. There are very few yardsticks against which we may measure our development, which make the whole area free to claim whatever progress you think you have made. With the stages of one-pointedness clearly defined, we are instead given those yardsticks whereby we can actually measure our progress. And I tell you - it is very sobering!

These are the stages of focus:

When we start to work on our ability to concentrate or to focus - we close our eyes and immediately experience that our awareness is being drawn to outside events through sense-impressions, and it's really difficult to hold a focus on the object we have chosen as our focus point. This is the first stage.

After that, with training - either by focusing on the breath or focusing on an object - we will start to experience moments when we manage to hold on to our chosen focus point (on the breath, a Buddha statue, a cross, a prayer or whatever) more easily. We experience losing the focus point all the time, but nevertheless, it is more easy to hold it, and also more easy to recreate it in our mind.

The third stage occurs when we manage to hold on to the object for a little longer. We may start to feel that we become less restless, more still and the powers of distraction have less hold on us. We may also start to understand that it is the accumulated time in focus that really develops one-pointedness and our capacity to experience bliss.

In the fourth stage we are able to focus on our object for maybe three or four minutes uninterruptedly. At a certain stage we will then experience a feeling of something that is sometimes called 'nectar', 'raining down' from above our heads. This is a wonderful but also a precarious state, because when 'the rain' starts and we get a glimpse of this golden state of reality, it is so overwhelming that many believe this is the experience of enlightenment. Which of course it is not. It is just that instead of coming from the personal sphere, this nurturing energy originates from someplace vast and beyond the personality. That is all it means, but because of its attractive luminous quality it easily becomes a huge distraction.

Again it is the witness position and the process of dis-identification that gives us the key to proceed further. We have to let go of the feeling of bliss, and return to being aware of our object again. Spirituality can't be amassed, it only really becomes a reality in the act of letting go.

If, when this nectar is available and becomes more and more of a reality for us, we manage to let go, and always return to our centre, we will begin to experience that through letting go we will open up for an increasingly richer flow. If on the other hand we try to intensively seek bliss and think something like; "What did I do the last time that was so right that it produced the feeling of bliss?", and try to repeat this, the experience of bliss

will not return. We must completely forget that bliss is even possible. The moment we forget this and get reabsorbed in the
breath or the object, the flow of bliss re-emerges and it may even
sometimes appear by itself.

I find the insight of the importance of letting go extremely
valuable because it reappears as a necessary ingredient and fruitful attitude in our personal development.

For example, if you work with forgiveness, you must learn to
let go of pride and self-righteousness. In an emotional situation
where forgiveness is required, this will never take place as long
as we hold on to pride or self-righteousness. In order for warmth
and merging contact to re-appear, which is true state of forgiveness, we have to let go of all aspects of our ego-reactions.

Through all the stages I have just mentioned, we are still
operating within the personality, meaning the body-mind organism. It is of utmost importance to understand what this body-
mind organism really is in the big picture since in the end we
will find that it is the identification with our personality that
really prevents us from experiencing God or the Absolute.

When bliss states have started to appear in our consciousness
and we repeatedly manage to let go, we will experience more and
more 'rain' of nectar. And if we manage to become dis-identified
with the experience of bliss - and this is the secret - to not identify with the content of our mind – then the next stage will
appear by itself.

At this stage we leave the object of focus we have been using
so far and shift to focus on the feeling of bliss itself. We begin
to use the feeling of bliss as the object of our meditation, without becoming identified with it. And in time this becomes more
and more stable until we begin to experience that the feeling of
the nectar, the feeling of being deeply absorbed, the feeling of
bliss will appear more and more often in our everyday life. It will
appear spontaneously - in the supermarket, in the shower, in the
loo – everywhere.

There will now come a period where the effect of our effort
must become clear. Any effort or wilful action on our part makes
our personality come into being again, and it becomes obvious
what a hindrance and reduction of consciousness that is. The
more we acquire effortlessness as an attitude, the more we
become as 'a feather on the breath of God'.

The next stage after that is where we experience that bliss or
limitless presence just happens by itself completely effortlessly.
This is the stage of continuous being. In certain traditions, this

stage of bliss is the end stage – a view I personally don't share. It's an intermediate stage. The real usefulness of this stage of bliss is not bliss itself, but the fact that it produces in us an ability to penetrate illusion, the apparent reality of things. Someone who had reached this stage of continuous being was in ancient times called a sage.

To be able to let go of bliss as the goal of spiritual endeavour, it is necessary to understand what it means to penetrate apparent reality. This in turn enables us to investigate and understand the universal laws governing the created universe, kept alive only in the endless tension between opposites and existing only in mind.

One-pointedness creates the capacity to penetrate the apparent reality that we perceive through our senses. With one-pointedness we can penetrate apparent reality. This releases wisdom, an uninterrupted continuous flow of consciousness that is experienced as a brilliant clarity penetrating to the core of existence and at the same time suffused in love and understanding. In traditional mysticism, this ability to penetrate is then used as a means to investigate every possible aspect of human experience. With the ability to penetrate, we will find that what we see is not really what we see. One story that is often used to demonstrate this phenomenon is about someone walking along a mountain path and suddenly seeing a snake. The common reaction to seeing a snake is fear - so of course he jumps back. Then the moon comes out and he sees that what he reacted to was not a snake, but a coil of rope. Then comes the all-important question: "Where is the snake that created the fear?" or to put it in more everyday terms, how do I know that the reality I see in life is 'a rope' and not a 'snake'?

This may sound like a small thing, but the reality of this is that this question of 'ropes and snakes' touches the very core of existence. Our ability to penetrate simply develops our capacity to distinguish between reality and illusion.

When we penetrate into all aspects of life this way, everything leads to the realisation that anything we put to the test and investigate, ends up being just an illusion. This is existentially absolutely frightening since as we go along we realise that everything we investigate does not really exist. We look closely into 'snakes', but all we really find is 'ropes'.

In the end there is only one thing left, and we have to ask: 'Who is asking the question?' In putting our 'I' to the test this way we may experience that the self - the entity in us that asks the question - does not exist either. At that moment the person-ality 'explodes' or implodes and the reality of the Void or the Uncreated or God or whatever you would like to call it is realised as the only true reality.

What I am trying to point out by going through all these stages is that our innate tendency to look for bliss in the end turns out to be one of the greatest obstacle to liberation, regardless of the level we are presently working on.

In inner work the heart has a special position because it is the only part of us that is represented both in our personality and in the void. What we call relative compassion is really the training ground for approaching what we call absolute compassion. That is why all mystical traditions indicate that a compassionate attitude towards our fellow beings is always at the heart of their teaching. This is because, when the 'personality bubble' breaks open, the essential experience is compassion - a complete non-separation with everything.

We're living in a time when the traditional knowledge has outplayed its active role. Each of us now plays an important role in establishing the new spirituality, which is more and more emerging. Asia is heading towards the materialistic society we in the West have had for the last few hundred years. I believe now it is us who have the responsibility to work towards establishing a new spiritual tradition. Among other aspects it has to be based on our ability to follow our hearts in our work and in our life. If we also, among other qualities, acquire one-pointedness and the capacity to penetrate apparent reality, I believe we will be able to establish a new authentic occidental spiritual tradition based on the core that always has been the foundation of all spiritual traditions.

What emerges from the process I have just described are basically two things - the capacity for love and compassion and the capacity for presence, and in my experience they are one and the same.

So, don't waste time!
Thank you.

How Breathwork Blends With Emotional Therapy

JACQUES DE PANAFIEU

Jacques de Panafieu was the first to introduce Rebirthing to France. Since then he has supervised thousands of sessions. He talks about his personal development that followed as a result of getting interested in Breathwork.

I have to take many deep breaths to accept all your praises. I'm very glad to be here with all of you, and I would like to share with you some of my experiences. And I will start with a somewhat personal aspect, but which is directly connected to what I want to talk to you about.

I had my first Rebirthing experience in 1974, at a time when Rebirthing was completely unknown in France. The encounter occurred during a bio-energy seminar, and for two years I thought this had been a bio-energy experience. Then a friend, Dominique Levadou-Feuillette, came back from a stay in the United States with Leonard Orr. She quickly set up a first Rebirthing seminar, which I attended. And from then on, our entire history with Rebirthing started up very quickly. We began by organising therapy groups, followed very quickly by trainings. This is the short version of how I ended up training twenty year-groups of rebirthers, or approximately 500 people.

Three months after this experience with Rebirthing, I had an experience of intensive enlightenment seminars. I was completely fascinated and excited by this technique as well and since then I have always worked with Breathwork, Rebirthing, and work on the intensive seminars and clarification simultaneously. Today I would like to speak about blending of these two approaches, in particular in the field of working with emotions.

To characterise these two approaches, I would say that Rebirthing for me is on the side of nature, of life, of the mother, of fusion, and of cosmic love; whereas the intensive seminars on clarification are to work on the spirit, the law, the father, responsibility and love and connection with another. A form of sharing that is not as cosmic. I have used these two approaches since the beginning, and I still do nowadays, what American Indians call walking with both feet. Because one of the two feet is directly connected to the right brain - rebirth - while the clarification work in the intensive seminars works more with the left brain. But there comes a time when both join up again and become one. In other words one may start off from one extremity or the other, and achieve a form of unification.

I was able to observe, as you probably also have noticed, that enlightenment experiences occur with Breathwork. During intensive seminars for example, I have seen participants re-experience their own births, just as it happens in Rebirthing, with an exceptional characteristic. During intensive seminars we have forty-minute sessions, during which people take turns to listen or speak for five minutes at the time. The person enters into their birth process, five minutes later there is the sound of the gong, and it's the other participant's turn to speak. The extraordinary is that the person who is reliving his or her birth, with the organic manifestations as well, can stop the process, wait for five or ten minutes and bring their attention to their partner, then start back up again five minutes later, at exactly the same point in their birth process where they had left off. This is quite a fascinating indication of the power we have over our own emotions as individuals. Because from my point of view, organic work is even deeper than emotional work.

There is a common point between these two approaches also, which is the fact that they are both mutual. I work a lot with mutual Rebirthing - in a group setting - so that each person always has a partner. In intensive seminars or in clarification, we also work in pairs. To give you an idea of my experience, I must have accompanied or supervised something like thirty thousand Rebirthing sessions, and spent 750 days leading intensive semi-nars. So I would like to think that I have a certain amount of practice in this area.

Before I continue on the subject of emotions, I would like to go back a little bit and talk about what happened with Rebirthing right at the beginning. Originally the people who came were somewhat like you. They were adventurers who were ready to commit themselves radically to this new invention which Rebirthing was. They were practically all psychotherapists at the beginning and they entered into the process of rebirth with a lot of ease. Then, when Dominique Levadou's book was published, people who had not had the same type of previous experience started to get interested. We became aware at that point that for certain types of people, Rrebirthing was very difficult, and in certain cases counter-indicated, or at least premature. This led us to develop what I called "rebirth-therapy", in other words an experience that is different from pure Rebirthing.

When it comes to emotions I see two great categories; firstly the emotions that we often encounter in Rebirthing - love, joy, exaltation, sharing, desire, and emotions which are grounded in life, in the here-and-now. Secondly there are other emotions, such as; fear, anger sadness and despair, which are connected to the past. People who are able to spontaneously enter into emotions of the first group, are quite apt for Rebirthing. People who are not tend to encounter difficulties.

If we examine the way in which these emotions have been blocked, I will offer you a hypothesis. Starting from the notion of direct communication and indirect communication, the child presents itself through direct communication with its surroundings. He or she expresses his or her needs, desires, feelings and love. But unfortunately, in most cases, this direct or simple communication with others is just not heard or received properly. Then two things occur. On the one hand, emotions get locked up. In bio-energy for example, it is considered that some people have a gap here, which indicates that they at a certain point have been on the verge of exploding out of despair, for not having been heard or been accepted. At that point, their muscles and bones have been modified, in order to lock up these emotions and feelings. This is what happens on an organic level, but at a mental level - and both are connected - there will be what we call fixed or frozen attitudes in clarification. A fixed attitude is a reactive formation to the difficulties people encounter on their life path.

I will give you some postulates or conclusions about life or oneself, which may make up a person's philosophy about life. The following is a case story from Rebirthing. I had a friend who was born without the help of a midwife or a doctor. It was her father who delivered her. But since she was slippery - as all newborn babies are - he let her slip down, drop down. What she instilled in herself at that moment, was that "men let us down", "men let women down and let me down among other women". In her life, even though she was intelligent, beautiful, charming, etc., she later got a history of men who successively let her down or abandoned her. Here is another example. Here again a father is involved. When he saw the head of his child come out, and the midwife still had not arrived, he pushed her back inside. Subsequently, in a therapeutic process called the tunnel of birth, where several people make up a tunnel and the person relives the equivalent of a birth process by crawling through all these people, the woman in question stuck her head out, when it was her turn to come out, and went right back in. This surprised her so much, that she asked her mother about how she had been born. Her mother - as often happens - had never told her about her birth. But the postulate, the conclusion she had reached, based on this birth experience, was that she was always filled with energy to get things started. Mysteriously, after a few hours in certain cases, or a few days, or a few weeks, she would suddenly lose all interest, get discouraged and just give up.

There are a many other strategies that children set up for their own survival. I'll mention to you an example that really struck me. It was a client with whom I never did any rebirth because it was way too early for her. She gave me 900 negative sentences about the world and herself, during a certain type of process. During all of her life, she was convinced that the whole world hated her. It turned out that she had been born as an illegitimate child in a very religious family. Her entire family had blamed her for being the cause of the misfortunes of her mother who had not managed to get married, and for all the difficulties they had encountered. So, there you see the absolutely abominable situation of a child used as a scapegoat. The woman was educated but at the time she was unemployed. Then she suddenly found work, in a field that she loved, with quite friendly and welcoming people. She immediately became sick. For two weeks, she went into a very deep regression. She felt unable to go by the house of her childhood and would take a very large detour to go to her workplace. She even had to be accompanied to her work by her mother, still taking the detour route.

So you see the power of these fixed attitudes or belief systems, which in other techniques also are called the life script, or their indirect form of communication, personality. There is a definition of personality which I really like: "Personality is what enables others to always know what we're going to do next." In particular, children need to understand this but of course it applies to adults too. There is a situation for example which often occurs with alcoholic parents, which is that the child never knows in advance what the parent's reaction will be. The same movement, the same attitude will sometimes be congratulated, and the next day, lead to a slap in the face.

There are several consequences of this. One of them is

schizophrenia, which is one way to take into account a dissociated universe. Another is autism, which is completely retiring from the field of communication. These fixed attitudes or belief systems also bear on emotions. In certain families for example, boys are not allowed to cry, and in other families, or in the same families, girls are not allowed to get angry. In other families, one is not allowed to show either tears nor anger - all kinds of emotion are entirely forbidden. So, let's examine what happens if a person who has this sort of belief system, or fixed attitude, starts to do Rebirthing.

There is a whole series of situations, which you probably have encountered. First we have simply refusing to enter into what is offered: "I don't want to breathe." It's over. Other people will accept the proposition, but go to sleep. There are of course many different types of sleep in Rebirthing, but there is a quite particular sort of sleep which means "I won't go any further". It also happens that the person enters into a type of emotional frenzy. For example I had a Spanish client who was a very powerful psychiatrist. What he was seeking in Rebirthing, was to go beyond the unbearable. He also had a whole other set of beliefs on the value of extreme situations, of paroxystic emotions. Letting go was a notion he just could not understand. There are also certain subtleties that appear, and it is that certain emotions are presented instead of other emotions. I mentioned girls who were not allowed to get mad. Their anger often expresses itself through tears, Men may manifest their sadness or despair through fits of anger. The person may also express their emotions, and continue to express them, but more and more mechanically. They go through the same motions, the same yells and the same movements are repeated throughout one session, or from one session to the next. It may be experienced as a momentary relief, but it doesn't settle the problem in a conclusive way, and it may even reinforce the problem. So emotions can be fixed attitudes or rather not fixed attitudes any-more but fixed states directly connected to the fixed attitudes.

About ten years ago I ran a seminar here at this location. It was a double seminar, an intensive seminar and a Rebirthing seminar. Up till then I had thought the normal order of things was first to rebirth and work on emotions etc. followed by the intensive seminar with its spiritual dimension. But for practical reasons, the order got turned around at this particular training. We started with the intensive seminar, and then moved on to Rebirthing. It turned out to be much better for all sorts of reasons. One of the obvious reasons was the quality of trust that set in amongst the participants. But there was also another factor that came into play. During the intensive seminars, we work fundamentally on dis-identification. Most of us unconsciously identify with one side or another, in particular with our bodies.

I'll give you an example that really struck me. A woman was absolutely shocked that the first question someone asked when we talked about somebody giving birth was "how much the baby weighed." It was as if we were reducing this person, this individual, to a few pounds of flesh. I could see her point that this indicates the extent to which our entire society identifies a baby mainly with their body.

Once we have done the work of dis-identification, which starts by conscious identification, or in fact with unconscious identification, then conscious identification, then dis-identification. At that point, when emotions come up in Rebirthing, they're a lot more pure.

I'll give you another example of how a fixed attitude can greatly complicate the work of liberation through breathing. For example, a person can be convinced that all men are pigs, or that all women are bitches. When this person encounters a difficult relationship with one person in particular, all men or all women come to add on their weight to his or her problem. This really greatly slows down the process.

The seminars last at least three days. They begin at 6 in the morning and finish at eleven P.M.

Outside the sessions there is complete silence. The initial question is "Tell me who you are?" During thirteen sessions a day, the participants will meet thirteen different people, and introduce themselves in their own truth to their partners. In the beginning the participants give indications of identity - birth date etc. - they give qualities, flaws, they recount their life-stories. Then very slightly they start to mention their emotions, often there is a stage of void, a vacuum, then emotions come back in a much more intensely.

As they pursue the work, it's like peeling the layers of an onion. At a certain point, the person will say, "I am nothing", then they'll switch to the opposite polarity and say "I am everything". Pursuing the work, they'll become aware that they are neither nothing nor everything. All the layers of identification get purified, one after another, until the moment when one experiences what one truly is. The answer is the same for all the participants, even if each of them expresses it slightly differently. It's the most subjective thing in the world. Nobody can answer in your place, of course, but the words used to describe the experience are always the same, in every country.

There are other questions later on: "Tell me what life is?" and "Tell me what another is?" And there, once again, all of the answers are identical for all the participants. In general there is an experience, of which nothing can be said, because it is way beyond words. At that moment when the person comes out of the experience, he or she gives a name or a tag. There is a re-identification, but it's a slightly wider, freer identification than the previous one. A few very rare people remain in the non-identified state. But Charles Berner, who is the creator of this technique, and of clarification, says that in the ultimate stages, we have to dis-identify ourselves even from our soul, since it is something that is still personalised.

As regards the difference between pure Rebirthing and rebirth-therapy I would say that as far as the breathwork itself is concerned, it is the same thing. The different is the surroundings but there are no strict boundaries between the two approaches. There is maybe one aspect which we take into account in rebirth-therapy, namely the phenomenon of transference and projections.

So how can we use clarification to dissolve fixed attitudes and remove the obstacles, which prevent the person from freely entering the experience of breath? To answer this I will make a slight philosophical detour to give you this basic hypothesis or presuppositions.

We, as non-physical individuals, capable of choosing, constitute the foundation of everything that exists.

The man with the pre-destined name Jeff Love, with whom I learned the technique of intensive seminars - wrote a book called The Quantum Gods. One of his fundamental hypotheses is that the factor that enhances therapy work, is that a person has been completely heard. Whereas in life, and in thousands of situations, our cycles of communication are never completed. Therefore our minds are clogged with billions of uncompleted communications. So the position of the clarifier is to be completely welcoming of what is being presented. The alliance of both is much more than simply adding them up. The thing we most need generally is being acknowledged and recognised. So this way of listening without intervention, without agendas, is an enormous relief. Of course, the clarifier may intervene to accelerate the process, but will always remain in this perfectly respectful position.

I will give you the guidelines we use to untie the fixed attitudes. It is important to know that these are guidelines that only can be used after a certain time. If you say to person "what you say is a belief, it has nothing to do with reality", he or she would chase you out with a kick in the butt. So, it is necessary for a person to be ready to accept that what they considered up to now as being an absolute truth, is nothing but a belief. There are a whole series of preliminary steps before reaching that particular stage. I'll go through them very quickly to give you an overview of the various stages:

The first stage is the capacity for the client to speak about him or herself, to mention everything that concerns him or herself without any reluctance.

The second is to help solving problems, since most problems are directly connected to communication between human beings. If a person is incapable of communicating, her or she will never be able to solve any kind of problems.

The third level of clarification is related to guilt and shame - shame is even deeper than guilt. We have realised that certain people slow themselves down in their own process, and refuse to grant themselves success or happiness, because they feel guilty.

The two instructions that the clarifier gives are:

"Tell me something you have done and that you think you should not have done, according to your own evaluation." And,

"Tell me something that you did not do that you think you should have done, according to your own evaluation". These are extremely powerful instructions, which make it possible for a lot of cleansing to occur. It's only after these various steps that a person will start work on their beliefs. The work is based on the notion of polarity.

I return to the example of the young woman who had been an "illegitimate" child, and everything she suffered. For her everyone was mean and dangerous. Her reality corresponded exactly to her beliefs. This is what is referred to as "self-fulfilling prophecies". A person may be terrified of other people. When he goes out on the streets, he wears armour and a sword. The person who meets him tells himself: "This person is dangerous", and returns home to get his own armour and shield. So the first person says, "I was right after all to come out with my armour, since he is wearing armour too." We may laugh at this oversimplified example, but in how many real life situations do you think we introduce ourselves in a way that triggers exactly what we are afraid of, what we feel and expect? When a person has a fixed attitude such as "Everyone is mean", everything that is similar to that belief comes and gathers up around that belief, and the belief system builds up. Everything which does not resemble the belief is then stored away into the unconscious. And according to clarification, that is what the unconscious is - the opposite polarity.

In our work, we start to help the person discover what the fixed attitudes are that create a handicap for them in their life. There will probably be a long list and the participants will be asked to choose the one item which is the most dangerous or handicap-inducing. We'll then ask them to formulate the exact opposite belief or attitude. This will generate another list and from it we will chose the one that is most opposed.

Then there will be what we call "pondering", a kind of balancing from one polarity to the other.

We will ask the person to form the idea of being in the state of "everybody is mean" and ask how they went about forming that idea. Then we will ask the person to form the idea of being in the state of, "Everyone is beautiful, everyone is nice" and ask how they formed that idea. Then we start up again at the beginning and swing back and forth from one to the other. There comes a time in the process for the discoverythat: "I am the one who is creating my attitudes and my beliefs." At that moment there is a very significant feeling of liberation and relief.

The person will reach another very important step where we will ask the question, "Tell me what you are trying to communicate about yourself to others by using this attitude?" There will be a whole series of messages, but the basic messages that we come to, after going through the entire process, are: "Love me", and then the deepest, the ultimate message: "I love you all". At that point we invite the person to address all the people in their surroundings to communicate the real message. Then we will have recovered the direct communication that I mentioned in the beginning. When a person enters into the Rebirthing at that moment, they will enter with a level of fluidity and awareness that will enable them to go much further and much quicker. I have presented a kind of standard case where we have all of the clarification work followed by Rebirthing. In reality most cases will be a little bit of one and then a little bit of the other with each type of work enriching the other. Here is something very interesting - the notion of instruction. In the words "tell me" there is the underlying idea of "You are going to tell me". The alliance is set there in the first words, "Tell me". This is much more comfortable and pleasant than straight forward questions. Questions are always a form of pressure, whereas "tell me" opens up a space for sharing. If, during the clarification, emotions come up, we have a certain way of dealing with them. For example, we may ask the question, "Tell me what is happening for you right now", or "Tell me what state you are in right now". These are ways of relatively dis-identifying oneself from emotions. Because many people also are afraid of being overwhelmed or submerged by their emotions, it is reassuring to give them tools which enable them to encounter emotions is reassuring. To talk about emotions without getting carried away - especially for those people who are at the beginning of their work - has a positive effect. I did an exercise with some actors that is quite exciting as far as de-identifying from emotions is concerned. The instruction is: "Enter into anger, for example, without any story, without telling yourself your own story and without any, or very little, external manifestations, and when a signal is given, enter into joy, sexual desire, fear etc". What is suggested for the participant is to observe how he or she enters into that particular state - how they change their way of breathing, how they change their posture, their inner disposition. There is a kind of inner flexibility that appears which makes it possible to let go of a state, to enter into another state, and to understand how we create this. This goes in the direction of liberation from emotional conditioning. When all the emotions from the past have been cleared away through Rebirthing, the person will enter spontaneously into all these beautiful emotions that Rebirthing can bring about. This is basically the philosophy of our combined work. As far as Rebirthing is concerned, I do not set any particular number of sessions. It could be just one session. Sometimes, after a particularly strong session, I may tell the person not to set another appointment straight away. I tell them to go and check out the effects of what they have just discovered in their own life. If, on the other hand, I had taken out my diary right away and said, "And now for the next session, etc.", it would be as if I was denying the importance of what the person has just experienced. In the beginning of our practice of Rebirthing we used to say, "Ten sessions". But the unconscious programs itself according to the planned duration. In particular

the manifestations of negative transference sometimes cling on
to these programs. At one point for example the person might
say, "How come? I've already done ten sessions, and I haven't yet
found the man of my life. I've been cheated!"Once for example
in a clarification group, I heard the words, "I want my money
back". One of the men with whom I was working - one of the
greatest clarification specialists - used to tell his clients during
his first years of practice that he would refund all the money the
client had paid him if he or she was not completely satisfied after
six months. He explained to me why "That way, I only took on
to work with people that I was really able to help". This is
important for a young psychotherapist. He really did excellent
work in each of the sessions and nobody ever asked him for their
money back. After two years he considered his work to be
good enough, and he stopped doing it. I think it's a beautiful
proposition.

Inner Qualities of a Professional Breathworker

TILKE PLATTEEL-DEUR

Tilke Platteel-Deur has been practising and teaching Breathwork and the dynamics of relationship, since 1979. After intensive training in the Psychology of Selves with Hal and Sidra Stone, she incorporated the Voice Dialogue technique, as they developed it, into her work. Together with Hans Mensink she has created the Institute for Integrative Breath Therapy, (Das Institut für Ganzheitliche Integrative Atemtherapie). They offer a basic three year training and students have the option, after having worked at least a year as a practitioner, to take a fourth year to learn to become a trainer.

Some history

After I finished High School, in 1956, I went to the '*Rotterdamse Dans Academie*'. Modern Dance was what I loved most. I took exams in it and I taught it. All movements in this type of dance, the Martha Graham style, are built on breathing. The technique uses the inhale to stretch the body and the exhale to contract the body and the movement evolves out of the exhale. This technique helped me enormously to get a deeper contact with my body, my feelings and with life itself.

In 1978 I had my first Rebirthing session. It was a revelation. It felt like coming home in my body and in myself. I understood on a very deep level the contractions and the stretching that I had been doing all those years at the dancing academy. I knew with a strong inner knowing how my body had been meant to move, and what it was capable of. I had a strong sensation of oneness, of being connected to something that I felt was the source of my being. I felt that I was love. I experienced my inner God. I was elated.

I didn't have the slightest idea what had happened to me, but I felt certain that something very important had occurred, something that was going to change my life. The thought that popped into my mind was: "This is going to be my second career, no matter what".

In those days we just knew that 'it' worked, but not exactly how it worked. So, when I started to give sessions myself - after some rather superficial training - I was everything. Everything except a professional. I was simply acting on Leonard Orr's positive feedback and on his idea that having had about ten sessions was enough to start working. Today I know that it was not. I was a pioneer in those days, and God saved me hundreds of times from all kinds of disasters.

Having been a professional dancer however, I knew very well about the advantages of having a good technique. Since there were no long term training programs in those days, I started to travel around the world to try to get some technique and knowledge together. As Richard Bach says: "Teach what you need to learn." I worked, I learned, I got paid, and I slowly learned what was to become my new work - work which would become a very fulfilling part of my life.

Today, after having trained several hundred therapists over the last 18 years, I most strongly recommend people not to start working the way I did, but to get a really good, thorough training.

The beginning
When I met Hans Mensink, in 1979, we were - at least on the outside - total opposites. Nevertheless we decided to work together, after we discovered, during a short conversation, that we shared the same vision of creating a 3-year training program. There were two main reasons to do so:
1. Getting breathwork out of the corner of charlatanry.
We were so enthusiastic about the deep effects of this simple technique that we wanted to help ourselves and others to learn to use it in a well founded way, a way that would give credit to it.
2. Our own growth.
All around us we saw trainers giving short workshops, lasting between two and five days. They would bring their participants up to a high level of energy and then leave. As a consequence they were never able to see how people sometimes would fall into a pit, simply because the insights they had achieved were not integrated into their normal daily lives in any way.

We noticed a great danger in that, both for the participants in the trainings and for the trainers themselves. In order for trainers to grow and take on their own process, they need to give people the opportunity to get to know them really well and to give them honest feedback. Ideally as well as they know their students so they will get honest feedback from them. That takes time!!!

So we started a program which grew organically over the next six years into the three-year training we wanted.

Today I can say; "Yes, I am a pro." I don't claim to have mastered absolutely all the qualities mentioned here. I am still working and learning. And that's mainly because I do a lot of private work, for myself and with my clients. As a therapist, you have to get "It" into your flesh and blood. Because it's work that you do with people of flesh and blood and it's the kind of work that is done with blood, sweat and tears. So you need to study, to practice and to widen your knowledge. But most importantly, you need to do your own personal process of inner growth. Ultimately, you will be known by the content of your life and by 'who you are' more than by what you say or even do.

Live, what you teach, it makes you reliable.

THE QUALITIES OF A PROFESSIONAL BREATHWORKER

LOVE and LEARNING through LOVE	Trust
	Self discipline
	Authority
	Integrity
	Attention, Veneration
	Service
	Acceptance, Tolerance
	Purposefulness
	Humour

TRUST

Trust comes with learning and experience. Trust comes with the inner work you do and with learning craftsmanship. Both are equally important. So studying and learning, and trusting the inner power make the work easy, safe and pleasurable.

The *Course in Miracles*, Manual for Teachers states it very clearly:

> *"Trust is the foundation on which the ability of God's teachers to fulfil their function rests. The teachers of God have trust in the world, because they have learned that it is not*

*governed by the laws the world made up. It is governed by a
Power that is in them but not of them. It is this Power that
keeps all things safe. It is through this Power that the
teachers of God look upon a forgiven world." (p. 8)*

Because we are human, most of us have not reached that
state of mind yet. Therefore we need practical skills. There are a
few skills I consider absolutely necessary:

1 A profound knowledge of breathwork, 'How to play the
   breath'. I am still grateful to Leonard Orr for teaching me to
   play the breath like an instrument.
2 Besides that, you have to have techniques to work through
   "emotional stuff". You need a frame of thought, an
   intellectual understanding of the work you are doing. You
   need to understand how to work in the direction of
   stabilising an adult personality. "An aware ego" as Hal
   Stone calls it. And you need to have a stable understanding
   of transference and counter-transference.
3 You need to really understand that this work is about
   integrating our judgements about ourselves and about life,
   and how integration works and can be brought about.
4 You need to be able to do Inner Child work.
• If you were to grade yourself on your intellectual understanding and on your technique, between 1 and 10, 10
   being the most excellent, what would it be?
• Do you need to study and/or practice more?

DISCIPLINE

Discipline means to become your own disciple. That means to
stick to your purpose and to clear away the problems you may
encounter. It is not a question whether it is because you are a
little sluggish or because there is some 'outside' obstruction.
Listen to your inner voice and listen to the good advice of people who have more experience. You won't lose face by asking for
advice and listening to it.

• Do you have a certain routine to help you to stay grounded
   and centred?
• Are you open to feedback and do you ask for it?

AUTHORITY

Being your own divine inner authority means to hold to your
authenticity. Don't try to copy someone else. Be yourself. Find
your personal style.

As I said before, you can't 'float' on your experience, you'll always have to develop, to study, and to take sessions. Grow inside and out. Your growth process always goes on. If you neglect this, your inner child will feel so insecure that your so-called authority will melt away. Maybe it is a pity, or may be it is fortunate that we have chosen a profession that doesn't allow us to rest on our laurels. So take supervision. And practice, practice and practice even more.

Get to know yourself through and through, especially your vulnerability. As you'll often work with the vulnerable child of your clients, you had better be comfortable with your own!

And it's just as basic to get well acquainted with your anger and rage. When your anger is disowned, and not well known to you, you could be a threat to the inner child of others. Your anger, which is mostly a cover up of fear, would come out in a rather cold, polite and withdrawn way.

- Do you take sessions on a regular basis and/or supervision?
- Do you give to yourself what you're giving to your clients?

INTEGRITY   HONESTY   MODESTY

Learn to distinguish your own signals that warn you when you're going to make a mistake. If we are really honest, we all know when we're doing something that is unethical, dishonest, hurtful, etc. Sometimes we just don't want to hear this clear inner voice, but that's all together a different story.

Be honest to yourself and to others. Communicate if there's something that you feel incapable of. Modesty means knowing your own boundaries, your strengths and your weaknesses.

Don't make yourself bigger than you really are, and don't make yourself smaller.

Don't mess around with your clients sexually. You are mainly working with their inner child. Acting on their sensual, or sexual, feelings is like having sex with your three year old!!!!

- Are you honest about your "weaknesses"?
- Do you communicate when you feel that the work stagnates?
- Do you send someone on to somebody else if necessary?

ATTENTION   VENERATION

Focus your attention on your client, in a loving, supportive and accepting way. You should come from a point where you know your client has got all the resources s/he needs to move further. You just need to be there to help him to remember. You don't need to "work hard." Lean backward and smile inside, in total appreciation for what you see happening in front of you. Whatever it is, it's always a miracle that we're able to create what we create. Whether it is positive or negative.

- Close your eyes and imagine giving yourself exactly the kind of attention you would give to your clients.
- Smile inside and breathe a little, appreciate yourself for being the creator of your life.

TO BE OF SERVICE

Willingness to be of service is essential to our professional attitude. It means, neither more nor less than to fulfil your function towards someone. It doesn't mean being servile or submissive. It is an attitude of being proud to be able to do the work you do, and doing it well.

- Are you willing to make exceptions and work for free just because someone is in need and you are willing to be of service?

ACCEPTANCE

You need deep trust to be tolerant and accepting. Acceptance and trust are only possible if you're really working on your own inner process. If, inside of us, there still is a thick layer of non-evolved - which means not-worked-through - material, we will be judgmental about the same kind of stuff in others. Then we can't be in acceptance, so we can't work with that person.

So again it is essential to get to know the shadow sides of your personality. Life will present you with plenty of chances to do exactly that. Because every time you are irritated about someone or you find you are putting someone on a pedestal, you have a "disowned self" right in front of you. If you can start to see that as a gift and an opportunity to learn, rather than something unpleasant you are on your way to being a more complete human being.

- Ask yourself honestly:
- Do I ask for supervision, or do I work on it in a session, each time I feel 'upset' by someone?
- Do I look at what it has to do with me and my beliefs when there is a problem in my life?

SINGLENESS OF PURPOSE

To know your purpose in life will help you tremendously to stay on your path. For me, doing my work is not my life's purpose, but it is the means for me to fulfil my life's purpose. It is the best way I know in the moment to express myself.

Life will always put you to the test in the form of placing obstacles on your path. Don't let yourself be distracted, but simply move forward. For that you need discipline, but you've got that already, right?

- Do a little exercise. State as clearly and precisely as possible, your purpose for this lifetime.

This may take you some time to think about.

HUMOUR

Humour is a sure sign that you've stopped being identified with one part of your personality. As long as you are identified with something inside you, there is always an atmosphere of wanting to be right and of seriousness. The moment integration takes place and identification stops, there is room for humour and laughter.

When integration happens, tension is released. We stop feeling the desperate need to be right. It causes more possibility of choice. There is room for different opinions.

Humour, supported by a deep acceptance, allows us to look in appreciation at the creations of others and ourselves.

Ask yourself honestly:

- Can I really laugh about myself when I've made a mistake?
- Can I forgive myself and say "Sorry"?
- Am I amiable to someone who makes a mistake?

There is a nice theme to work on!

LOVE, LEARNING THROUGH LOVE and BEING TOUCHED

The capability to be touched and moved by another person is a sure sign that your heart is open. It's OK to shed some tears, even when you are working, when you see how someone has a deep insight or revelation.

If there is no real sense of love for the person you are working with, you can't work.

In the Bible Jesus stated it quite clearly: "There are these three, hope, trust and love. But the most important of those is love".

Love is the most important, essential ingredient to succeed with our work. (This probably goes for all types of work). When we notice we are 'plugged in' about something or someone, our flow of love is distorted. Our connection with that person is disrupted. We can't see clearly anymore. The relation is not working, the therapy won't work either.

We need to be willing and prepared to learn through our feelings of uneasiness as well as by our deep longing for harmony and love. If we are willing to do just that, we will, in a very fundamental way, be able to contribute to the spreading of more consciousness and more love on this planet.

The holiest spot on earth is where an ancient hatred has become a present love.

BIBLIOGRAPY

1. Stone, Hal and Sidra (1985), *Embracing Our Selves: Voice Dialogue Manual,* Marina del Rey, California: Devorss & Company, 1985.

2. *A Course In Miracles:* Foundation of Inner Peace,1985

Chapter 6

Breathing into Society

Beyond the Coercive Organization

STEVE MINETT

Steve Minett has had three areas of focus in his life; academic research and teaching in the social sciences, participation in "Therapy-New-Age-Human-Potential" activities and working in business, especially in marketing communications. His ambition is to build bridges between these three areas, and he is currently working on developing "Breathwork for Business".

This paper opens with the following four propositions:

1 Traditional, conventional organisations are inherently coercive. (I am going to argue that coercion is essentially built into the structure of conventional organisations. We will also see historically why this has come about.)
2 Organisations use coercion to resolve internal conflicts. (Conflict resolution is, of course, a necessary function of all effective organisations.)
3 Developments in the contemporary environment of organisations are now making the use of coercion functionally counterproductive. (In other words, the coercive organisation is now functionally in decline because of changes in organisational environments.)
4 Consequently, organisations now have a need to find alternatives to coercion to resolve internal conflicts. (What mechanisms are organisations going to use to solve internal conflicts if they give up coercion?)

By way of an overview, I have divided the paper into four parts; the first part is called "What is Coercion?" This looks at the difference between 'power' and 'coercion'. There are lots of terminological problems here, so I want to formulate definitions which differentiate between power and coercion. The second part deals with the reasons why organisations adopted coercion as an essential ingredient of their structure. Another way of putting this is to try to answer the question which classical economists have posed for centuries: "Why do economic organisations exist?" In other words, why aren't all economic activities structured by contractual relations in markets, which is what happened before modern organisations evolved (and perhaps maybe what we are heading back to). The third part addresses the question why coercion in organisations is becoming counter-productive. Here, we will look at the changes in organisational environments. The fourth and final part considers the alternatives to coercion. Here, I want to introduce the idea of a 'self-selected value community' which I am going to argue can serve as one alternative to the conventional coercion-driven, economic organisation.

Part One: What is Coercion?
What does the word 'power' mean? This is an interesting question because, as Pfeffer and others have pointed out, 'power' is commonly used in everyday language but when asked to define it most people find the task difficult. It's one of those classes of phenomena which are easy to recognise when seen or experienced but difficult to verbally define. Social scientists, (starting with Robert Dahl in the 1950's) however, have come up with a fairly consensual model of what it means to have power.

This is a very simple model involving two actors A and B. The idea here is that A exercises power over B by getting B to do something which he or she otherwise would not have done. In this model B wanted to do X and because A intervened B did Y instead. Notice that it is not enough that this should be the case; it is also necessary that A should have intended B to do Y. In other words, power is being able to achieve your intention in terms of altering other people's behaviour. This is a very simple model of power: power is altering behaviour in an intended way.

Let's now consider the various ways in which one actor may attempt to alter another actor's behaviour. Perhaps the most obvious method is to offer the other actor an incentive and, in a money economy, the most obvious incentive is money. Another powerful motivator in human relationships is personal love. 'Spiritual love', or the power of ideas and values can be a third motivator - if actor A persuades actor B through rational arguments or through having a charismatic personality that actor A's ideas are worth implementing then actor A can change actor B's behaviour. Finally, however, there is coercion; trying to enforce changes in behaviour via the use of threats. This move-ment from incentives and motivators to threats is one of the great divides in power theory: there are clear and essential differences in quality of relationship between the two behavioural approaches. (I will later argue that these differences are now crucial for modern organisations.)

Coercion also comes in different varieties: there is illegitimate coercion - coercion that is specifically ruled out by social rules, such as all forms of criminal coercion (e.g. individuals threatening others with guns and knives, etc..). All societies, universally, proscribe such activities. On the other hand, there is also legitimate coercion: some forms of coercion are permitted by societies and even regarded as a good thing. Obviously included here are the actions of governments pursuing 'law & order' often carried out against some of its citizens: the police and the military can use coercion in legitimate ways. In fact one definition of an effective state is, "the agency that can exert a monopoly of legitimate violence over a particular territory". So the idea of legitimate coercion is very deeply embedded in modern societies. It is the use of legitimate coercion within organisations with which this paper is concerned.

Another perspective on the definition of coercion can be gained by considering a spectrum of power relationships. At one end of this spectrum is what can be called 'free-exchange' relations and at the other end is coercion. The idea is that there are various dimensions to this spectrum: firstly, 'exist costs', i.e. the cost (to actor B) of leaving the relationship - these are low at the free-exchange end and high at the coercion end. Secondly, 'alternatives'; there are many in a free exchange type relationship and there are few in a coercive relationship. These other two dimensions contribute to 'dependency' (which is a concept closely related to power; the more dependent B is on A, the greater the power which A has over B). Dependency is low in free-exchange and high in coercive relationships. We can look at some examples: spiritual love, it could be argued, is close to the ideal of free-exchange relationship. The cost of leaving (or entering) the relationship are minimal because the alternatives are maximal, in the sense that spiritual love is universalistic - every living person (or indeed being) is a potential respondent in this type of relationship, there are no exclusions, and dependency - if it is true spiritual love - is very low: We do not engage in spiritual love with each other because we need things from each other but out of the purest of disinterested motives. Personal love, on the other hand, can often be at the other end of the spectrum. There is often a lot of dependency in the phenomena of personal love and it can be a very unbalanced relationship if one person is in love with the other and not vice versa.

These extreme illustrations raise the question as to whether there is a smooth continuity of degree along the spectrum between them, or whether there is a real discontinuity between free-exchange and coercion - in other words a qualitative rather than quantitative difference between the two types of relationship. And, in fact, I am arguing this later case: I do see coercive relations as different in kind from other forms of power relations and the key distinction I wish to introduce concerns the ability to impose 'inescapable costs'. In other words, a technical definition of coercion can be formulated as follows; a situation in which actor A can impose inescapable costs on actor B. The core point here is to make a clear distinction between coercive and 'incentive-persuasive' forms of power: in all forms of the latter, the targeted actor, B, is required to exercise judgement as to the outcome of the proposition which s/he is being offered; take for example a money incentive. There may be a number of alternative sources of money. They may be willing to offer more than actor A, but are they more trustworthy? etc. Again, where love is the motivator, there is always questions as to whether actor A 'really' loves you, by how much? And do you actually love actor A? etc...etc.. and so on. In all these cases actor B has a number of real decisions and independent choices to make. This, of course, also applies where actor A tries to persuade you to adopt his/her ideas and values. You have to make judgements, you have to make assessments on your own account to decide whether you want to be influenced by somebody else's ideas and values.

Power relationships based on persuasion and charisma tend to be somewhere between the free exchange end and the middle of the spectrum, depending on the personalities and maturity of the individuals involved, especially where rational arguments are involved. These types of relationship can be located closer to the free-exchange end where people are enabled to make rational and considered choices and where there is a free market in ideas and values. When it comes to relationships based on money-exchange, we tend to move further towards the middle because, in a monetary economy, money-exchange is usually connected with high levels of dependency: people are dependent on money in order to survive and have a good standard of living in a money economy. Therefore people who have large monetary resources can exercise power over others. Although, in a free market situation this power should be mitigated by the existence, for the dependent actor, of alternative sources of money.

Another way to illustrate the spectrum is to give two extreme examples from either end: for the free-exchange end this would be a street market - an open market where goods are available on display. Here 'information cost' (as the economists call it) is very low. People are free to examine the products; to pick them up, smell them, etc.. so that they can gain all the information they might need to make a purchasing decision, and as long as there are large numbers of sellers with different products to offer and a large number of customers with money to buy, it should be a free-exchange situation with very little coercion involved. The opposite end of the spectrum might be imprisonment, where (by definition) one group of actors are denied opportunities.

When it comes to coercion, however, the essence of actor A's strategy is to minimise actor B's choices: the more effective the threat the less choice actor B feels him or herself to have. This becomes doubly the case if actor A is exercising legitimate coercion, i.e. coercion accepted by the wider society. Then actor B's alternatives are effectively doubly reduced. If you are faced with criminal coercion, you can always appeal to the police or the wider society for protection. But if society legitimises the particular act of coercion to which you are being subjected, that option is denied you. Given this account, it may be redundant to comment that, overwhelmingly, people do not react well to being coerced; it provokes fear, resentment and rebelliousness. (Obvious though this may be, it is worth stating here because this will become significant when considering why coercion in organisations is now becoming dysfunctional.)

Part Two: Why did Organisations Adopt Coercion?
Having thus defined coercion, we can move on to consider how and why organisations adopted it. If we go back far enough in time, say about 200 years, there weren't economic organisations of the size and type we are familiar with today. Economic activity was carried out by market relationships contracted, largely, between individuals and families. These were often stable, long-term relationships based on established patterns of economic activity. Our next example, we see two merchant capitalists (perhaps in the textile trade) maintaining relationships with local craftsmen and artisans who would carry out particular types of work for them. One of the merchants is more successful and becomes richer. Along with his growing superiority in resources, he sees an opportunity to reserve the

dependency he feels on the skilled workers of the area, a dependency he has heretofore shared with his closest competitor. The idea that these workers also work for his competitor poses a threat to this greater merchant, for example, in terms of what they charge him for their labour and because his business has become dependent on their special knowledge and skills: these workers could potentially exert power over the greater merchant because they had an alternative merchant who might offer them more money, etc... So, in order to protect himself against the risks posed by this dependency, he decides to cut them off from other sources of income by setting up a formal economic organisation and making a boundary around their relationship: in other words, he engages them in a contract of employment, thus cutting off their relations with all other owners of capital. In other words, he monopolises their labour time, skills and knowledge.

This is one of the main explanations for the origin of modern organisations. There are also efficiency arguments, but my point here is that this sequence of developments ensured that coercion would be built into the structure of formal organisations: the owner reversed his dependency on free-exchange relations by making his workers 100% dependent, for their income, on him. He was then in a position to coerce them (with societal legitimacy) by threatening to reduce their income to zero - a threat which he was now structurally enabled to carry out at any time, as both parties to the employment contract were aware.

Given this 'origin in coercion', it was perhaps not surprising that organisations then went on to develop the classical hierarchical organisational form, with which we are all too familiar; a single individual at the apex - the boss, the decision-maker of last resort - and beneath them a descending power hierarchy with many levels, depending on the total size of the organisation. In terms of function, the classic idea is that information flows up the organisation from the bottom, where the operations of the organisation are actually carried out. The information passes up, through the formal channels of communication to the boss at the top. The boss at the top, having analysed the information, then passes down commands, again through the formal structures, to the operatives at the bottom, who are then supposed to fulfil and comply with these commands. This is the classic structure of organisations that we have lived with for the last 150 years or so, and because organisations have been getting bigger and bigger, the hierarchies have been growing taller and taller.

There are, of course, a number of obvious problems with this traditional-conventional model of organisations: as regards the upward flow of information, there is a lot of scope for distortion and concealment by the individuals who compose the communication channels to the top. They are quite capable of distorting and concealing information that does not suit them. If it is going to make life difficult, they may well distort it or conceal it. This is closely connected with the idea of 'telling the boss what the boss wants to hear'. Such is often the fate of dictators; the information they receive has far more to do with what their subordinates believe that they want to hear, rather than with what is actually happening at the bottom of their organisations. This practice is clearly dysfunctional for an organisation which needs to make frequent and effective adaptations to its environment.

There is a similar problem with regard to commands coming down. If people lower down in the organisation don't like the commands that the boss is giving they can engage in evasion and manipulation. They can simply ignore some commands if they think it is going to make their lives difficult. They may simply evade implementing the command - do nothing and it can be very difficult to ensure that commands get implemented in a very tall and hierarchical organisation. So these are the problems of the classical organisation. For a long time we have lived with these problems without much distress because we lived in an environment of comparative stability and predictability.

Part Three: Why Coercion is Becoming Counter-productive
Now, however, the use of coercion in organisations is becoming counter productive. This is because organisational environment is becoming chaotic; change in this environment is becoming chaotic and unpredictable. Markets, for example, are becoming more and more fragmented by customer segments; different types of customers are constantly evolving - it is no longer a case of one type of soap or shampoo. As we all know, these days you have to make 20 or 30 different types of shampoo for people with different types of hair. You have to make different types of soap for people with different types of skin. You have different types of soap in Europe than you have in Asia or in Africa or North America. The same thing with cars, or

whatever product you care to mention, they have to be customised to fragmented segments of the market. Customers are becoming more and more demanding in terms of ultimately individualised products. This is obviously putting enormous pressures on investments in productive processes and personnel training. Such economic changes are happening much faster and the general trends are much more unpredictable than was the case just ten years ago.

All this can be described as 'turbulence' and the environments of organisations are now much more turbulent than they have ever been before. Organisations need to react much quicker, to be nimbler on their feet and more flexible than ever before. Their reaction time has to be minimised and, indeed, their behaviour needs to become generally much more pro-active. Given all this, the cumbersome equipment of the conventional hierarchical power structure, with all its problems of distortion of information and evasion of commands, etc.., becomes much less tolerable: at some point, it becomes in fact, functionally intolerable as a means of ordering organisational behaviour. I would suggest that for many economic organisations we have now reached or exceeded this point; for many contemporary organisations the traditional-conventional hierarchical pyramid has become dysfunctional and obsolete. And, of course, many organisations are actively looking for alternatives.

If we look more precisely at the environmental pressures driving contemporary organisational change, we can discern more exactly the nature of the change objectives which organisations are striving to achieve. Firstly, organisations have to get closer to markets: meaning that information from markets can no longer be filtered up the organisational hierarchy. It must get to the actual decision-makers faster so that they can respond to markets faster. This requires shifting decision-making down-wards. This, in turn, requires employee initiative and responsibility. Consequently, we are in a situation where employee obedience is no longer enough. It is now not enough that employees should simply obey commands - organisations now want the 'hearts and minds' of their employees as well. This, in fact, represents a true 'revolution' in organisational behaviour; the trend towards the use of coercion as a means of controlling behaviour has gone through a 180 degree revolution and is now moving in the opposite direction.

We are now, therefore, moving back towards the free-exchange end of the Power Relations Spectrum . Since about the 1970's, I'd argue, this movement has been perceptible: since around this time, the traditional authoritarian manager has been in decline and there have been various attempts to make organisations flatter and more flexible and responsive. The pyramid has been flattened out. There are still 'top managers' but the idea is that they are much 'closer' to the bottom of the organisation. Much of the formal channels and rigid patterns of communication and command have been done away with: people now communicate flexibly. Everybody in the organisation communicates with everybody else as and when necessary.

Secondly, the boundaries of the organisation have become much more porous: first of all, and especially at the bottom where the organisation interfaces with the market-place, so that information can pass from markets into the organisation, quickly and effectively, and can reach everybody within the organisation. Also, in terms of the functions of the organisation, there is a greatly increased use of external suppliers and sub-contractors for functions such as; manufacturing, catering, printing, and many other services. A lot of the activities which organisations traditionally have done internally, using employees, are now being sub-contracted to external, independent individuals and-or other organisations. This includes the whole phenomena of consultancy, of which there has been an enormous growth. 'Consultants', of all exotic varieties, now provide advice or temporary services not only to top managers but also now to various other levels within the organisation. Many of these 'external' relationships turn into established patterns. As a result, a lot of individuals who would traditionally have been clearly 'outside' the organisation, become deeply involved in long-term relationships with individuals 'within' the organisation: it's no longer quite so clear who's an 'insider' and who's an 'outsider'. But, of course, these people are also engaged in economic relationships with other organisations as well. (I'm going to argue that what we may in fact be witnessing is the 'de-construction' of the conventional organisation and a movement back to contractual relations in the marketplace - where we started 200 years ago.)

Let's look more closely at the current organisational struggle for the hearts and minds of its employees: firstly, at the individual level, there are the various methodologies that business theorists and management gurus have developed to win this human relations battle for management. 'Empowerment' is, perhaps, the most famous and widespread of these. In a nutshell, I'd argue, that the central concept of Empowerment is to get employees to act like entrepreneurs; in other words, to take initiative, to take responsibility and to take risks at work much more than has conventionally been the case (see Ellis & Minett, 1997). This, obviously, requires high levels of commitment by employees to the organisation's goals, values and vision.

The problem for contemporary organisations in trying to implement programs such as Empowerment, De-layering, etc.. is that the top managers trying to achieve this are at the same time (and perhaps inevitably) keeping their other hand tightly clutched around the 'coercion lever', which enables them to maintain control over their organisation: they are offering the organisation's warm hand shake of commitment in return for the employee depositing his/her heart and mind in the organisation's safe keeping, while at the same time they are (with their other hand) hiding the hand-gun of coercion behind their backs. The message to the employee, which is really hardly even 'hidden' in the structure of the situation, is as follows: "we would like you to personally commit to our organisation. We, on the other hand, are going to retain our legitimate right to expel you and/or threaten to expel you from this same organisation any time that we (top management) judge that your behaviour, attitudes, opinions, etc.. do not contribute positively to the development of this organisation. (In the event of any dispute about this, we guarantee that we will win and you will lose.)"

This position of top management's is, I would argue, self-contradictory: they are asking people to commit at the heart level to an organisations which may well within a month or so fire them - nobody having a guaranteed job anymore. This is the downside of the situation of most modern organisations. While they are trying to develop these very high levels of psychological involvement and engagement by individuals they retain their coercive power in the sense of being able to deprive people of their livelihood by firing them. This has a dis-inspiring and de-motivating effect. It also undermines the growth of trust, which is essential for effective communications.

Part Four: What are the Alternatives to Organisational Coercion?

This brings us to a consideration of the alternatives. Here, I would like to introduce the concept of the 'self-selected value community'. This may represent the organisational future, or at least one trend in the organisational future. If we extrapolate from the notion that the conventional organisation is in the process of de-constructing itself, there will come a point where the organisational boundary may dissolve to the point where it can be justly claimed that the 'organisation' has ceased to exist. Most organisations may have a long way to go before they get to this point, but I think you can see it coming. There may be several routes to this 'organisational dissolution': some organisations already claim to have a 'clover leaf' structure: the top managers, in such organisations, form a nucleus from which all its activities are sub-contracted. Eventually, these 'nuclear' individuals may decide that they will simply form partnerships, based on contractual relations, and essentially the formal organisation will disappear entirely. Another, less comfortable, route could be embarked upon by people who have been 'shaken out' of formal organisations. Driven by the difficulties of finding conventional jobs, they may form this type of informal structure simply in order to escape from the miseries of unemployment.

Other routes can be imagined, but what they will all lead to is a group of individuals with relatively stable patterns of economic behaviour, forming a sort of virtual organisation or an organisation based on their preference to do business with each other. This is what I call a 'self-selected value community'. My argument is that the criteria people use to select who they wish to work with are ultimately based on shared values: sharing values with another person is very close to the idea of trusting that person.

The 'community' aspect of this concept involves the idea that, having had some 200 years of formal organisations as the basis of economic activities, we are now moving back to communities instead. In the old days, of course, it was 'organic' communities, based on local geography, which played this role. Today such communities have largely been broken up by social and economic forces, so clearly this is a new form of community which is being envisaged. Organic and self-selected communities differ in a number of ways and they both differ from formal organisations: the basis of membership in the organic was birth right - an individual enters an organic community by right of birth. Formal organisations, by contrast, use instrumental selection as their method of entry; the organisation selects you. You select the organisation to a certain extend in that you apply for a job with it, but the ultimate decision on your inclusion rests with the organisation. The method of adaptation in the organic community is socialisation: in infancy by your family of birth and childhood, and early adulthood, by various institutions such as schools, churches, clubs, etc.. You are socialised into adapting to the culture, the values and the behavioural patterns of your community of birth. In an organisation this is achieved by 'select and expel'; organisations select those people they believe will conform to their cultural norms, their values and behave in the way they desire. If they make a mistake in this selection procedure, the solution is expulsion - any individual who (contrary to prediction) does not behave in the way desired will be expelled from the organisation.

Socialisation can be seen as a limited form of personal growth, in the sense that it requires individuals to change themselves in order to adapt to the needs of others. The idea here is that, with the increasingly complete triumph of formal organisation, the 'select and reject' method has ousted the limited form of personal growth represented by socialisation from many areas of life: for example, religious communities and, to a lesser extent, 'organic' political communities use personal growth as a method of adaptation. Both of these forms of community have tended to wither in the era of formal organisation. An even more striking example is marriage: traditionally, adaptation within marriage was required to be based on personal growth. Now, however, marriage in most western societies has moved very far, and very rapidly, towards the select-and-reject model: if there is a failure of adaptation between the marriage partners, you simply reject that partner and select another one and perhaps go through this process several times.

The emergence of self-selected value communities would reverse this trend: the basis of membership will be self-selection based on mutually shared, personal values. The method of adaptation will be personal growth. By consciously removing the select-and-reject option, people in this new organisational form will have to adapt to each other, the only other alternative being to voluntarily leave the organisation

Let's now look at how the personal growth method could work to resolve conflicts. We can start with a fairly conventional model of how thinking in organisations is structured. At the top is a vision; a clear vision that brings people together. Visions, however, though often intensely experienced are always essentially private. In order to be brought into the public world they have to be expressed in symbols, such as words. Conventionally, this is done in a mission statement. The common 'problem' with these is technically known as 'motherhood and apple pie' - mission statements are conventionally very general assertions of good intentions with which all participants can agree; nobody is offended and no 'hard choices' have to be made.

Below this things get more difficult: what are the core values of the organisation? How do the individual participants interpret these? How are the interpretations to be implemented in organisational actions and communications. The ideal of the pyramidal form is that there should be integration and consistency from the vision at the top right down to the actions and messages coming out of the organisation at the bottom.

It is, of course, in this area, between vision and action, that there is a great potential for conflict because when people get down to the nitty gritty details of how the vision and mission are going to be implemented, they tend to disagree. There can be many reasons for this; personal psychological histories, egoism, different cultures, different languages, different world views and so on.

So, here we have the challenge of intra-organisational conflict resolution: organisations need to be able to resolve their conflicts if they are going to act effectively in the real world. As we have seen, coercion is a very effective method of solving these intra-organisational conflicts; the boss, in an authoritarian hierarchy, decides what the organisation is all about, what its values are and what it should do. S/he may listen to individuals lower down in the hierarchy but ultimately s/he will decide. If anybody disagrees with the boss's decisions they will be told to be quiet and if they refuse, they will be expelled from the organisation. This is a very effective (though potentially sub-optimal) way of resolving such conflicts. If, by definition, the self-selected, value community pledges itself not to use the structural coercion of being able to expel people from the organisation, how then is it going to resolve its internal conflicts?

There are a number of 'negative' alternatives. The most basic is chaos and disintegration leading to 'organisational death'. Another is the rise of cliques and factions creating an informal intra-organisational power structure. If two or more factions have approximately equal power, this could lead to internal power struggle and ultimately result in schisms, splitting the organisation into two, or more, separate organisations. The problem with this as a 'method' of conflict resolution is that once an organisation has split in two then those organisations may become subject to the same forces and you have further schisms amongst them until the 'organisations' are all reduced to one individual. Another alternative is to return to coercive methods of solving problems. A variant of this which might afflict self-selected value communities is the cult. (I regard this as a coercive form in the sense that it involves high levels of dependency both by the followers on the cult leader and by the leader on the followers, see discussion in part one.)

The positive alternative, I would suggest, can be called the 'collective personal growth organisational transformational' route. What would this consist of? It would have, I'd argue, a number of attributes: it would be both liberal and radical. Liberal in the sense of Gorbachov's word 'Glasnost' - that is open and transparent; openness of information and debate within the organisation and acceptance of open dissensus. This would clearly differentiate this type of community from both a conventional organisation and a cult. 'Liberal' would also include tolerance and respect for individual integrity. The radical element, again to use Gorbachov's word 'Perestroyka' - encompasses a willingness to change both at the individual and organisational levels. This should be underpinned by a faith in progress through collective structural change. These elements taken all together can create the basis for a 'field of transformational collective consciousness'.

We can first observe that this is not necessarily a new phenomenon: traditional religious centres such as ashrams and monasteries may well have in the past and even today nurture this kind of collective consciousness amongst their members. It can have transformational effects both for individuals and for the collective community in which they participate. A major difference for the self-selected value community would be that this consciousness would be value-open and not linked with any particular religious tradition. Two essential elements in creating and maintaining this transformational collective consciousness would be, firstly, collective transformational practice and, secondly, heart-centred discourse. The first of these requires that all participants in the organisation are collectively engaged in some type of developmental technique. This could be meditation, Breathwork, inner voice dialogue, or any of the various self-development techniques available today. As regards heart-centred discourse, a key element would be what I am calling here 'peer-to-peer' communication; i.e. no special individual statuses, no hierarchical distinctions between people in the organisation. People may be differentiated by functional role, they may be responsible for administration, or for certain tasks, etc.. but they have no higher status, in term of discourse, than any other individual in the organisation.

A second element of heart-centred discourse is what I am calling 'plumbing the psychic iceberg': this means communicating not just at a rational level but also - and openly - via all the other personal communication channels which exist between human beings. Many of these were blocked by the ultimately coercive nature of traditional-conventional organisations, where reference to the differences in structural power between individuals, or mention of emotional conflicts between individuals were taboo. As were the open acknowledgement of personal interactions between the child-adult and adult-child levels in different individuals. All of this was taboo in conventional coercive organisations, especially of course where there was a difference in hierarchical positions between the individuals involved. The essence of heart-centred discourse is to make all these levels of communication transparent to all involved. In this way 'acknowledged' or official communication can move closer to the real communication that goes on between people in organisations, and this, in turn, can contribute greatly to organisational efficiency.

Sharing the Breath

WILFRIED EHRMANN

Dr Wilfried Ehrmann is a psychotherapist from Vienna who integrates breathwork, counselling and systemic approaches in his practise.

I would like to invite you to join me and play with some models that can give us some ideas about how to share the breath with society, in a broader sense than we have done so far. Though we often think that Breathwork is avant-garde in the field of consciousness growth, there is an obvious gap between reality and vision which has to be looked at. I want to give a few ideas in this direction.

1. Historical process structures in psychotherapy

It seems that history has its own time structures. For example, we tend to be shocked by the rigidity and intolerance of the rules set up in fundamentalist countries found in the Islamic world. But looking back at our own history, we have to admit that their forms of social regulation are similar to those used by us in the medieval ages. Around the Christian age of 1300 or 1400, today's Islamic revolutions would have been considered as modern social technologies. The age of the Moslem religion is 1377. A civilisation seems to need a certain amount of time to grow in terms of power structures and individualisation, apart from a general development of the human consciousness.

Looking at the history of psychotherapy and growth work, we can find the following parallels.

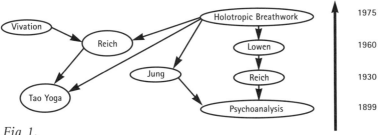

Fig 1.

After 25 years of psychoanalysis, Freud's theories were still harshly criticised both by the scientific establishment and by large groups in society. But with the help of his growing circle of talented and committed students and his own continuous publications, the ground was prepared for the irresistible rise of psychoanalysis as one of the most important contributions to modern way of thinking and reflecting

After 25 years of Reichian bodywork, Reich had to face trial and prison, where he later died. But the techniques and theories had already spread and attracted enough supporters and disciples who would develop efficient teaching structures. This freed Reich's inheritance from odd elements and laid the foundation for a successful growth of bodywork. In the seventies, the seeds Reich had planted unfolded and formed many different approaches and methods. A new paradigm in psychotherapy arose and slowly found its way into the concepts of psycho-therapy.

Rebirthing has been practised around 25 years now. After some years of incubation, it started out with stunning vehemence in the beginning of the eighties. Every workshop leader returning from Poona[1] would let his people lie down with the words – "let's go, breathe, breathe as much and as fast as you can". Compared to the immense practical impetus and momentum, the theoretical background remained barren and poor. The explanations consisted of a few concepts, more or less arbitrary collected from East and West that somehow seemed to fit in.

A common explanation of a Rebirthing session is that the power of the breath breaks barriers which normally protect suppressed feelings and transforms them into experiences of happiness and bliss ("integration into ecstasy")[2] according to Leonard and Laut. In this process the mind has to be put aside as its main function is to reinforce the barriers of suppression. Concepts in eastern philosophy that suggest control and restriction of the mind are therefore appreciated in Breathwork theory.

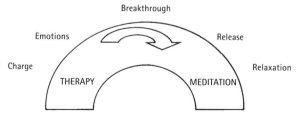

Fig 2.

1   Poona, refers to the ashram run by the Indian guru Bagwan Shree Rajneesh [later known as Osho]. The ashram was very popular with western disciples, and Rebirthing was practised as one of the spiritual techniques. Editor's comment.

2   Jim Leonard & Phil Laut, Rebirthing. The science of enjoying all of your life. Trinity Publications, Cincinnati 1983, p. 66).

Examining the structure of a typical Breathwork session, it is easy to find an immanent explanation for the mixture of eastern and western concepts in Breathwork theory. The power of Breathwork is in fact partly due to the mix of East and West, therapy and meditation in the practical process itself. In a one-hour session we often go through pain from childhood experiences to reach a state of high openness and sense of unity. We bring up material of therapeutic contents and move on to release it, often with blissful relaxation as a result.

As we usually focus on the conclusion-phase in the Rebirthing session, we tend to underestimate the therapeutic process that has preceded this meditative state. The concepts surrounding Breathwork are often derived from the final part of the session, stating that the mind should be transcended, in the same way as the goal of meditation is the containment of the mind. But therapy often has to build up, or educate the mind - explore and structure it. The relationship between meditation and mind is in many aspects as unexplained as the relationship of emotions and mind.

Breathing is simple - the message is simple (free your breath). Truth is simple, so we may conclude that breathing is the truth. We may also ask if there is an illusion of simplicity around breathing. Is there fear of complexity involved in the concepts of Breathwork?

2. Evolution and chaos in society
In the western tradition, we find two major general concepts for understanding society.

2.1. The first model describes that a more or less linear growth of awareness, consciousness, reflection and perfection is the driving force of mankind. This idea was especially formulated by Hegel and Marx, and later taken up by Ken Wilber who tried to include eastern spirituality in this model of evolution[3]. Wilber describes levels of consciousness, first accessed by individuals, which over time become part of society's common sense. It is evident that more and more people in today's society are looking for experiences that in earlier cultures were reserved for experts. The word 'esoteric', which original meaning is exclusive and secret, has changed meaning to the contrary. These days you can buy the secrets of the ascended masters in every railway bookstore.

---

3   Ken Wilber: Up from Eden/The Atman Project, Shambala Publications 1999

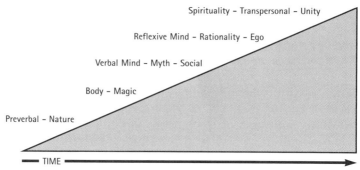

Fig 3.

Breathwork includes this linear model of progress because of the simple fact that we ask clients to breathe high up into the chest, to draw the energy up. Especially the resolution oriented part in Breathwork corresponds with the idea of linear progress (cf. Wilfried Ehrmann:). Breathwork never limits the goal to clear up the past. It always focuses on the open way to spiritual experiences and to higher forms of consciousness. Orr describes Rebirthing as Yoga for the west and considers it a quicker way to the divine. Many Breathworkers would agree with Deike Begg, who writes in her recent book: "The ultimate purpose for me in my work as Rebirther, therefore, is to make contact with this divine power that dwells deep within each and every one of us."[4]

This is the way of the sage.
2.2. The second model is sometimes called the post-modernistic concept of society, representing the liberal attitude of 'anything goes. It is nominalistic, in the sense of late medieval philosophers like Occam, who made a razor sharp distinction between sensual experience and mental conceptualising.

In this line of thinking, society is not made up by innate growth from one level to the next, with the former transcended and overcome by the latter, but consists of uncountable drafts constructed by individuals and groups in order to structure their environment. Modern constructivism, which also is a leading paradigm in many therapeutic approaches, states that everyone creates his/her own reality. According to Wittgenstein: We perceive the reality in the way we describe it[5].

We find these 'anarchistic' tendencies in Breathwork too. Anything can come up in a Breathwork session, there is no predictability. Order is built (by a certain breathing rhythm) and

4   Deike Begg: Rebirthing. Freedom from your past. Thorsons, London 1999, p. 178

5   Ludwig Wittgenstein: Philosophical Investigations, Prentice Hall 1973

gets destroyed (by another), chaos is welcomed and should be appreciated. The destruction of fixed ideas through the power of breath is one of the strong ingredients of Breathwork. Like the example from chaos theory that says that the rise of the smoke of a cigarette can only be predicted in its form by a length of a few centimetres. From then on, there is no possibility of calculating the way the smoke will take into the air as there are too many influences that interact among themselves simultaneously.

In a similar way, virtually all systems of the mind-body get involved and begin to interact in non predictable ways, as soon as we start to change some parameters by changing the breathing pattern. It is possible that images of early childhood can come along with images of former lifetimes, images of daily life experiences intermingle with traumatic incidences at birth, sometimes consecutively, sometimes overlaid.

The anarchy moves on to the level of concepts, as pointed out above. Ideas from Reich and Lowen, Buddha and Babaji go together in a flow of thoughts and explanations. Levels are easily changed among Breathworkers, and clients sometimes have to struggle to understand them. Some of the ideas are often considered as unquestionable truths, like the concept of 'Thought is creative'. At a closer look it is obvious that this is an anarchistic concept.

And this is the way of the fool.
We can go in all directions - and we usually do simultaneously. And we can find treasures in every direction. We need the second model to correct the first one. Evolutionary models tend to produce megalomania in those who consider themselves being on higher levels, and minority complexes in those who think they will never make it. Power and dependency structures are often justified by the supreme rights of the more evolved, and a lot of desperate striving can arise when people try to climb the ladder in order not to be among those who eventually will perish because of their meagre development. But we also need a correction to the post-modernistic relativity, which in the end leaves everything up to momentary impulses.

Maybe the wisdom of the Buddhist koans is the ultimate way – To go for enlightenment by forgetting about it.

3. The place of Breathwork in society
An essential task of IBF could be to define and redefine the place

of Breathwork in society, to develop and to represent it. We can do this best by intensifying the interaction with the neighbouring fields:

- Medicine
- Complementary Medicine
- Psychotherapy
- Social Work
- Education
- Esoteric
- Spirituality

Each one of these fields have their own way of breathing and their own language. When sharing the breath, it is important to recognise the breath in the field in which we are sharing - to speak each other's language - and not to presuppose experiences we bring in, that may not be common or understandable from the outside. This is the way to avoid rejection, misunderstanding, scepticism and unfair criticism.

4. Psychotherapy and Breathwork
To give an example of this interaction, I'd like to compare with the bridge from Breathwork to psychotherapy.

Psychotherapy has proven to be a successful brand in society, with a respectable performance next to classical medicine, through adapting some of their standards and paradigms, and yet, step by step emancipate from their power system, as well as from their naturalistic concept of man.

Historically, Austria has had, and still has, a mayor impact in this development. Not only has it given birth to psychoanalysis and some other disciplines derived from this approach. Austria has also introduced the first legal structure for psychotherapy and is playing a leading role in founding the European and the World Association for Psychotherapy, as well as organising two World Councils.

When interaction is fruitful, both sides have an equal input and outcome. Here are a few items of exchange:

What can Breathwork offer to the world of psychotherapy?
- A holistic understanding of healing
- A basic mechanism which is easy to internalise, relatively easy and substantially changeable
- Access to birth and early childhood by reaching "kino-

gramms" (early body memories)[6]
- Easy transfer to daily life, connection to self therapy and meditation

What can Breathwork learn from psychotherapy?
- Relationship dynamics (including transference and counter-transference and rules of abstinence)
- Classification of psycho-dynamic disorders and appropriate methods
- Ongoing theoretical discussion on a philosophical and praxeological level
- Numerous techniques for exploring and healing the psyche

What does psychotherapy require as entrance criteria?
One key to western society is science. It has been successful for three centuries by inheriting religion as central social institution to provide a deeper sense of life. Science means logic, common sense in a scientific community, intersubjective proof and reality construction, containment on essentials ("prinicipia non sunt multiplicanda praeter necessitatem" - principles are not to be multiplied beyond necessity) etc.

Rejecting the realm of science is like jumping over the development levels of the rational ego. This can lead to an outsider position of incompetence and ignorance. So we need to acknowledge the interrelatedness of scientific thinking and heart-opening feelings - and the insight that both of them are necessary for growth.

Building bridges from Breathwork to psychotherapy will build a bridge to society so that the breath will flow in a broader stream into society. To be able to do this, we have to work on our communication skills and find ways to reformulate our language.

Sharing the breath with society also means sharing the language. (Wittgenstein: "Our language is as complex as our body.") That includes a careful formulation and reformulation of basic concepts - context related. In therapy we adjust how we speak and breathe to match the client. We have to do the same with other sections of society.

Some examples:
1) 'Rebirthing' is the most obvious example of a word that leads to misunderstanding and distrust. Many people ask if it is a way to explore former lifetimes; some see it as a cult and

6 cf. George Downing: The Body and the Word. A Direction for Psychotherapy, 1994

others as an effortless and immediate way to a new life. Rebirthing is a Breathwork technique. It is therefore more correctly described using this term.

2) Another example is the term 'hyperventilation' that is often used in connection with Holotropic Breathwork or Rebirthing. It evokes unpleasant associations to the medical profession and gives mainly uncomfortable associations for ordinary people. I suggest that this term is best left to the medical profession and only for clinical use. Although the accelerated breathing in a Breathwork session may have similar symptoms to the hyperventilation syndrome, it arises from totally different circumstances and is resolved in completely different ways. So it should not be mixed up with the traditional form of HV.

3) The term 'heart' is often used in connection with heart-opening and heart-centred, sounds familiar to many but is considered as esoteric and unscientific by mainstream psychotherapy. You can read highly informative and complex books on psychotherapy, which do not include the word "heart" once.

4) The term 'energy' seems to be an almost irreplaceable concept in Breathwork. But it can trigger rejection in some other psychotherapeutic approaches that would criticise the vagueness and ambiguity of this term[7].

5. Fundamental Values

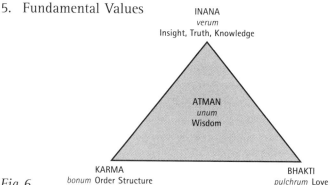

Fig 6.

Let us create a new model for bridgebuilding by using a model of polarities of fundamental values from early Yogic writings

7   cf. George Downing: The Body and the Word. A Direction for Psychotherapy, 1994

that has its parallels in scholastic philosophy.

If we see this map as a table with three legs rather than a pyramid, we can see that all three angles need equal weight to keep the table in an even and flat position. I think, we agree that Breathwork has its starting point and a seat in the realm of BHAKTI. Heart-opening is what attracts many people to this approach, and heartfulness is a basic quality in this conference.

Still we haven't moved sufficiently in other directions. This could cause some remittance from other areas of society. So far Rebirthing has had difficulties building up an effective organisation, and we are still facing problems when we introduce new impulses for structuring IBF more efficiently. The knowledge and scientific background for Breathwork is still weak. It can also be the case that some of us want to escape knowledge or avoid order because they adore the spirit of love and beauty as supreme value.

As this model also is used in systemic therapy, we must keep in mind that each angle of the triangle needs appropriate care and respect in order to keep the whole thing in balance. When we trust the centre - when we trust wisdom - there is no need to be afraid that any of the beauty and heart-openness will be lost when we open up to knowledge and order. On the contrary, we can enrich our capability of love by embracing more of the spirits of this world.

What does this mean in terms of Breathwork and breath-therapy? For successful therapeutic work, structure is as important as heart-opening, reflection and insight as supportive as the sweetness of breath. As the centre of all is spirit, in the form of wisdom, the ultimate goal is to arrive there. But the way is less linear that paradoxical. In order to help the client to more inner stability and clarity, we will need some kind of verbal interaction to connect experience with knowledge. The predominance of non verbal interaction, which is a good tool for exploring early childhood experiences, has to be brought into good balance with structure and reflective insight, so that the whole person - the preverbal child and the verbal grown up - is included in the work.

There are schools of Breathwork that concentrate on each of the angles. We can see that the polarities are included in the breath in the various areas of Breathwork:

Order:	Pranayama	control
Love:	Rebirthing	flow
Insight:	Breath-therapy	reflection

If we concentrate on the fractal structure of self-resemblance, inherent in this model, we will discover how everything is interrelated. It is no exaggeration to state that each breath carries society in itself.[8] Every Breathwork session is affected by society. Vice versa applies as well, of course.

There is also a dynamic movement in these polarities of fundamental values. I'll explain one way to connect which is my personal way:

I come from a family with good order, directed by rigidity. I went to university to gain more knowledge. It helped me to find a distance to my family and discover an important part of my own way. My first intense loving relationship helped me to see the limitations of the reflective mind. I ended up building up a new order, in form of a family with two children. Problems in the relationship brought me to therapy where I to start with mainly got intellectual insights but also to deeper feelings. The first Breathwork session gave me a kind of cosmic opening to a universal form of love which guided me on a new way and brought me to look for new forms of order ...

You can see the wheel of life, the cycles that guide you through a day, a year, a whole life in a fractal way. There is no use in stopping at any point, the movement is always there since it is the nature and the essence of life.

6. Success formula for sharing the breath with society

I'll end this lecture by proposing a 'success formulary' which hopefully will help us to integrate more with society and thus open up a bright future for sharing the breath with society.

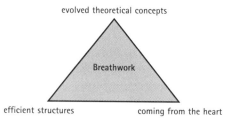

What I think will make Breathwork successful in the future is that it comes from the realm of love and heart with an efficient working structure and well-evolved theoretical concepts.

We are a tiny fragment in the global society. We have an important message. Whether we can add a piece of salt to this earth depends on how we convey our message in terms of power and differentiation - and all this can be found in our breathing.

8 Cf. Klaus Neubeck: Atem-Ich, Stroemfeld/Nexus, Basel/Frankfurt a.M. 1992, who claims that every notion and every thought is directly represented in a certain pattern of movement of the diaphragm).

Spiral Dynamics:
Breathwork & Social Evolution

JIM MORNINGSTAR

Jim Morningstar, PhD, ABPP, is a clinical psychologist who was one of the first 12 certified Rebirthers in the 1970s. For the past 14 years, he has been the director of Transformations Incorporated, which includes the School of Spiritual Psychology and Creative Consulting and Counselling Service in Milwaukee, USA. He is the author of the books, Spiritual Psychology, Family Awakening and Breathing in Light and Love.

I want to share with you one of the most useful tools I have encountered for understanding conscious evolution on our planet, Spiral Dynamics. This tool has helped me realise and explain the importance of Breathwork (Morningstar, 1994) as a means of social integration at this point in human history. Spiral Dynamics is simply a framework for understanding how we grow and gives excellent clues as to where we are going. Breathwork is the tool for bringing about change and integration particularly suited to our current place in the cosmos.

Spiral Dynamics had its roots in the levels of consciousness research begun by an American psychologist, Claire Graves, in the 1950's. Frustrated by the conflicting jumble of theories of human behaviour, he set out to illuminate the core motivational beliefs of humans on the planet. His research spanned several decades. His results began to correlate with data from other world-wide projects co-ordinated through the United States National Institute of Health. The beauty of his work is in its blending of simplicity, reaffirming universal principles we know, and complexity, collecting data from incredibly diverse areas of human knowledge. Canada's MacLean Magazine reporting on Grave's work in the late 1970's called it 'The Theory that Explains Everything.'

Graves, a professor at Union College in New York, died relatively unknown in 1986. I had the privilege of meeting him in the 1970's. Like many geniuses who are perfectionists, he never published his complete work. That is because he was always discovering new refinements and exploring new horizons such that he saw his work as never complete. Also like many geniuses, the publishing and application of his work was later accomplished by his students. Two such enterprising followers, Beck and Cowen (1996), coined the term Spiral Dynamics and applied its principles to social change. They were hired by the government of South Africa, for example, to assist in the transition from apartheid. The theory has been successfully applied to the areas of social welfare, education, business management and marketing. My interest is in the area of psychotherapy and consciousness growth. It helps me select which healing approach is appropriate with which individuals, under which circumstances. It makes obsolete questions like what is the best form of government or best system of education or best form of therapy. But more than this, it indicates what is most likely to be effective with whom and when.

Graves asked a wide variety of individuals over a long period what motivated their life choices. Two broad groups always emerged: those who touted self-expression, those who favoured self-adaptation, those who were more yang and those who were more yin. Among the self-expressionists are those who favour winning at all cost and those who take a more measured reasoned approach. Among the self-adapters were those who professed submission to a Higher Authority and those who promoted conformity to the will of the group.

So far this is fairly common knowledge. What made it more interesting is the predictability of how and when people made changes in their beliefs. Not surprisingly most people tended to take on the belief system of their family. However, a great revolution in belief systems is happening. Growth on our planet is evolving at an exponential rate. When open system individuals grow, they always go from an adept to an express system or vice versa in a predictable order.

These changes in belief systems are not about what people think, but rather how they think. This involves using different parts of the brain, stimulating different body chemistry and engendering whole new sets of behaviours. Each stage of growth builds upon the preceding one at the same time that it refutes many of its major tenets. At any one time we are a combination of many differing systems of belief, but there tends to be a major or nodal system through which we are interpreting our life.

Figure 1 shows that as we progress psychologically, we adapt higher systems and are still influenced, to a greater or lesser degree, by those we have grown past and those we are growing toward.

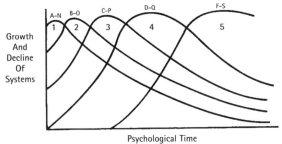

Fig 1.

Figure 2 is a symbolic representation of the concept that each stage in growth (each widening circle) involves more areas of the brain (area of X's + 0's) and takes us further into our universe (dotted line circles). It also lists the conditions for consciousness changes. First, we must have the biological equipment, not be severely brain damaged. Second, we must address and successfully solve the challenges at that stage of growth. In tribal life, for example, I must learn the customs and rituals of my clan and glean the advantages they bring. Third, there must be some dissonant stimulus to my current belief system that attracts me. In the Saintly system, for example, I begin to notice those who are not waiting till the hereafter to enjoy their rewards, and who do not seem to be immoral people to me. Fourth, I must get insight into how I could live differently than in the prevailing system, envision myself in a new life as it were. And fifth, I must then overcome the barriers, inner and outer, that the current system has to my growing beyond it. I have to do the work, in other words.

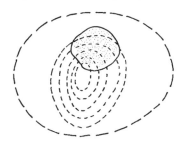

Representation of Adult Personality, A complex of Bio–social Ecological Systems

Conditions of Change

1. Biological Equipment

2. Solution of Existential Problems
   (Readiness)

3. Dissonant Stimuli (Impetus)

4. Insight

5. Overcome Barriers

Fig 2.

A – F = Different "Dynamic Neurological Systems"
N – S = Qualitative Variation in State of external Affairs
A – N, B – O, etc = Existential States
Xxxx's, oooo's s = Qualitative Difference Designations

Figure 3 graphically portrays another facet of our human growth patterns - they are seldom in a straight line. As we progress, we reach plateaux then often seemingly regress before we grow further. If we are growth oriented, we can fully contain our spirit within any belief systems only so long, till we reach a point of moral crisis. In the Pragmatic System, for instance, I may no longer believe that just accumulating more goods or money is truly fulfilling to me. I may seem to be left without moorings, then I cannot subscribe to my old beliefs, but I do not have a fully integrated new set yet. This is when we often see people in therapy or Breathwork. They are looking for help in making sense of an expanding universe (to them it may seem disintegrating). This is represented by the dips at the end of each plateau (a, a', a"). Some people get stuck in these dips for years or perhaps lifetimes. During this period I search often through old forms of doing and explaining life. These can be old adapt self forms if I am growing into another yin system, e.g. old time religion. They tend to be old express self forms if I am growing into yang system, e.g. using 'Atilla the Hun' tactics for corporate management. In the end, these will not suffice and I reach a point of behavioural crisis (b, b',b"). At this point, I hit rock bottom, really let go and start to put together a new life based on the new principles I am learning. Given the success of this integration, I reach a new plateau and spend time there mastering this level and the challenges it brings.

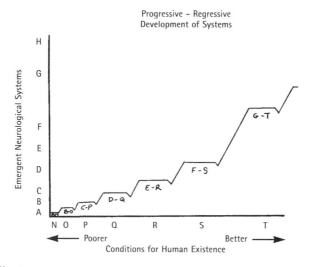

Fig 3.

Even this explanation of growth is greatly oversimplified. Figure 4 shows what happens when there is growth without all five factors for change being present. We can make a Horizontal Change when there is dissonance within our current system, e.g. Religion A appears hypocritical to me, but there is no Insight into a new level of consciousness. So I convert to Religion B which has a different set of authorities and doctrines, but essentially still subscribes to a black and white system of right and wrong. What I think has changed, not how I think. Oblique change happens when I take on some higher level characteristics, but do not solve all the problems for existence at that level and/or do not have complete insight into a new way of being. I might choose Religion C which affords me more opportunity for self-determination, but still limits my vision through some restrictive doctrine. True Vertical Change indicates I am experiencing my world in an entirely different way.

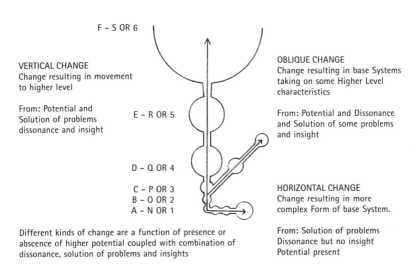

Representation of the Three Basic Forms of Change When Higher Potential for Change is Present

F – S OR 6

VERTICAL CHANGE
Change resulting in movement to higher level

From: Potential and Solution of problems dissonance and insight

E – R OR 5

D – Q OR 4

C – P OR 3
B – O OR 2
A – N OR 1

OBLIQUE CHANGE
Change resulting in base Systems taking on some Higher Level characteristics

From: Potential and Dissonance and Solution of some problems and insight

HORIZONTAL CHANGE
Change resulting in more complex Form of base System.

From: Solution of problems Dissonance but no insight Potential present

Different kinds of change are a function of presence or abscence of higher potential coupled with combination of dissonance, solution of problems and insights

Fig 4.

A less linear model of growth is shown in Figure 5. Each system incorporates the one before. We can always go back to and use the strengths (or weaknesses) of a prior system when called for. In a crisis I may revert to 'more primitive' forms of behaviour which may be entirely appropriate or even life saving.

I may not say 'excuse me' or take a vote before going to get the fire extinguisher in an emergency.

Nesting Aspect of adult Personality Systems

When new system takes over, lower level system is subordinated in the new system.

When lower level system dominates that part of higher level system emerged operate in service of lower level system

This is an example of a centralised level six system with developing level seven and eight systems

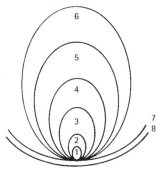

Fig 5.

Graves outlined motivational thinking and value systems for each of the levels of existence which we are about to review. Table 1 is presented just to hint at the greater complexity of each level should you wish to look further into them. I have added a middle column on learning systems which is relevant to how we learn at each level and consequently what forms of therapy will be effective with individuals at various stages of growth. In another work I have delineated the development of twentieth century psychotherapy modalities as change agents (Scholz, 1973). For our purposes here, the development and role of Breathwork in the transformation of world consciousness will be highlighted.

Level of Existence	Existential State	Nature of Existence	Learning	Motivational System	Type of Thinking	Value Means Value	System End Value
2nd Being	H–U	Experientialism		Experience	Differentielistic	*Experiencing*	Communion
1st Being	G–T	Cognitive		Existence	Systemic	Accepting	*Existence*
6th Subsistence	F–S	Sociocentric	Roter Social Learning	Affiliation	Experientalistic	Sociocentricity	Community
5th Subsistence	E–R	Materialistic	Sign Gestalt Perceptual	Independent	Objetivistic	Scientism	*Material*
4th Subsistence	D–Q	Saintly	Avoidant 2-Factor	Security	Absolutistic	Sacrifice	*Salvation*
3rd Subsistence	C–P	Individualistic	Operant Conditioning	Survival	Egocentric	Exploitative	*Power*
2nd Subsistence	B–O	Tribalistic	Classical Conditioning	Assurance	Autistic	Traditionalism	Safety
1st Subsistence	A–N	Automatic	Imprinting	Psychological	....	Values purely	reactive

"Ontology recapitulates Phylogeny" is an old dictum indicating that each of us in our development relives the growth of our species. As a child we grow through automatic, tribalistic, heroic and saintly systems, repeating the stages of thousands of years of human development in the first seven years of life. Now we are perched on the threshold of a tremendous change in planetary consciousness which is simultaneous with the new millennium. The moral crisis has been reached and we are ready for a new level of integration, or recycling as recent Balkan wars have threatened. Breathwork as we have witnessed facilitates a profound increase in conscious awareness which not only heals our past, but helps us build a new global spirit. Let us look at the reasons why this technique is particularly suited to what our society needs and what our responsibility is in this critical process.

In traditional therapeutic terms, anxiety and compulsive behaviours are characteristics of yin (adapt self) systems whereas acting out and impulsive behaviour are associated more with yang (express self) systems. Breathwork as a holistic technique has been able to do what few other change agents have done, that is to bridge all the systems of our past and open the neurological circuitry for higher levels than group consciousness has been ready to integrate until now.

Theme for existence associated to each existential state:

1. A – N   React naturally to imperative physiological needs so as to reduce the tension of them. No concept of cause and effect.
2. B – O   Live in accordance with established tribal ways.
3. C – P   Express self for what self desires regardless of the consequences lest one feel ashamed
4. D – Q   Sacrifices the desires of self now in order to get reward later on in some other realm
5. E – R   Express self for what self desires but in a rational, calculating way without feeling shame or guilt
6. F – S   Sacrifice what one desires now in order to get reward now in the form of acceptance by and approval of others
7. G – T   Express self as self is inclined but not at the expense of others
8. H – U   Sacrifice the idea that man will never know what it is all about and go on living

Problems of existence represented by each letter:

N   Achieving stability of imperative Psychological systems
O   Achieving basic safety in a non-comprehended world which seems full of spirits
P   Awareness of existence as an individual; how to live against the fact of death
Q   Reasoned knowledge leading to control of the physical universe; How to conquer threat and want
S   Comprehension that human subjectivity is a reality not a myth to be cast aside; how to live in a world of abundance for human wants
T   Restoring ecological balance disturbated by the knowledge accured; how to restore disturbed universe
U   Truly accepting the reality of ever broadening realms of consciousness; how to live when having, but never really knowing life.

Let us review the eight levels of consciousness as we know them to date. Beck and Cowen (1996) have added the dimension of the spiral to this model which may appear hierarchical in its presentation thus far. Indeed no one level is better than another. Countless humans have lived happy and fulfilled lives at each level presumably because they came here to address the lessons that level had to offer. These lessons tend to come around again and again, but with increasingly expanded awareness as we grow. Beck and Cowen use colours rather than numbers for each stage. Rather than belief systems they use the concept of meme, "self replicating patterns of information that propagate themselves across the ecologies of mind." (1996, p 30) For simplicity, however, I will refer to eight levels. Here I will quote from their work Spiral Dynamics (1996).

"BEIGE 'Survivalistic' MEME 1st Awakening Graves Code: A-N
    Basic theme: Do what you must just to stay alive

Characteristic beliefs and actions:
- Uses instincts and habits just to survive
- Distinct self is barely awakened or sustained
- Food, Water, Warmth, Sex, and Safety have priority
- Forms into survival bands to perpetuate life

Where seen: The first peoples, newborn infants, senile elderly, late-stage Alzheimer's victims, mentally ill street people, starving masses, bad drug trips, and 'shell shock.' Described in anthropological fiction like Jean Auel's Clan of the Cave Bear ." (Beck & Cowan, p 45).

Help at this level would be CPR or intravenous feeding. All assistance is here directed toward keeping the individual breathing as we are often called to do as Rebirthers when 'unconsciousness' sets in.

"PURPLE 'magical' MEME 2nd Awakening Graves Code: B-O
    Basic theme: Keep the spirits happy and the 'tribe's' nest warm and safe

Characteristic beliefs and actions:
- Obey the desires of spirit beings and mystical signs
- Show allegiance to chief, elders, ancestors and the clan
- Preserve sacred objects, places, events, and memories
- Observe rites of passage, seasonal cycles, and tribal customs

Where seen: Belief in guardian angels and Voodoo-like curses, blood oaths, ancient grudges, chanting and trance dancing, good luck charms, family rituals, and mystical ethnic beliefs and superstitions. Strong in Third-World settings, gangs, athletic teams, and corporate 'tribes' (Beck & Cowan p. 45).

Notice their inclusion of 'guardian angels.' Lessons at this level return I believe in level eight which is the threshold of where we are now as a planet. Help at level 2 involves classical conditioning procedures because they intervene at the human brain stem level. Background anxiety from birth is the underlying condition of most humans on earth. Rebirthing literally reconditions trauma to the breathing mechanism which verbal therapies cannot reach (Morningstar, 1994). It thus prepares our brain for higher order functioning which we cannot talk ourselves into.

"RED 'Impulsive' MEME 3rd Awakening Graves Code: C-P

Basic Theme: Be what you are and do what you want, regardless

Characteristic beliefs and actions:
- The world is a jungle full of threats and predators
- Breaks free from any domination or constraint to please self as self desires
- Stands tall, expects attention, demands respect, and calls the shots
- Enjoys self to the fullest right now without guilt or remorse
- Conquers, out-foxes, and dominates other aggressive characters

Where seen: The 'Terrible Twos,' rebellious youth, frontier mentalities, feudal kingdoms, James Bond villains, epic heroes, soldiers of fortune, 'Papa' Picasso, wild rock stars, Atilla the Hun, William Golding's Lord of the Flies, and Mighty Morphin Power Rangers." (Beck & Cowan, p45).

Helping techniques at this level include operant conditioning procedures, 'shaping' behaviour or deconditioning phobic responses. Again these are precognitive interventions and address deep level habit patterns, e.g. addictions, and fears e.g. phobias. Helping here requires altering the active reward-seeking behaviour of those being helped. Because Rebirthing is not 'done' to someone like Pavlov's dog was trained, Rebirthees learn to shape primitive behaviour patterns and decondition deep-rooted fears in sessions themselves with the assistance of the Rebirther.

"BLUE 'Purposeful' MEME 4th Awakening Graves Code: D-Q

Basic Theme: Life has meaning, direction, and purposes with predetermined outcomes.

Characteristic beliefs and actions:
- One sacrifices self to the transcendent Cause, Truth, or righteous Pathway
- The Order enforces a code of conduct based on eternal, absolute principles
- Righteous living produces stability now and guarantees future reward
- Impulsivity is controlled through guilt; everybody has their proper place
- Laws, regulations, and discipline build character and moral fibre

Where seen: Rev. Billy Graham, Frank Capra's It's a Wonderful Life, Puritan America, Confucian China, Hasidic Judaism, Dickensian England, Singapore discipline, codes of chivalry and honour, charitable good deeds, the Salvation Army, Islamic fundamentalism, Garrison Keillor's Lake Wobegon, Boy and Girl Scouts, patriotism.(Beck & Cowan p 46)

At this level more co-ordinated functioning between the sub cortical forebrain and the brain stem along with an abundance of adrenaline makes the avoidance of punishment a very powerful motivating factor. It is said that if there are no aversive consequences at this level, there is not learning. At this level I first learn to avoid punishment and am rewarded later. Delayed gratification is actually a great advance in our civilisation over the Atilla the Hun quest of immediate gratification of the previous level. Guilt, penance, expiration confession are all important steps in development. But if this has been inflicted too harshly or dogmatically, it hinders later growth Many Rebirthees engage in a form of confession and expiration as they release guilt. Some even utilise the pain of tetany in a healing way to get beyond the fear of pain despite the Rebirther's attempts to avert it. Part of the Rebirthee knows what is needed for his or her healing.

"ORANGE ' 'Achievist' MEME 5th Awakening Graves Code: E-R

Basic Theme: Act in your own self-interest by playing the

game to win

Characteristic beliefs and actions:
- Change and advancement are inherent within the scheme of things
- Progress by learning nature's secrets and seeking out best solutions
- Manipulate Earth's resources to create and spread the abundant good life
- Optimistic, risk-taking, and self-reliant people deserve their success
- Societies prosper through strategy, technology, and competitiveness

Where seen: The Enlightenment, 'success' ministries, Any Rand's Atlas Shrugged, Wall Street, Rodeo Drive, The Riviera, emerging middle classes, the cosmetics industry, trophy hunting, Chambers of Commerce, colonialism, TV infomercials, the Cold War, DeBeers diamond cartel, breast implants, fashion, J.R. Ewing and Dallas." (Beck & Cowan, pg. 46).

Psychoanalysis grew out of helping people transition from the prior Saintly System (4th Awakening) to this more cognitively reliant Pragmatic System. The authoritative doctor allowed guilt ridden patients to bring their libidinous id (level 3) out from the Victorian rule of their superego (level 4) and be guided through the rational ministry of their ego (level 5) Facilitators who are at the next level of growth are best in helping others overcome the barriers of the prior level. In the 5th level we see the advent of many cognition therapies which teach us to think rationally to a better life (Ellis, Kelly) or to communicate more clearly to improved family systems (Satir, Jackson). Rebirthing uses affirmations to retrain the brain with its increased neo-cortical development at the level toward more clear and healthy thinking and self-talk patterns. (Scholz,1973)

"GREEN 'Communitarian' MEME 6th Awakening Graves Code: F-S

Basic Theme: Seek peace within the inner self and explore, with others, the caring dimensions of community.

Characteristic beliefs and actions:
- The human spirit must be freed from greed, dogma, and divisiveness

- Feelings, sensitivity, and caring supersede cold rationality
- Spread the Earth's resources and opportunities equally among all
- Reach decisions through reconciliation and consensus processes
- Refresh spirituality, bring harmony, and enrich human development

Where seen: John Lennon's music, Netherlands' idealism, Rogerian counselling, liberation theology, Doctors without Borders, Canadian health care, ACLU, World Council of Churches, sensitivity training, Boulder (Colorado), Green Peace, Jimmy Carter, Dustin Hoffman in The Graduate, animal rights, deep ecology, Minneapolis-St Paul social services, the music of Bruce Cogburn, Ben & Jerry's Ice Cream company." (Beck & Cowan, p 46-47).

At the sixth level there is a more refined integration between lower appetative centres and higher cognitive processes. People learn here through observation of others rather than having to make all their own mistakes. This yin (adapt self) level recognises the authority of the peer group. The advent of group therapies and consciousness raising groups is especially meaningful at this level. The therapist is not looked to as the authoritative answer giver. Solutions come more from group process. The Rebirthing movement started amid this level of growth in our world and still reflects the importance of group dynamic in heightening the growth of Rebirthees.

"YELLOW 'Integrative' MEME 7th Awakening Graves Code: G-T
Basic theme: Live fully and responsibly as what you are and learn to become

Characteristic beliefs and actions:
- Life is a kaleidoscope of natural hierarchies, systems, and forms
- The magnificence of existence is valued over material production
- Flexibility, spontaneity, and functionality have the highest priority
- Knowledge and competency should supersede rank, power, status
- Differences can be integrated into interdependent, natural

flows

Where seen: Carl Sagan's astronomy, Peter Senge's organisa-
tions, Stephen Hawking's Brief History of Time, W. Edwards
Deming's objectives, Paul Newman's version of stardom, chaos
theory, appropriate technology, eco-industrial parks (using each
other's outflows as raw materials), early episodes of TV's
Northern Exposure, Fel-Pro,Inc. (a gasket manufacturer), Fred
Alan Wolf's 'new physics' Deepak Chopra's Ageless Body.(Beck
& Cowan, p 47).

The seventh level marks a new tier in the spiral of human
consciousness, coming from a being motivation rather than a
survival mentality. Learning here is more with the whole person
than any one part or parts of the brain. Gestalt techniques and
those which bring into play non-verbal and non-linear
processes often open the door for guidance from other
dimensions of our being. Here is where the use of Rebirthing has
had a great impact on our evolution. Although frustrating to
those who want to capture its essence in a formula, it is its very
ineffable nature in which lies its value. Rebirthees are drawn to
it because it does not define them in survival terms, but liberates
the spirit to be and express fully.

"TURQUOISE 'Holistic' MEME 8th Awakening Graves Code: H-U
Basic Theme: Experience the wholeness of existence through
mind and spirit.

Characteristic beliefs and actions:
- The world is a single, dynamic organism with its own
  collective mind
- Self is both distinct and a blended part of a larger,
  compassionate whole
- Everything connects to everything else in ecological
  alignments
- Energy and information permeate the Earth's total
  environment
- Holistic, intuitive thinking and co-operative actions are to
  be expected

Where seen: Theories of David Bohm, McLuhan's 'global village,'
Gregory Stock's Metaman, Rupert Sheldrake and morphic fields,
Gandhi's ideas of pluralistic harmony, Ken Wilber's 'Spectrum of

Consciousness,' James Lovelock's 'Gaia hypothesis,' Pierre Teilhard de Chardin's 'noosphere'.Beck & Cowan p 48.

This is our cutting edge. People at this level register a different physiology, often standard deviations different from others, i.e. less core anxiety and operating from a different ground of being. Helping at this level entails not doing something to change someone, but being them as you both change. This requires a commitment of total being and removal of all illusions of separation. This higher yin (adapt self) stage to which we are evolving necessitates a global transformation toward the divine feminine if our old male models are not to become top heavy and lead to a collapse of our support systems. Rebirthing has paved the way for this breakthrough level for many. It is imperative that we reach a critical mass of being at this level to tilt the balance of world consciousness. Breath is the thread which runs through the physical, emotional, cognitive and metaphysical systems and brings them together as no other element can. Love and light are also universal principles and healing forces, but they are otherworldly without breath. It is only through breath that love and light can transform the beings of this planet.

We are called as Rebirthers to open our hearts and minds to all who seek this transition to a higher level of being. We are called to train other Rebirthers and to serve as direct agents for the Spirit of Breath. All other therapies can be combined with and used with Breathwork to increase their effectiveness. Only Breathwork, however, has spanned the healing spectrum of the twentieth century from classical conditioning of the brain stem to embracing of our eternal spirit. It is not a 'new age' discovery. Breathwork is a timeless truth that has been awaiting this point in our evolution to re-emerge because we are now ready to integrate all our levels. Breathwork is a holistic marriage of the Divine Male and Divine Female as is experienced in each complete cycle of inhale and exhale. We need every level of our being and every person on our planet to effect this transition. Some will not participate consciously, but we need many more to be conscious. We are given an incredible opportunity to change the face of our planet or to revert to primitive forms of struggle for individual power and survival. Every Breathworker has received a calling to do this work by the Spirit of Breath. This is the greater plan of social evolution. It is our privilege and mission to embrace our highest and share our breath with all our brothers and sisters now. There is only One Breath.

BIBLIOGRAPY

1. Beck, Donald Edward and Cowen, Christopher C. *Spiral Dynamics*, Blakwell Publishers Inc, Cambridge, Mass., 1996.

2. Morningstar, Jim *Breathing in Light and Love*, Transformations Incorporated, Milwaukee, WI, 1994.

3. Scholz, James A. *Therapy According to Levels of Consciousness*, Unpublished Manuscript, Milwaukee, WI, 1973

4. Lecture given at the Global Inspiration Conference on the 6th of June 1999 in Spain

The Psychology of Selves

TILKE PLATTEEL-DEUR

Tilke Platteel-Deur has been practising and teaching Breathwork and the dynamics of relationship, since 1979. After intensive training in the Psychology of Selves with Hal and Sidra Stone, she incorporated the Voice Dialogue technique, as they developed it, into her work. Together with Hans Mensink she has created the Institute for Integrative Breath Therapy, (Das Institut für Ganzheitliche Integrative Atemtherapie). They offer a basic three year training and students have the option, after having worked at least a year as a practitioner, to take a fourth year to learn to become a trainer.

Introduction

From the time I started to do Breathwork, the technique fascinated me. Merely by using breath there was a great deal that I could accomplish for myself, and later in my work with clients as well. Nevertheless areas remained where I was unable to understand and explain why and how certain dynamics worked. This was especially true for the dynamics in relationships. Since our life is mainly relationship, in one form or another, I felt the need to find a frame of thought through which to understand the work I was doing on a deeper level. I also wanted tools to make its practice easier.

Because the universe seems to provide us with answers to questions that we put out, I was very lucky to meet Dr. Hal Stone and his wife Dr. Sidra Stone-Winkelman in 1981 in Amsterdam. They were there to introduce their ideas on the Psychology of Selves, and the Voice Dialogue technique that they had developed. After Hal's first lecture I felt so thrilled about the simplicity and brilliance of his ideas that I started to study with him and soon after that we - my working partner Hans Mensink and I - incorporated the 'Psychology of Selves' into our training. Hans and I have been teaching together since 1979. Our 'Institute for Holistic Integrative Breathwork' offers a three-year training program in which we train people in Breathwork, Voice Dialogue, Polarity work and NLP. This training enables the students to learn how to work with other people and to guide them through a deep process of personal growth.

The Psychology of Selves is a frame of thought that helps us to understand the human psyche better. Its essential idea is that the human psyche is composed of many parts or sub-personalities. The idea that the psyche consists of many different parts is not new. Freud, C.G. Jung, Moreno and Perls, among others, each used this idea in their own specific way.

Hal & Sidra Stone however, took this concept and transformed it into a simple, easy and fun technique, which enables us to get into personal contact with our many different voices by talking directly to them. This happens in such a way that we not only experience these voices as lively parts of our personality, each with their own feelings, wishes, behaviour, and so forth, we also learn how to stay aware of these different energies or sub personalities when they operate in our lives and in our relationships.

In the traditional meaning, the ego has always been seen as the decision-maker of the psyche. In the Voice Dialogue technique it becomes clear that what we refer to as 'ego' is often the ego being identified with a combination of sub-personalities. The concept of the 'Aware Ego' as the Decision-Maker who gets his information both on an awareness level and on an experience level, is, however, unique. I will explain this later more precisely.

We found the Psychology of Selves to be an easily under-standable frame of thought and the Voice Dialogue technique an ideal method to use alongside and in combination with Breathwork. It proved to be the very clear and simple concept we were seeking to support us in our work on our own process and with our client's processes on an emotional, energetic and mental level.

Consciousness and the 'Aware Ego'

From Hal Stone I heard - maybe for the first time - an accept-able and workable concept of the word 'Consciousness'. Many of us have used the word consciousness to describe what we experienced in meditation. I now think that awareness - mean-ing the capacity to witness - is a better word to describe that state. When, later, many of us became involved in all kinds of personal growth work like encounter, counselling and Rebirthing, we were very much into pure experience, and then we called that 'consciousness'. Hal brought these two, awareness and experience, together. I like to say it this way:

Consciousness is both the experience and the awareness of the different energies we experience in life. Out of experience and awareness an aware ego emerges. This aware ego isn't something static but is continuously in the process of becoming more and more aware.

This process can be imaged like this:

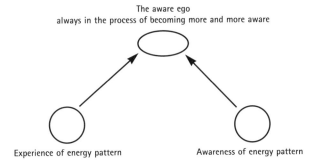

Fig 1.

Example
When I stand in front of an audience to give a lecture, I am distinctly aware of, and experience physically clearly, at least two very opposite energy patterns in myself. You could even call them 'Voices' because they seem to be talking in my head.

One is the professional part of me that is able to address an audience and tell them something interesting. I call this my 'Inner Teacher'. The other part is a very vulnerable and shy 'Inner Child', a small girl in me that is afraid when she sees so many strange faces and who would like to hide in a little corner with someone she knows well and trusts.

If I tried to give my lecture from the energy space of the 'Inner Child', I would not be able to talk at all because of her shyness. If I spoke through the other voice I would be identified with the voice of 'The Teacher', trying hard to get it right and probably creating a lot of resistance in my audience, because I would be too severe and not playful at all.

But if I could use the teacher and be aware of my Inner Child's vulnerability I would be lively and authentic.

I will explain the way, in which all our different parts come into existence how we can befriend them and learn to embrace them, and most importantly, how they influence our relationships.

The Psychology of Selves

We can say that the soul chooses a body in order to learn certain lessons that can only be learned in the body. Imagine the immensity of the soul, with all its knowledge and its feeling of being connected with its origins, becoming trapped in a small baby's body. The soul's unique quality of being is like a psychic fingerprint, as Sidra Stone puts it [1], carrying every special aspect of our being. It is the part of us that makes us undeniably unique.

In the womb we feel at one and as one with our mother. While our body grows, the soul gets 'hooked' more and more onto the body. And then, during birth, we experience a deep sense of loss and separation. This is not only on account of our separation from our mother. Because the body is our only frame of reference and because we are very much identified with the vulnerability of the body, it is as if we 'forget' our connection with soul. Therefore we experience birth as separation from our source. This separation feels totally real and makes us feel very vulnerable. And in fact after birth we are vulnerable, we can't take care of ourselves and we do depend on others to be fed, cleansed and taken care of.

At birth we seem to forget our uniqueness and everything we planned to do here on earth because the enormous shock of the transition, the pain and this feeling of loss and separation are too overwhelming.

In order to become strong enough to survive, we have to develop the many parts of our personality that come into existence to protect our vulnerability. These different parts or, as I have called them before, 'voices' may not be who we are deep inside but we need them because our need to protect our vulnerability is immense. We cannot simply be our unique self as little children. We have to develop a certain set of 'Primary Selves' to make it possible for us to belong to our families, our religion and our country. We have to have a system of behaviour that allows us to 'fit in'. We need these Primary Selves that give us a measure of power to control our surroundings and to survive in this world. If we do not develop a certain power, we would be constant victims to everybody and to the circumstances of life.

Let's have a look at some of the voices that start to develop very early in life.

---

1   Hal & Sidra Stone, The Psychology of Selves, p13

The System of Protection and Controlling

The system that develops first is the part we call the 'Protector-Controller'. This part helps us to develop ways of controlling our surroundings. We cry when we are hungry or wet, and we learn very fast that people come to help us when we scream. As we become older this is the part that makes the rules. It tells us how to behave and how to fit into our family, society and even country. It makes us into more or less adapted people and it will always look for means to make us safe in the world.

For example

While we are still young, daydreaming may be a great way to escape from troublesome situations in our family. As a schoolboy or girl we may be scolded for the same behaviour because our teacher expects our continuous attention.

The ways we behave are often based on past situations. They may sometimes seem impractical and even strange today but in the past they have been the best solutions we were able to come up with.

In fact we can look upon the Protector Controller as the head of a group of voices that are all protecting us. We call them the 'Primary Selves'.

THESE PRIMARY SELVES INCLUDE:

The Protector

My Protecting Voice will say things like this:

"*You better watch out how you behave*".
"*Be honest and nice, otherwise people will not like you and you might feel hurt*".
"*Be strong, it doesn't help to whine and complain*".
"*Take care, that you earn enough money so you can live well and be respected*".

The Pleaser

In the first weeks of our life a nice smiling, cooing little part starts to emerge. We call it 'The Pleaser'. It notices that when it smiles, people around us are friendly and loving towards us. Later on it will say something like:

"*I know how to tune into people and feel what they might need*".
"*I want to be nice to others, then they are going to be nice to me*".

"I am happy when other people around me are happy and when I smile they will like to be with me, so I will feel loved and safe".

This is a wonderful and very useful energy to have but if it starts to run our life it will make it very hard for us to sometimes say 'No' to other people when we need to.

The Perfectionist

This is the part that refines our way of dealing with life. It wants us to become better and better in everything we do. It hopes that if we become perfect, everybody will love us. The trouble with this voice is, no matter how hard we try, we will never be able to live up to its standards. Like many of the Primary Selves, it has learned from one or both our parents how they wanted us to become perfect as our parents are the role models for many of our Primary Selves.

The Perfectionist' might say:

"You have to practice really hard so you learn how to speak that language properly, otherwise people won't take you seriously".

"When you dress up, you better get the tiniest details right. I like you to look just perfect".

The Pusher

In order to accomplish more and more, and to accomplish it even better in life we bring some nice pusher energy into our group of sub-personalities. My Pusher sounds like:

" I want you to do this and that before you can relax".

"You should get up earlier in the morning to accomplish everything that I have in mind for you."

My pusher, often together with my perfectionist, is largely responsible for all the books I buy that are lying in high piles on my bedside table, waiting to be read!

If we didn't have a bit of this pusher energy, we would hardly get anything done.

The Inner Critic

All those times that our parents, or caretakers, are not totally content with our behaviour and tell us so, we start to confine our energy in order to conform to their moral and social standards. What we receive in the form of criticisms from the outside world, soon becomes the stable foundation for a good strong 'Inner Critic'. This Critic is always busy criticising us and telling us that we are not good enough the way we are, hoping that if he keeps getting at us, we won't be criticised by others. Mostly I refer to the Critic as 'he' because many people experience this energy as being male.

My own inner Critic e.g. warns me when I did something unfriendly, incorrectly or dishonest by giving me a very itchy feeling around my stomach. Even when what I did is just a tiny little bit 'off track' my inner Critic will give me a tiny little itch. In the past I just got upset about that feeling. Today I have learned to listen to it and use it as a perfect barometer.

Together these Primary Selves form the so-called front side of our personality. They want to see us happy, and to avoid that we are hurt physically or emotionally. They think that if we are good and perfect, nobody will hurt us.

Because these 'Primary Selves' are so very important to us we need to honour them and not to try to get rid of them. They have been helping us throughout our lives, so they all have the right to exist. We should therefore not judge them.

On the contrary, we should really consciously get to know them, learn about them and learn how to use them to our advantage.

But what happens to that part in us that is connected to soul while growing up?

The lost Inner Child
It seems that we are paying a price by developing the strong parts that form our personality. Our Primary Selves cause us to lose contact with our vulnerability. And our vulnerability is the part in us that is closest to our uniqueness, our Psychic Fingerprint. It is like a doorway to our soul and therefore to our creativity, our life force and our connection with God. Losing this contact in order to grow up is paying a high price indeed.

Our vulnerable child energy, which is extremely sensitive, enables us to be intimate with other people, and so it is very important for us to rediscover it in the course of the inner work we do with ourselves. The Primary Selves stand between us and our deeper contact with other people. Having our vulnerability and our Inner Child available to us enriches our relationships. It seems a paradox. We need our strong parts to get along in life but we also need to wake up to who we really are and stop just being our Primary Selves in order to be whole again.

We can easily imagine how different parts in a personality will be more developed than others in different families and cultures,

Example
In a very intellectual family it might be expected that in order to fit in, the children would develop a certain set of primary selves that helps them adjust and live well inside their family, such as: being intellectual, well-behaved, diligent, aiming for success, etc. But what will happen to the other side of their personality?

This question brings us immediately to the opposite of the Primary Selves; the Disowned Selves. Let's explore them.

The Disowned Selves
Disowned Selves, or the less developed Selves - because they did not have the chance to develop - are the counterpart of the Primary Selves. They are a group of energies that have been kept away or repressed unconsciously because they did not fit into our family system.

When we grow up and develop our power and responsibility on one side, then on the other side, there will be parts that are weak, scared, vulnerable, lazy, shy, etc.

This system obeys a law, which is;

The degree to which we identify with the Primary Selves on one side is exactly the degree to which we will disown on the other side, the equal and opposite energy in an equal and opposite way.[2]

This is the same as in physics. When you have an action on one side you get an equal reaction on the other side. This means, when we are very identified with power, our vulnerability will be proportionately disowned.

But also: If we are highly identified with being loving and caring, like the prototype of the good mother, that part in us that is more selfish and knows too well how to see to it that we take good care of ourselves will be disowned.

Example
Carla grew up in a very intellectual family where the emphasis was on becoming a strong, intelligent woman. She studied architecture and was rather successful at the technical side of her work. She could deal very well with the men on the construction site. But in the area of design she often felt blocked. And in her relationships it was difficult for her to become intimate with a partner. During her therapy we first explored the parts of her that were in control of her life. Then we started to make contact with

2   Hal Stone, Tape on the Psychology of Selves

her vulnerable child, a little girl who had often been hurt and who was never allowed to show people how shy she was. We also discovered a very magical little girl who liked to daydream and visualise all kinds of beautiful pictures and places, who was not allowed to be that way because; "one can use one's time much better that that". When she started to allow this energy to be more present in her daily life, she started to discover the designer side of herself, which gave her great pleasure and satisfaction.

In the same intellectual family I mentioned before, it is very likely that there will be at least one child who will carry the so-called 'Disowned Selves' for the rest of the family. This child will be the rebel. It might refuse to study, or to be tidy, or to be perfect, etc. It will develop the energies that are opposite to those that his family is used to and he will 'carry' them for the other members of the family.

In each of us there are disowned energies that were not useful in the family we grew up in. These are energies that - had we developed them - would have caused us to receive less love and appreciation than we needed in order to survive. In some of us this might have been the 'Sensual Self', or the 'Intuitive Self'. Often our 'Angry Part' will be disowned because few of us had the opportunity to express our anger freely as a child. But also archetypal Voices like our 'Aphrodite', our 'Wise Man' or 'Wise Woman', our 'Warrior' may be lost to us in our growing-up process.

Most important, through our growing-up process our inner child who carries our sensitivity and intuition and who is the key to being intimate with others is lost to us.

Some examples of how we can identify a 'Disowned Self'.
Imagine a man who is highly identified with being a responsible father, the provider for his family, a hard worker and very successful. He is the prototype of 'The Responsible Father'. This man may have a son who is the total opposite: irresponsible, lazy and rebellious. And... the father will hate his son for being that way! If the father could explore the parts of himself that are less compulsively responsible, and know how to relax and take it easy, his son would not as easily activate the 'Responsible Father' part, and they would have fewer and less serious difficulties.

A mother who is very neat and formal may wonder how it is possible that she has got a daughter who is sloppy and busy seducing all the young boys in her High School. She will think that it is all her fault, and try even harder to do everything 'right' and will be very surprised that all her efforts have the opposite effect, and push her daughter even more into the opposite energy. If she could make peace with the part within herself that sometimes longs to be free and seductive, she would not be so upset about her daughter, and her daughter might even have fewer tendencies to be so different from her mother.

A man who is spiritual, kind and sensitive with a very flowing energy, may find himself falling in love with a woman who is intellectual and strict. She will be withdrawn whereas he is open and vulnerable. Because they really love each other, they will not understand why they have arguments. They will wonder why they are so unhappy, not being able to see that they are caught up in opposite parts, both defending their positions and viewpoints. If he could develop his intellectual part some more, and she the part that is easy going their difficulties would be less.

Each time we are strongly identified with a sub personality we feel righteous about our opinions because we don't have access to other points of view.

I am not saying that we should become these disowned parts. If we actually did, our Primary Selves might become very anxious. Becoming those parts would be like bouncing from one extreme into the other. Nor should we try to kill or get rid of parts we don't like very much in ourselves as well as in other people.

We have to understand that when we try to get rid of some part in ourselves - or in someone else - it is one of our Primary Selves trying to get rid of the opposite side in us - or in the other person.

What we do need to do however, is to get acquainted with our disowned energies to the degree that we experience them as true parts of ourselves. When we meet these opposites in other people in our normal daily life, it is a sure sign that we are meeting some unknown part of ourselves projected onto the other person. We seem to attract people who really carry our opposites for us. It is like a law: what we deny, we attract.

What's more, the best place to meet our Disowned Selves seems to be in our closest relationships. In that sense we can look at relationship as being a very important teacher.

Example
This whole system of opposite energies that can get us into huge conflicts became very clear, when my working partner Hans

Mensink and myself started working together.

Hans had just come back from India, where he had visited Baghwan. He was spiritual and identified with freedom and with not being very conventional. He meditated a lot, did tarot readings, lived mainly with his guitar, and had hardly any money.I was married with two children, living a seemingly stable life in a nice, big house. Although I had taken a training as a professional dancer I was still the rather conventional type.

We met and couldn't stand one another at first sight. But during our first conversation, which lasted, perhaps, for just half an hour, we discovered that we shared the same vision. We both were enthusiastic about Breathwork and we wanted to create a thorough training for it that would take three years. We longed for Breathwork to become an honoured way of working therapeutically, and to become socially acceptable. This shared vision brought us together and has been the driving force that helped us to solve every difficulty that we encountered in the time we have worked together.

That was twenty years ago. We really had to work hard to integrate many of our opposites in order to be able to work together as well as we are still doing today. In the beginning, we would often sit together for several hours to get our relationship straightened out after we had worked for a few hours. What I had to integrate inside myself - and not to judge in him - was the part of me that was more flowing, looser and less conventional. Hans had to learn that his conventional part was not as bad as he had thought. We also needed to learn to recognise in each other the signs that would tell us that the other felt vulnerable.

When we feel vulnerable we tend to fall back into our well-known Primary Selves for protection and lose contact with our vulnerability. One could say that a conflict in relationship always comes about between a disowned part like a 'Vulnerable Child' in one person, and a strong Primary Self like a 'Severe Father' in the other person, and can be cleared through awareness of these energies.

To sum this up:
> The part that seems to upset or irritate you in your partner, is the part that needs to be integrated inside your self.
> The part that seems to upset or irritate you in your partner, is the part where he/she needs help and is not easily able to ask for it.

Now, let's get some taste for what these Disowned Selves inside us look and feel like.

Exercise
Who is it in your surroundings that you get angry at, that you cannot stand or that you feel irritated with a lot? What is the most striking quality in that person that 'sets you off'?

Take the first answer that comes into your mind. And yes, that's what you are looking for, a nice Disowned Self.

Who is it that you admire and/or overestimate a lot and whom you think of as being better than you are?

Again take the first answer that comes to mind, and there you have found another Disowned Self.

It is rare, but it may happen, that having done a small exercise like this, we get a revelation, which makes it possible that we claim the disowned part on the spot and integrate it. But normally we will have to do some real work in order to get to know the disowned energy well enough to experience it as a part of us. Integration really means to reclaim a part that has been disowned as a real part of us. Then we have that energy available to us in our normal daily life.

If we suppress, disown certain energies very strongly over a longer period of time, our whole system will be affected by it. Energy is going to be expressed somewhere and in some way or another. This even may happen in the form of an illness.

The real work that has to be done is to rediscover our vulnerability. In reclaiming our vulnerability and in honouring our Primary Selves, we discover the real power that being in contact with vulnerability and source brings. The moment we are no longer identified with one side, whether it be the power side or the vulnerable side, we are on our way to develop a more aware ego. Then we have the Disowned Self and the original Primary Self available to us.

As long as we are identified with power, we are not really making a choice. It is more like power is choosing for us. As long as we are identified with vulnerability we don't have much choice either. In both cases we don't have any possibility of taking a different point of view. It simply is not available to us. What is disowned is disowned and therefore neither visible to, nor noticeable by us. But when we start to separate from our Primary Selves, or perhaps I could say, to get a conscious relationship with our Primary Selves, everything becomes different. When we integrate the disowned Selves then - as Hal

Stone puts it - we have to carry the tension of opposites as well as the burden of choice.[3]

We have to embrace both sides and learn how to handle the different energies inside ourselves.

Summary
- As I already said before, the work is not just about feeling the different voices. It is about getting to know them and to appreciate them for what they are and what they do for us.
- The work is about developing an aware ego that is in a continuous process of becoming more and more aware. Then we have more freedom of choice.
- Through an aware ego all the parts are able to express themselves better and in a more congruent way. Even parts like our 'Intuitive Self' or our 'Spiritual Self' that we prefer to consider as 'good' are better and more safely filtered through an aware ego.

Example
When we are identified with our spirituality and we let it come out through our power part then we are in danger of misusing our spirituality. We all know what can happen when people channel power through their spirituality while being identified with it. We get the worst type of guru-guru behaviour!
- All this leads to carrying more responsibility in the choices we have to make in life. The time is past where we can lean back in a so-called 'faith in God' and just put our sense of responsibility into God's hand.
- It means, we really have to be able to carry our responsibility for what we have to do here on this planet, the way we do it and, sometimes - even more importantly - for what we should not do.
- When we have developed an aware ego we actually can carry that responsibility.

Our way into Society
In groups of people that are devoted to personal growth we often see that the conventional part, the intellectual, or the business part in people seems to have been forgotten and replaced by a more flowing, intuitive and often caring and loving energy. Basically there is nothing wrong with that. It is just that by denying where we came from, we are as unbalanced as we were when we started out on our path of growth. Many of

3 Hal Stone. Tape on the psychology of Selves.

us have become so absorbed with our spiritual path that we tend to forget that we had a conventional part to begin with. The real consciousness process is about rediscovering the disowned parts, loving and honouring them and bringing them back into our lives so we can use them appropriately.

The moment we want to bring Breathwork into society and give it the place it deserves, we have to know how to carry the energies that are required in, and by our society. We can't hope to be received on a management level if we are not really befriended with the kind of energy that is called for on that level.

Our 'Conventional Self' is like a good old-fashioned energy that is conventional, well-groomed, well-behaved, and has a stable knowledge and understanding of our work, its theory and practice, etc. This does not mean that we have to throw away our intuition, our sensitivity or our caring heart. It's just the opposite. We take our 'Intuitive Part' and we add our 'Conventional Part' and use them both together, so that we will be received in society as honoured guests who have something of importance to contribute in an intelligent and loving way.

When we integrate our conventional part and come well prepared to make the move to bring Breathwork into society, our conventional part will be satisfied and happy and our Inner child will feel safe. When we prepare ourselves thoroughly there is less chance that people in society will judge us or be embarrassed by us. This will lessen the chance that we get hurt. Then we really honour and take good care of both sides inside ourselves.

The Spirit of Breathwork

Appendix:
Who is the International Breathwork Foundation?

Created in 1994 as the outcome of the first Global Inspiration Conference, the International Breathwork Foundation (IBF) is a world-wide network of Breathwork trainers, practitioners and other individuals interested in sharing up to date information about Breathwork and its diverse theories, techniques, practices, schools and trainings.

The IBF has an open, respectful and inclusive spirit of all nations, races, religions and spiritual traditions and does not adhere to any specific tradition, religious or otherwise.

The stated purpose of the organization is "to promote a heart-centered approach to Breathwork, its theory and practice, for the expansion of consciousness and for personal and global transformation."

The IBF functions as a non-profit organization and receives its primary funding from an annual membership fee of $100 US (or 100 Euros). Members receive priority admission and a reduced conference fee at the annual Global Inspiration Conference, a quarterly newsletter reporting on latest developments in the field of Breathwork around the world, a quarterly breathwork magazine of their choice, and listing in the IBF website directory and calendar of events.

An annually elected administrative team and a host of national coordinators work throughout the year to implement the purpose of the IBF within their countries and elsewhere in the world. Members of the organization regularly contribute their knowledge and experience to the IBF data-base which contains extensive information on Breathwork literature and publications, as well as Breathwork related events occurring around the globe.

Breathwork trainers from several countries are currently collaborating together in their national trainings, pooling their knowledge and resources to create innovative Breathwork training exchange programmes between their cultures and respective Breathwork traditions. They are working towards the creation of an internationally accredited professional Breathwork training, which will allow students to undertake training modules in several countries of their choice and with a selection of allied trainers around the globe. The standards for international accreditation of breathworkers are being based on guidelines for professional practice and on-going development established during meetings held at previous Global Inspiration conferences.

The annual Global Inspiration Conference serves as an international meeting ground for IBF members and other people interested in Breathwork. The conference attracts breathworkers from many diverse cultures and Breathwork traditions, and therefore offers an outstanding opportunity to exchange views, teach and learn, and receive inspiration from like-minded colleagues in the field of conscious breathing.

All are welcome to join the IBF network and creatively participate in a global activity which promotes and honours the breath as a simple, safe and gentle, and yet very powerful transformational tool.

For more information on the IBF's activities you may visit the IBF website at - http://www.ibfnetwork.org

To know more about becoming an active member of the IBF network, please contact the IBF Public Relations department - Carol Lampman - bconscious@aol.com

- or your nearest IBF National Coordinator:

Nemi Nath, Australia & New Zealand
- breathe@breathconnection.com.au Tel: 61 266 897 455

Wilfried Ehrmann, Austria
- atman@compuserve.com Tel: 431 369 2363

Veronique Batter, Belgium
- vbatter@be.packardbell.org Tel: 322 358 4607

Annette Weber, Denmark
- anw@post9.tele.dk Tel: 45 3393 8287

Kaupo Save, Estonia
- creates@hot.ee

Claire Le Saget, France
- claire.le.saget@wanadoo.fr Tel: 33 1 3024 7365

Catherine Dowling, Ireland
- dowling_catherine@hotmail.com

Robin Lawley, Italy
- robinlawley@tiscalinet.it Tel: 39 06 907 9126

Tilke Platteel-Deur, Netherlands & Germany
- tilke@worldonline.nl Tel: 31 35 695 0093

Ewa Foley, Poland
- foley@foley.com.pl Tel: 48 2234 1706

Natividad Jimenez, Spain
- natividadjs@yahoo.com

Ankara Nygards, Sweden
- an-kara@algonet.se Tel: 46 247 229 53

Urs Baumgartner, Switzerland
- Baumgartner.Urs@bluewin.ch Tel: 41 41 780 8180

Brigitte Martin Powell, UK
- brigitte@powell-martin.freeserve.co.uk

Lyubov & Yuliya Umanets, Ukrani
- quattro@carrier.kiev.ua

Jim Morningstar, USA
- Mornings7@aol.com Tel: 1 414 351 5770

Viola Edward, Venezuela
- edwardconsult@cantv.net Tel: 58 2 977 2735